# LAND USE

## IN A NUTSHELL

### FOURTH EDITION

By

**ROBERT R. WRIGHT**
Donaghey Distinguished Professor of Law Emeritus
University of Arkansas
Little Rock

**MORTON GITELMAN**
Distinguished Professor of Law
University of Arkansas
Fayetteville

**WEST
GROUP**

ST. PAUL, MINN.
**2000**

To all students of
land use law

*

# PREFACE

This series of "nutshell" books was instituted by West primarily to serve the needs of law students, and this book on Land Use is written with that in mind. It is intended to be a succinct expression of the salient points to be found in this subject matter. The difficulty with being succinct, or for that matter in writing a book of this type, is that there is a tendency toward oversimplification and the avoidance of some of the more intricate and interesting aspects of the material under consideration. We feel compelled to make the same qualifying observation that Professor W. Barton Leach made in his article, Perpetuities in a Nutshell, 51 *Harv.L.Rev.* 638 (1938): "If this paper fails of its purpose it has, at least, eminent company. Lord Thurlow undertook to put the Rule in Shelley's Case in a nutshell. 'But,' said Lord Macnaghten, 'it is one thing to put a case like Shelley's in a nutshell and another thing to keep it there.' Van Grutten v. Foxwell [1897] A.C. 658, 671." Nonetheless, as an overview and as something of a summary of the material, this book should prove helpful not only to law students but also to lawyers and judges.

A caveat is essential in that regard. The subject of land use controls and urban planning is approached in different ways by editors of different casebooks.

V

The emphasis of some varies considerably from others depending upon the subject. While this book probably bears greater relationship to the Wright and Gitelman casebook and approach than to those of others, an effort has been made to discuss practically all of the subject matter contained in the leading casebooks. Therefore, even though the casebook used and the emphasis placed upon the material may vary, students utilizing this book should find coverage of most of the material discussed in class.

Student use of this or any other text should be on a periodic basis as different topics are considered. In this manner class discussion and the understanding of the material can be supplemented by the observations contained in this book. It will also prove helpful to re-read portions of the book for review purposes at the end of the course.

The field of land use is so rapidly developing, so diverse and so much affected by various fields of law and by new trends that viewpoints or approaches to the subject will vary depending upon the professor. In developing areas of the law, it is also not unusual to find differing interpretations. This should be kept in mind in considering this material in conjunction with a particular professor's approach to the subject.

Another comment is worthwhile in regard to the somewhat summary treatment accorded the subject in this book. It would have been more time-consuming, but easier in a sense, to write an extended trea-

tise.  Law professors are accustomed to writing law
review articles in which a fairly limited subject can
be thoroughly explored.  It is much more difficult for
us to reduce the material to a limited, relatively simple version.  It goes against our grain, so to speak,
since almost all of our legal writing has proceeded in
the opposite direction.  In place of writing a great
deal about relatively little, in this book we have written relatively little about a considerable variety of
material.  We trust that faculty, students and
lawyers who read this book will take that into account.

ROBERT R. WRIGHT
MORTON GITELMAN

January, 2000

\*

# OUTLINE

IX

## OUTLINE

*

# RESEARCH REFERENCES

Access Westlaw, the computer-assisted legal research service of West Group, to search a broad array of legal resources, including case law, statutes, practice guides, current developments and various other types of information. Consult the online Westlaw Directory to determine databases specific to your needs.

### Searching Land Use on Westlaw

With Westlaw, you can use the Natural Language search method, which allows you to simply describe your issue in plain English. For example, to retrieve state cases discussing historic preservation of churches, access the Multistate Real Property Cases database (MRP-CS) and type the following Natural Language description: historic preservation of churches

You can also use the Terms and Connectors search method, which allows you to enter a query consisting of key terms from your issue and connectors specifying the relationship between those terms. For example, to search for a form of the root historic in the same sentence as a form of the root preserv in the same paragraph as church (which will also retrieve the plural churches) type the following Terms and Connectors query: historic! /s preserv! /p church

## Use KeyCite® to Check Your Research

KeyCite is the citation research service available exclusively on Westlaw. Use KeyCite to see if your cases or statutes are good law and to retrieve cases, legislation or articles that cite your cases and statutes.

For more information regarding searching on Westlaw, call the West Group Reference Attorneys at 1-800-REF-ATTY (1-800-733-2889).

# TABLE OF CASES

### References are to Pages

# TABLE OF CASES

# TABLE OF CASES

\*

# LAND USE

## FOURTH EDITION

\*

# CHAPTER I

# THE CONTROL OF LAND USE: AN OVERVIEW

## § 1. The Past

Controls on land use are not an innovation of the 20th century. They existed in various forms in England long before we were a nation and in actuality extend back into the ancient English past. The earliest Code of Roman law, the Twelve Tables, provided for setback lines from boundaries and for distances between trees and boundaries. This was promulgated in 451–450 B.C.

Modern fiction has it that property rights have a certain absolutism about them. This stems largely from Blackstone's statement that property rights could not be violated "even for the general good of the whole community." 1 W. Blackstone, Commentaries 139 (1782). But he was speaking of the inherent right of Englishmen to own property—a fundamental, human right in Anglo–American society—and Blackstone himself stated in that regard that property could be used and enjoyed without control or diminution "save only by the laws of the land." Id. at 138.

What the "laws of the land" will permit in terms of controls on land use has broadened over the years, although interpretations have gone through times of extension and retrenchment as the development of the police power and the law of eminent domain illustrate. Societal and economic conditions have traditionally set the standards for a particular day. Industrialization in England led to limitations upon the use of wood for fuel. Population growth and urbanization without adequate requirements as to the quality of structures led to the Great Fire of London in the 17th century and beyond that to controls on the rebuilding of the city.

Controls on the use of land in America related also to particular conditions and circumstances. The cheaper and more plentiful the land, the less need there was either to compensate for controlling it or for any controls at all. In the earlier days when population was diffused and there was always more land over the horizon, it was also easy to indulge the populistic notion that property rights were sacrosanct and were somehow beyond the reach of society except in the most fundamental of situations in which landowners themselves came into conflict. Judge-made controls, such as the law of nuisance, were generally adequate. But as our situation became more complex, as cities formed and grew and reproduced like amoebas to become separate accumulations of people, property and governmental units, there arose the realization that more extensive public controls were required.

The early controls on land use in America extend back into the colonial period, but they were limited in nature and dealt with specific problems.

For example, one act of the Massachusetts Bay Colony sought to prevent farm animals from feeding or running at large on a certain island because the shrubs and grass were being destroyed and the owners and the public were being damaged. Another act in Massachusetts Bay provided for assignment of slaughterhouses, tallow chandlers, and certain other nuisance-like activities to particular areas of Boston, Salem and Charlestown. These were early examples of the exercise of the police power—the power to regulate on behalf of the health, safety, morals and general welfare of the community. These regulations were not difficult for the people to swallow because they dealt with clearly defined problems on which there would be general agreement because of the nature of the activity.

Throughout the 19th century in America, the police power developed with relatively little hindrance. The alternatives for a court considering a police power control were to uphold the act or declare that it went so far as to constitute a taking of private property for public use without just compensation. (This problem is discussed at length in the chapter on eminent domain and the police power.) The early cases, which were largely state court decisions, provided great latitude in the exercise of the police power. In Brick Presbyterian Church v. City of New York (N.Y.1826), the city denied the church the continued use of a cemetery when the city had many years before leased the property to the church for a church and cemetery and had covenanted with the church for such use. In Commonwealth v. Tewksbury, (Mass.1846), the Massachusetts Court upheld a statute which prevented landowners from removing sand or gravel from beach property. And in Commonwealth v. Alger (Mass.1851), the same court upheld a statute which prohibited erecting wharves beyond certain lines in the harbor even though the landowner who challenged the statute had received his land given for that purpose.

Although other cases were similar, these early decisions took the attitude that only a physical taking of property was compensable, and they compared the exercise of the police power by state and local governments to the nuisance maxim that no one may use his land in such a way as to interfere with his neighbor's use. (See generally on all of this, F. Bosselman, D. Callies & J. Banta, *The Taking Issue* 106–114 (1973).)

This broad interpretation of the police power was carried forward in the latter part of the 19th century by the United States Supreme Court. Although it recognized that permanent physical invasions were compensable, it denied compensation in at least one situation in which damage clearly resulted to a landowner from a public project. The most important case of that period, however, was Mugler v. Kansas (1887), which involved a brewery rendered largely worthless by a Kansas prohibition statute. Using the nuisance analogy, the court reasoned that police power regulations which greatly depreciate the value of property do not amount to a taking.

(See generally, Bosselman, Callies & Banta, supra 114–123.)

The importance of the police power, of course, is that it forms the basis for the enactment of direct regulatory statutes and ordinances—and, in particular, is the basis for the legality of zoning.

## § 2. The Contrast of the 19th and 20th Centuries

For all practical purposes, this 19th century law is largely inapplicable today. In Pennsylvania Coal Co. v. Mahon, (1922), Justice Holmes wrote that while property could be regulated, if regulation went too far it would constitute a taking. How far it could go was a matter of degree which had to be determined on a case-by-case basis. That the police power remained a viable tool was clearly indicated four years later when the Supreme Court upheld comprehensive zoning in Euclid v. Ambler Realty Co. (1926). But it was clear that the police power was not unlimited: it could not be exercised arbitrarily or capriciously; it could not be unreasonable; it could not be confiscatory. Although *Euclid* drew upon the earlier nuisance analogy, that analogy was no longer particularly applicable. The *Euclid* zoning ordinance went beyond the regulation of nuisance-like activities. How far zoning could go, however, was subject to the test in *Pennsylvania Coal*.

Nonetheless, the situation by the 1920's presented a rather interesting contrast with the situation in the 19th century. Except for a few cases such as Rideout v. Knox (1889), a Holmes opinion which

presaged his later expression in *Pennsylvania Coal,*
the 19th century expounded the virtue and sanctity
of the private ownership of property while permitting almost any exercise of the police power that fell
short of an outright taking. The first half of the
20th century presented a similar striking contrast
by expanding the uses of the police power in its
approval of comprehensive zoning while at the same
time the courts became more inclined to find that a
particular police power action encroached upon private property rights to the point that it constituted
a taking. As between the two, despite the dedicated
pronouncements of the 19th century relative to
property rights and despite the expansion of the
police power in the 20th century, the protection of
private property against governmental actions has
been greater in this century than in the last.

This is illustrated by some recent decisions. In
recent years the U.S. Supreme Court has altered its
view so as to accept the concept of allowing damages for a regulatory taking which does not involve
physical appropriation of property. In First English
Evangelical Lutheran Church of Glendale v. County
of Los Angeles (1987), the Court held that compensation can be awarded for damages accruing from
regulatory takings during the interim period after
the regulation had been imposed and before the
regulation ceased. This ordinance involved a prohibition against construction of buildings within a
flood protection area. In a related case, Nollan v.
California Coastal Commission (1987), the Court
held that the takings clause of the Constitution was

violated when the commission sought to condition a permit to rebuild a house on the plaintiffs' transfer to the public of an easement across their beachfront property. This situation is discussed at some length later in the book.

It is unclear how far the Supreme Court will go in declaring what regulations amount to a taking. It is clear, however, that if the regulation is deemed to deprive the owner of all economic use, as in *First English,* it amounts to a regulatory taking for which damages may be awarded.

Further, if the regulation, as in *Nollan,* extracts a property right as a condition for a building permit, then the regulation goes "too far."

The most recent U.S. Supreme Court case on this subject, Lucas v. South Carolina Coastal Council (1992), essentially ratifies the *First English* decision in holding that a total deprivation of economic use will amount to a taking for which damages may be awarded. *Lucas* advanced this and other propositions which will be explored more thoroughly later in the book.

Consequently, while the 20th century validated comprehensive zoning and expanded the limits of the police power, it also cautioned against regulation so excessive as to amount to a deprivation. Extending the remedy beyond the invalidating of regulatory laws considered arbitrary and unreasonable to include the allowance of damages for the period during which the regulation was in force could, if carried too far, have a deterrent effect on the extent of regulations applied by local governments.

## § 3.  The Inheritance

Land use controls today, however, retain a substantial inheritance from the past. The common law doctrines of nuisance and waste, as well as some others, remain available for use and are employed in the limited situations in which they apply. These controls are the subject of the next chapter. The police power, though not accorded the wide judicial berth of the 19th century, has expanded in a variety of ways. It forms the basis today not only for such purposes as zoning ordinances but also for recent environmental laws and regulations. City planning and the predecessors of the "new town" movement can be traced in rudimentary form back to the 19th century, although both flowered during the 20th century. Planning remains in a state of transition and growth, but even high school students are aware of the fact that the City of Washington originated as a planned city with particular attention being given to boulevards and traffic circles.

The feeling, popular in some circles, that planning and controls on land are somehow a break with the past and are in derogation of property rights does not therefore manifest a familiarity with the past.

## § 4.  The Present

This book deals almost entirely with the present state of the law and with current trends and problems. In addition to common law devices and the law of zoning, attention is given to planning and the planners, subdivision development, restrictive covenants, housing and urban development, aesthetics, natural resources, environmental problems, taxation, eminent domain and the police power, and energy and related problems. New forms of planning manifested in the zoning process, such as cluster zones and planned unit developments, are considered. To what extent can zoning be exclusionary? To what extent can aesthetics enter into zoning or planning considerations? What can be required of subdividers? How does taxation affect land use? What is the interrelationship between laws pertaining to the environment or to the regulation of natural resources and older forms of land use control? When is there a "taking" under today's cases? If there is a "taking," what are the remedies? What will be the interaction between environmental laws and the energy crisis? To what extent does regional and state planning exist and to what extent should it exist?

Although many of these questions and others are answered in large measure by the current state of the law, others are not yet answered and will not be answered for some years to come. Land use law is the most dynamic and constantly changing aspect of property law because it is an amalgamation of property law and public law. Public policy considerations affect land use law to a far greater degree than any other aspect of property law. Constitutional questions obviously play a part in that situation, and the scope and basis of constitutional review has been increasing in recent years.

Finally, it must be said that there is an interconnection between land use controls on the one hand and social, economic and constitutional trends on the other which is not usually found in traditional property law. Governmental and judicial bodies usually attempt to make land use policies responsive to emerging concerns and developing needs. Conflicts result from situations in which localities attempt to block or ignore those needs or from situations in which the response is challenged as an overextension of the police power. The complexity of urban problems and the growth of urban areas places constant tension on the land use process with the result that anyone undertaking a study of this field of law is like the pioneer approaching a new frontier. As he crosses one range of hills, there are still other hills beyond. The legal process, of course, is like that, but this course represents an intensification of that process to an extreme degree.

# CHAPTER II

## COMMON LAW CONTROLS ON THE USE OF LAND

### § 1.  Generally

While most controls on land use result from the actions of governmental units or private developers, the use of land can also be affected by judicial determinations. These are normally negative rather than positive controls which result from lawsuits involving narrowly focused issues. Generally speaking, actions of this type occur most of the time in these two situations: (1) lawsuits involving neighbors suing neighbors or a public official acting against a neighboring landowner on behalf of the public in general, and (2) lawsuits involving individuals who share the ownership of a parcel of land.

The first type of lawsuit involves an alleged nuisance, and the second type involves an action for waste.

### § 2.  Background of the Law of Waste

Actions predicated upon waste customarily involve persons who possess interests of one kind or another in the same piece of land. Persons who may be involved are life tenants and remaindermen, landlords and tenants, secured creditors and debtors (such as mortgagors and mortgagees), common or joint tenants in which one or more of the tenants are not in possession, beneficiaries and trustees, grantors and grantees, holders of the equitable title and holders of the legal title, and covenantors and covenantees. The majority view is that owners of contingent interests, such as possibilities of reverter and contingent remainders, may not bring an action for waste, but there is authority to the contrary.

If the party in possession commits certain acts upon the land which are usually but not necessarily alleged to be harmful to the rights of the party not in possession, the customary allegation is that waste has been committed. Suit may be brought for an injunction or damages or both.

The law of waste is quite old, and it assumed increased importance with the Statute of Marlborough in 1267 and the Statute of Gloucester in 1278. The early English law was very rigid with respect to the party in possession, but this rigidity has lessened in recent times. Because our situation was different, due to the large land mass and the need to clear and develop the land, American law after the early years was far less rigid.

Early English law permitted an agreement to be made that a lessee for years could hold the premises "without impeachment of waste," which allowed the lessee to cut down all the timber, for example. But in the Bishop of Winchester's case in 1638 (1 Rolle, Abridgment 380 (T, 3)), it was held that he could be enjoined because it was not in the public interest to lay waste to the timber. Equity could also enjoin wanton acts of destruction despite the use of that term. Vane v. Lord Barnard (Ch.1716). While the magic term, "impeachment of waste," was generally not employed in the United States, it was accepted that equity had jurisdiction where the remedy at law was inadequate.

## § 3. Types of Waste

It is common for a student or layman to think of waste as some act which harms or destroys a part of the property. This is the usual type of action—one involving an unreasonable act which produces or will produce permanent and substantial damage. Affirmative or voluntary waste, as it is known, is not the only type, however. Permissive waste is passive in nature and may result from the possessor's allowing the property to deteriorate without taking appropriate steps to prevent it. As mentioned, equity may enjoin threatened unreasonable or malicious acts of waste, and this is generally called equitable waste. If the change to the property results in increasing the value of the land, this is referred to as ameliorating waste.

## § 4. Voluntary Waste

An act which results in permanent and substantial damage to the property and is unreasonable constitutes waste on the part of the person in possession. Whether the act is unreasonable and whether the injury to the property is of sufficient gravity to amount to waste will involve consideration of the comparative rights and reasonable expectations of the possessor and the party not in possession. This "balancing of the interests" consideration also enters into the law of nuisance.

Generally speaking, it is not waste in the United States to clear land of timber for purposes of cultivation unless the value of the non-possessor's interest is diminished or the amount of timber cut is inconsistent with that required for good husbandry. Timber may also be cut for fuel, for fences, or as ancillary to farming operations. If the land was being used for timber purposes at the inception of the lease, or if the lease was for that purpose, there is no waste in cutting it. This also applies to the removal of soil or minerals. These can also be extracted without committing waste if necessary to carry out the purpose of the lease. However, in the absence of one of these situations, such activities would normally result in waste.

It is not considered waste simply to change the appearance of land, such as from open land to cultivated land.

Modern cases generally allow alterations to structures, or occasionally the destruction or replacement of existing structures, if the value of the property would be enhanced. Thus, ameliorating waste is usually not waste in the sense that it would give rise to an action at law or in equity. A situation of this type may result when conditions have changed quite substantially in the neighborhood where the property is located. In the leading case of

Melms v. Pabst Brewing Co. (1899), the Wisconsin Court upheld the removal of a house and the leveling of a lot by a life tenant on the basis that there had been a radical and permanent change in surrounding conditions which justified the action taken.

## § 5. Permissive Waste

A possessor can be held responsible for poor husbandry resulting from inaction on his part. The duty of care is that of a man of ordinary prudence. Aside from allowing open land or cultivated land to diminish in value, permissive waste can result to structures from failing to make repairs or otherwise protect the premises against deterioration or destruction. Permissive waste can result in almost any situation when there is a failure by the possessor to act to preserve the property when he is found to have a reasonable duty to act.

## § 6. Remedies

Although statutes may vary somewhat, an action for waste normally involves a suit at law for damages, an equitable action for injunctive relief, or a combination of the two. It is not uncommon to seek damages for acts already committed and to ask for an injunction against future acts. The usual allegations in equity with respect to irreparable harm and the inadequacy of the remedy at law are required to secure an injunction unless a statute provides for some other test. Some statutes provide for temporary relief if acts of waste are threatened or are being committed.

The measure of damages, in general, is the amount by which the acts of the possessor have diminished the value of the interest of the party not in possession. This is not easy to measure in situations in which a long period of time will elapse before the plaintiff is entitled to possession. Where a life tenant is in possession, actuarial tables are sometimes employed to determine the probable duration. The amount of recovery is also affected by statutes, some of which allow double or treble damages in situations involving malicious or wanton conduct.

In one case involving the use of a building as a smallpox hospital, it was held that this was an injury to the reversion and that the plaintiff should recover the resulting diminution in value for every valuable use to which the building might reasonably be put.

## § 7.  Background of the Law of Nuisance

The law of nuisance began to develop shortly after the Norman Conquest, and in the late 12th century, the royal courts began to handle such disputes. The early dual relief of damages and specific abatement was superseded by trespass on the case, allowing damages only, which forced the plaintiff to seek injunctive relief in equity. Most of today's nuisance cases seek injunctive relief coupled with a prayer for special damages.

Unlike an action for waste in which the parties each possess an interest in the same piece of property, a nuisance action involves a suit by a neighboring landowner or by a public prosecutor suing on behalf of the people seeking to control or limit the use of land owned by the defendant. The basis of the suit is the maxim, *sic utere tuo ut alienum non laedas,* which means that no one may use his property in such a way as to injure his neighbor (or neighbors in the area generally). A claim of a nuisance thus involves the assertion of something in the nature of a negative interest—the interest of an adjoining or nearby property owner in not being adversely affected by the misuse of the land in question. It is somewhat comparable to a judicially created restrictive covenant in which each landowner is burdened by the limitation.

## § 8.  Public and Private Nuisances

A private nuisance is an unreasonable interference with the use or enjoyment of land without there being a trespass or physical invasion. Practically speaking, it will be asserted by A in a suit against B, in which A alleges that certain acts by B constitute a nuisance as to A and his property. These acts may or may not affect other property in the area.

A public nuisance has wider-ranging implications. It is of sufficient magnitude to affect adversely the health, morals, safety, welfare, comfort or convenience of the public in general. Water pollution, air pollution, the storage of explosives under dangerous conditions, a house of prostitution, the emission of loud noises or bad odors, and obstruction of public ways, are examples. Statutes will in some instances define what constitutes a public nuisance.

A nuisance may be both public and private at the same time. In other words, activity may be sufficient to constitute a public nuisance and still substantially interfere with the use of adjoining land to the point that a landowner may bring an action predicated upon allegations of a private nuisance.

All nuisance actions do not result from affirmative acts. A landowner may fail to maintain his property in a reasonably suitable condition, as in the case of a failure to maintain a horse lot or a pig pen or a dog kennel, or of a failure to prevent the danger of fire with respect to tall grass and brush during dry weather. An ultrahazardous use of land, whether intentional or due to neglect, could impose absolute liability permitting injunctive relief.

"Private nuisance" refers to the property interest or extent of interests affected rather than to the type of conduct.

From a strictly legal standpoint, a physical invasion of property gives rise to an action of trespass. But trespass and nuisance sometimes are difficult to distinguish. Gases, odors, dust particles, chemical particulates, and noise waves are invasions which produce trespasses in a technical sense, but the cases normally deal with such problems through nuisance doctrines.

## § 9. Nuisances Per Se and Per Accidens

A nuisance per se is simply an activity or structure which constitutes a nuisance in and of itself. It may be defined as such by statute or it may constitute an immoral or extrahazardous activity. Obviously, a nuisance per se is often a public nuisance as well, and it may constitute a private nuisance. Most nuisances per se have resulted from the courts declaring them to be such on numerous occasions, such as funeral parlors in residential districts.

A nuisance per accidens is a nuisance in fact, *i.e.,* it must be proven to be a nuisance. It would probably not constitute a nuisance under all circumstances. Most of the allegations of private nuisances involve alleged nuisances per accidens, but a nuisance per accidens may be alleged on behalf of the public as well. The burden of proof is on the plaintiff to show that the activity or structure complained of is sufficiently obnoxious or sufficiently interferes with the use of his land that it amounts to a nuisance.

## § 10. Nuisances in Rural Areas

Whether an activity or operation is considered a nuisance will vary depending upon its location. Not every activity that would constitute a nuisance if located in town or in a fairly well-settled area will be considered a nuisance in the open country or even on the fringes of a city. On the other hand, some operations are so noxious that they have difficulty finding a place to hide.

These situations often lead to application of the "balancing of hardships" or "balancing of the equities" doctrine. In an old California case, cement was being manufactured in an area close to the quarries when the surrounding area was developed for growing citrus fruits. The cement dust was ruining the citrus trees and affecting the homes of the plaintiffs. The court felt that despite the loss which would result from closing the plant, to permit the cement company to continue its operations would amount to a taking of private property and could not be permitted. Hulbert v. California Portland Cement Co. (1911). By contrast, in a fairly recent Arizona case, there was a conflict between a developing urban area known as Sun City and a large cattle operation, and the court balanced the hardships by requiring the cattle feedlot to be moved to more distant land of the defendant but also requiring the developers to indemnify the feedlot owners for damages and expenses resulting from the injunction. Spur Industries, Inc. v. Del E. Webb Development Co. (1972). Both of these cases involved operations which had sought isolation from other activities.

Another more modern case which contrasts with *Hulbert*, supra, is Boomer v. Atlantic Cement Co. (1970), which illustrates another attempt to balance the equities. The opinion in *Boomer* focused on the economic consequences in shutting down a plant which was polluting the air but which involved a $45,000,000 investment and the employment of over 300 people. Since there would be heavy economic loss in closing the plant in contrast to a relatively slight loss to the nearby landowners, the court chose to award permanent damages. The dissent argued that this amounted to an impermissible private taking for private use. In any event, *Boomer* and *Spur* represent the modern trend of the cases in making every effort to balance the hardships in order to avoid severe economic loss to the wrongdoer.

Although these cases do not illustrate it, operations which put forth large amounts of dust and gases or which emit foul odors are much "safer" from potential injunctions if they are located in open or rural areas. Cases involving emissions of this type have often held in favor of the industry or have given the plant a chance to improve its conditions. Moreover, in some cases damages have been allowed without enjoining the operation as in *Boomer*.

Even in rural areas, however, it makes a difference if the alleged nuisance is interfering with residential use as opposed to agricultural or commercial activity. If the area is viewed as residential in nature, even though it is rather sparsely settled, injunctive relief is more likely to be granted. But if the area is basically open country, the mere fact that there is a house or two in the vicinity will generally not suffice for injunctive relief in the absence of substantial interference or an extreme situation. Thus the Tennessee Court refused to enjoin a proposed crematory in a largely rural area, although the decision was based partly on the con-

cept that a mere possibility or fear of future injury
is not enough. State ex rel. Cunningham v. Feezell
(1966). Cases involving racetracks and drive-ins
demonstrate varied results depending largely on
how substantial the court views the impact on the
complainants and how the court chooses to balance
the equities. Cases involving pigs, cattle and other
such animals illustrate the importance of the question of whether the area is rural or is in the process
of becoming residential.

The Restatement of Torts indicates that factors
to be considered in nuisance cases include the ade-
quacy of the injunction and other remedies, unclean
hands or laches on the part of the plaintiff, the
relative hardship to the parties, the interests of
third parties and the public, and the ability to
frame and enforce the decree. If there will be a loss
of jobs, loss of purchasing power, loss of taxes, and
substantial harm to the owners of such an industry,
these factors should be taken into account in assess-
ing the public interest. Obviously, consideration of
such factors would lead to a balancing of the equities.

## § 11. Nuisances in Residential Areas or on the Urban Fringe

Nuisance situations become more obvious when
the area is well-established as residential in nature.
In fact, mixed uses and the relative lack of control
over development have been factors which have
affected the denial of injunctive relief in areas on
the urban fringe. Even in situations in which a solid

residential development is affected, as in the Sun City case, the tendency is to try to balance the hardships or permit the defendant to take measures to correct the condition.

These cases involving the fringe areas of a city often present the problem of "moving to the nuisance." One of the oft-cited cases on that subject, however, Bove v. Donner–Hanna Coke Corp. (1932), involved a house which had been built in an industrial area. Although the house was built before the coke plant, the court denied relief stating that this had been an industrial area for many years and that the plaintiff knew that when she bought the property. In the Sun City case, the court noted that if the developer were the only party harmed, it would feel justified in following that doctrine, but that people who had bought homes from the developer should not have to suffer. The key to the moving to the nuisance rule seems to be that if someone intentionally and knowingly locates in an industrial area or the like, the doctrine applies; but if there is a natural growth outward by the city until it begins to be affected by an alleged nuisance, then the doctrine does not apply.

This concept also affects the cases previously discussed relative to locating in a rural or agricultural area. If that is intentionally done, a homeowner should not then be heard to complain that the adjoining farm has cows or pigs which smell bad. (Of course, the result would be different if the situation had changed or intensified after the homeowner moved in.) Some states have adopted so-called "right-to-farm" laws designed to protect agricultural operations from nuisance suits.

A related issue is whether a federal law provides the exclusive remedy when a plaintiff is seeking relief on the basis of state nuisance law. In Marshall v. Consumers Power Co. (1975), the court found that the Atomic Energy Act was for protection against radiation hazards and did not preempt state nuisance law concerning other aspects of construction of a nuclear power facility.

If an area is not clearly established as residential, and contains mixed uses, courts will not normally enjoin such activities as gasoline stations, junkyards and funeral homes (although they will enjoin particularly noxious or harmful uses). The same result will likely occur if an area is in transition from residential to commercial. Even where an area was predominantly residential, the Pennsylvania Court decided to limit the operations of a grocery store rather than keep it out. Essick v. Shillam (1943).

Despite the dictum in the West Virginia case of Parkersburg Builders Material Co. v. Barrack (1937), courts will generally not issue an injunction based on aesthetic considerations alone. The funeral home cases, however, present certain aesthetic overtones since they seem largely predicated on the mental attitudes of the public. Funeral homes can be enjoined as nuisances in neighborhoods which are exclusively, predominantly, or essentially residential. By contrast, in the absence of a health hazard of some type, cemeteries are normally not subject to injunction. Other types of operations which are deemed particularly unpleasant or threaten the mental health and property values of people in the neighborhood are also sometimes enjoined. Examples include a mental sanitarium, a venereal disease clinic, and "halfway houses" for paroled convicts (although there are seemingly contrary decisions on the latter). Normally, a mere fear of future injury from an alleged nuisance per accidens is not enough for injunctive relief. But that rule does not apply to funeral homes and certain other operations which produce mental apprehension that the courts feel is genuine and common among average people.

Some nuisance cases seem to turn on the attitude of the judges toward the particular situation. The funeral home cases probably mirror that to some extent. Institutional homes of various kinds are also illustrative. "Halfway house" cases involving homes designed to help rehabilitate felons and move them back into society may have similar facts but different results. One case may enjoin the use because of the view that there would be a significant decrease in property values in the area, while another may say that there is only apprehension of lessened property values and no evidence to that effect.

A recent case involving construction in residential areas which has been given substantial attention in casebooks involved the question of whether a neighbor who was otherwise in compliance with zoning and other city regulations would have to construct his house in such a way as not to interfere with the solar collectors on his neighbor's house. Prah v. Maretti (1982). The court held that he would because the obstruction of the sun's rays would constitute a private nuisance. The court discussed, but did not expressly adopt, the English doctrine of ancient lights although the result is the same. The case is based on the reasonable use doctrine of the Restatement of Torts, Second. A long dissent pointed out, among other things, that Maretti had already moved his house over ten feet to accommodate the solar collector.

It seems dubious that most courts would follow *Prah*. The court cites but does not follow a Florida case in which construction was permitted which cast a shadow on a neighboring hotel's swimming pool. Moreover, in People ex rel. Hoogasian v. Sears Roebuck & Co. (1972), the court refused to enjoin construction of the Sears building which, it was alleged, would interfere with television signals in certain areas of Chicago.

## § 12.  Nuisances in Commercial and Industrial Areas

As indicated previously, there is usually little relief for someone who intentionally locates in an industrial area. But conflicts arise between otherwise lawful businesses or types of industry when one emits offensive odors or dangerous gases which affect or endanger the health of people working or doing business in the vicinity. Sometimes a commercial operation will be located apart from other businesses but gradually come into contact with the business area as a result of normal growth. This situation can lead to an injunction if, for example, the operation gives off offensive odors.

Many of the situations in industrial districts today are covered by air and water pollution statutes and regulations. However, unless a statute expressly states that the remedies under it are exclusive, the mere passage of it is generally not enough to divest courts of their common law jurisdiction over nuisance actions.

In considering injunctive relief the balancing doctrine applies, and courts may consider the comparative economic impact which will be involved. It is not unusual for courts to take halfway steps by requiring the defendant to clean up its operation, or make adjustments in it, or conform to the most modern methods and utilize modern technology in an effort to diminish the effect of the activity.

## § 13.  Public Facilities

Country clubs and public parks have been sued in nuisance actions because of errant golf balls, litter, crowds, and noise. Plaintiffs have at times been unsuccessful because of the requirement that the interference with the use and enjoyment of property must be substantial and continuous. An occasional interference is not sufficient to establish a nuisance. As in other instances involving "moving to the nuisance," courts are unlikely to extend relief to those who elect to live adjacent to a golf course, park, or playground. However, damages suffered as a result of the defendant's negligence in operating the facility or supervising others can result in liability independent of a finding of nuisance.

If construction of a highway has blocked access to a right of way or has otherwise interfered with a property owner's use of his land, a proper remedy might lie in an action for nuisance. One court even held that the remedy of summary self-help abatement (without breach of peace) is available to those who suffer from nuisances created by public entities as well as from those created on private land by private citizens.

## § 14.  Nuisances in Zoned Areas

The fact that an activity of a certain type is permitted in an area under the zoning ordinance does not mean that it may not be enjoined if it develops into a nuisance. The Colorado Court stated that the fact the zoning permits such an operation means that it cannot be considered a *public* nuisance. Green v. Castle Concrete Co. (1973). Actually, it would only be proper to say that it is not a nuisance *per se*. An otherwise legitimate activity could be conducted in such a way as to threaten the health or safety of the community in general and thus constitute a public nuisance. Obviously, it might also constitute a private nuisance.

Cases stating that a permitted use under zoning may still constitute a nuisance have involved such operations as funeral parlors, a taproom restaurant that attracted delinquents, a garbage dump, and a rock quarry. Some of these cases go beyond the idea that the key to whether a zoned business is subject to injunction depends on how it is operated. In the case of the funeral home, for example, the zoning was only given some weight as bearing on the issue and otherwise had no relevance. These are peculiar cases, however, and in few instances would an activity be enjoined from an area in which it could exist under the zoning law unless it had developed clear nuisance characteristics.

Some non-conforming uses which are permitted in certain areas because they predated the zoning can be eliminated by injunction if they constitute nuisances. However, the mere fact that they are non-conforming is not sufficient to justify injunctive relief.

Zoning laws and nuisance doctrine sometimes come into conflict with First Amendment rights. This is frequently the case when a zoning ordinance does not allow adult bookstores or when a neighboring property owner alleges that such a bookstore constitutes a nuisance. Until the materials in such bookstores are determined to be obscene in violation of law, the operation of the bookstore is generally protected. Statutes declaring these stores to be public nuisances have on occasion been declared unconstitutionally vague. The same problems arise concerning activities such as adult movies and stage presentations.

First Amendment questions also arise where the activities of religious groups are alleged to be nuisances or to violate zoning ordinances. The latter problem is discussed in Chapter VI.

## § 15.  Nuisance Doctrine and Environmental Regulation

When a jurisdiction has enacted a pollution control act, a question arises concerning whether the act provides the exclusive remedy as to the activities it is designed to regulate. If the legislation provides an exclusive remedy, plaintiffs may not bring common law actions for nuisance. The better rule is that such legislation be construed as providing remedies in addition to the common law action for nuisance unless the act specifically states that its remedies are to be exclusive. However, the United States Supreme Court, in City of Milwaukee v. Illinois and Michigan (1981), held that the Federal Water Pollution Control Act preempted the federal common law of nuisance.

A related issue is whether a federal law provides the exclusive remedy when a plaintiff is seeking relief on the basis of state nuisance law. In Marshall v. Consumers Power Co. (1975), the court found that the Atomic Energy Act was for protection against radiation hazards and did not preempt state nuisance law concerning other aspects of construction of a nuclear power facility.

## § 16.  Trespass or Nuisance

Aviation cases, in particular, point out the problem of classifying a nuisance as non-trespassory. Under the majority view in the United States which stems from Lord Coke and classifies an invasion of airspace over a property owner's land as trespassory, the airplanes would have to pass overhead on a regular basis. But since noise spreads in all directions, the noise is just as much of a nuisance whether the planes fly overhead or not. Consequently, a substantial number of states have held that a taking of property rights in airspace may occur as a result of nuisance regardless of whether there have been overflights. E.g.: Martin v. Port of Seattle (1964).

## § 17.  Other Judicial Controls on Land

In addition to the law pertaining to nuisance and waste, the judge-made or statutory law of lateral support, water rights, adverse possession, implied easements, drainage of surface waters, trade and agricultural fixtures, redemption and the rights of mortgagees, improvements by tenants, and duties in regard to fencing animals, all affect the way in which land can be used.

# CHAPTER III

## PRIVATE LAW DEVICES

### § 1. Generally

Even though many controls on land use result from the actions of governmental units, some very significant planned limitations result from "private" land use restrictions. Generally speaking, these create a right in the land of another. Unlike most of the common law controls discussed in the previous chapter, private law devices can be positive in nature as well as negative, since they compel a landowner to take affirmative measures as to the use of land subject to the restrictions. They are "private" in the sense that they are created by land developers rather than by public agencies.

Private law devices take several forms, and while courts sometimes confuse the terms as well as the nature of the various devices, it is important to understand how the devices differ from one another and the legal consequences which arise from the use of a particular legal device.

### § 2. Defeasible Fees

One way to impose controls on land use is by the creation of estates in land called defeasible fees. In the fee simple determinable, Blackacre is conveyed to the grantee for as long as a certain situation exists or does not exist, and if such prescribed use ceases or if the prohibited event occurs, then the land automatically reverts to the grantor and his heirs. The grantor and his heirs retain a possibility of reverter. In the fee simple upon condition subsequent, the land is conveyed "upon condition that" or "provided that" a certain condition perpetually is met or a specified event does not or is not permitted to occur, and if the condition is no longer fulfilled or the event occurs, then the grantee and his heirs have a power to terminate the estate (which is often called a right of entry for condition broken).

These estates usually encumber land titles needlessly, often adversely affect alienation, do not take into account unexpected future situations, and should almost always be avoided. They are not favored at law or in equity, and courts will construe such estates to give rise only to covenants whenever the language of the conveyance permits. In addition, the limited scope of such devices renders them practically useless for the creation of effective land use controls.

Some states have passed desirable statutes which extinguish possibilities of reverter and rights of entry after a specified period of time if the event in question has not occurred.

## § 3.   Easements Compared to Covenants

An easement is an interest in the land of another which is created by language of transfer, i.e., grant, reservation, or conveyance. Easements run with the land and can be affirmative, negative, appurtenant, in gross, implied, or prescriptive. Moreover, new types or new forms of easements or what are called easements are periodically created and recognized. Scenic easements are an example. The concept of "reciprocal negative easements" resulted from the use and recognition of covenants in deeds as binding upon all landowners in a neighborhood. These are not easements in the traditional legal sense based upon the usual terminology employed in these instruments.

More akin to this latter situation is the modern subdivision development. A land developer, having platted his subdivision into lots, blocks, and streets, imposes certain limitations on the use of all lots in the development. He will likely provide, among other things, for single-family dwellings with no detached outbuildings, for the dwellings to be constructed at least a specified distance from the street and from the side and back lot lines, for dwellings of a minimum square footage, as well as for an extensive variety of other limitations. These provisions are filed for record along with the approved plat and bill of assurance and constitute covenants which restrict the use of each lot. They are reciprocal in that each owner of a lot in the subdivision may enforce them against another lot owner. They "run with the land," in the sense that these rights continue upon the sale of a lot to a third party. Restrictive covenants are today generally considered interests in land. Although Arkansas declined to award damages for their breach in an eminent domain action, California and other states properly have held to the contrary. (Arkansas State Highway Commission v. McNeill (1964); Southern California Edison Co. v. Bourgerie (1973).)

While a restrictive covenant or a reciprocal negative easement may preclude someone from certain activity on a parcel of land, easements traditionally at law are affirmative and constitute a grant in the sense that they grant certain rights to A with regard to the land of B. One of the most common types of easements today is the affirmative grant to a utility company to run its lines across the owner's property.

Easements may be perpetual, for a specific term, or may be terminated by operation of law. An easement which is dependent on certain circumstances or is for a particular purpose may be extinguished if the circumstances no longer exist or if the purpose cannot be carried out. An easement could also cease to exist under the doctrine of merger, as when the owner of the easement acquires the fee title.

Recently, easements have also been used for public objectives such as for the preservation of open space, conservation, and the protection of scenic views.

The new Restatement of Property 3d (Servitudes) seeks to rationalize the semantic morass built up over centuries of judicial examination of easement and easement-like devices.

## § 4. Easements Appurtenant and in Gross

An appurtenant easement is connected with the ownership of nearby land, and its principal characteristic is that there is a dominant tenement, the owner of which benefits from the easement, and a servient tenement which is subject to the easement. For example, if A and B own adjacent land and A has a right of way across B's land, A has the dominant tenement and B has the servient.

An easement in gross does not have dominant and servient tenements because it is not connected with the ownership of nearby land. At common law such an easement was personal to the grantee and could not be assigned or inherited. There is a growing trend toward assignability, and commercial easements in gross are regarded as assignable by the Restatement. Easements in gross are traditionally not favored in the law, and an easement will be presumed to be appurtenant if there is any doubt.

Of course, an easement in gross may be made expressly assignable by the language employed. If it states that it is a grant to "A, his heirs and assigns," then it would be the intent of the grantor to make it assignable. Also, an express provision could be placed in the instrument stating that it was assignable.

Conservation easements are normally not appurtenant because generally there is no publicly owned land nearby which can serve as the dominant tenement. A scenic easement along a highway can be an appurtenant easement because the publicly owned highway serves as the dominant tenement.

Easements in gross are not altogether satisfactory for conservation purposes because the old common law rule that such easements are non-assignable prevails in some jurisdictions, although others have modified the rule by holding that such easements are assignable where the clear intent of the grant was to create an assignable easement.

Problems which have arisen in the area of conservation easements include those of notice of the easement to subsequent purchasers of the fee when the easement is not recorded, the possibility that it might terminate by court declaration of a change of conditions, and the control which the fee owner retains over the land. The owner retains any right not specifically granted.

## § 5. Implied and Prescriptive Easements

If a property owner sold part of his land to someone whose only access or only reasonable access to it was across the remaining land of the grantor, an easement of necessity would be implied to exist across the grantor's land. Equity will "imply" the existence of an easement in situations in which it would be inequitable not to do so. In this situation, however, if the grantee had other reasonable means of access to existing roads, the way of necessity would not be implied.

Some easements are implied because of the probable intent of the parties when, at the time of severance of the dominant and servient tenements, there was an obvious and continuous servitude burdening the servient tenement and favoring the dominant one.

Easements may also be acquired by prescription, or adverse use, for the required period. The use must be without the owner's consent and with his knowledge. A prescriptive easement can be acquired by the public as well as by private persons and can be appurtenant to other land or in gross.

Although the rule in England is different, in the United States there are no implied or prescriptive easements for light and air. Therefore, a property owner who wishes to build a building which would block his neighbor's access to sunlight or air is not restricted by any implied or prescriptive easement. However, in one case the court found that a landowner had stated a cause of action in private nuisance by alleging that a neighbor proposed to build a home which would block sunlight from the plaintiff's solar collector, even though the proposed home would conform to existing deed restrictions and ordinances. Prah v. Maretti (1982).

## § 6. Equitable Servitudes and Restrictive Covenants: Generally

Unlike easements, equitable servitudes are created by language of promise in the form of a covenant between parties. An action at law for damages can be brought for breach of covenants that run with the land, touch and concern the land, and involve privity of estate. Yet equitable servitudes render covenants enforceable in equity even when they do not run with the land on the theory that it would be unconscionable to permit a landowner who takes with notice of a restrictive covenant to avoid the covenant when the intent was clear that the burden should pass to him. Enforcement of equitable servitudes through injunctive relief is regarded by some as having no contractual basis even though the servitude itself arises from a covenant. It is based on the concept of notice as contained initially in the old English case of Tulk v. Moxhay (1848).

## § 7.  Real Covenants Running with the Land

Real covenants which are enforceable at law must run with the land, touch and concern the land, and involve privity of estate. Where there is doubt concerning whether a covenant runs with the land, a court will consider whether the original parties to the covenant intended for the covenant to be personal as to them or for it to run with the land. Clark v. Guy Drews Post of American Legion (1945). However, intent alone is not enough, and in order for a covenant to run with the land, it is also necessary to show that the covenant "touches and concerns" the land and that there is privity of estate between the party seeking to enforce the covenant and the one to be bound.

The requirements of touching and concerning the land and privity of estate are at times difficult to meet if they are narrowly applied. Courts have therefore been willing to look to the substance rather than the form of such covenants. Thus, a covenant to pay an annual charge on land to a homeowner's association was held to run with the land although under the common law rule, such a covenant did not touch and concern the land and there was no privity of estate between the homeowners' association and the defendant landowner. Neponsit Property Owners' Ass'n v. Emigrant Industrial Savings Bank (1938).

## § 8. Equitable Servitudes

If a covenant does not meet the requirements at law of running with the land, touching and concerning the land, and privity of estate, it may still be enforceable in equity under the concept of notice originally enunciated in the English case of Tulk v. Moxhay, as mentioned earlier. This concept is that if a party purchases land with notice of the covenant, he should stand in equity in no different position from that of the earlier owner. In short, it would be inequitable not to require performance.

Equitable servitudes can exist in a variety of ways: by a general scheme of development involving plat and covenant recordations, by inference of a general scheme as the result of the developer placing certain restrictions in most or practically all of the deeds (perhaps joined with his expression of intent to pursue a common scheme), by covenants contained in the original deeds, or by restrictions found in separate, usually contemporaneous, agreements among the owners of the lands. Under modern recording statutes, recordation of any instrument which forms part of the chain of title provides constructive notice of the servitude and enables it to be enforced in equity. In the case of a general scheme of development, inquiry notice may also be involved as discussed in this chapter.

Anyone involved in the building scheme, or anyone whose land is affected by deed or covenant, may enforce the equitable servitude against anyone else whose land is burdened.

The difference between equitable servitudes and real covenants which run with the land is of less importance today due to the modern practice of recording subdivision plats and restrictive covenants.

Retention by a developer of a power to eliminate or modify a restrictive covenant unilaterally or by subsequent agreement with one or more of his grantees will customarily be held to vitiate the restrictive covenants and eliminate any presumption of a common scheme of development.

## § 9.   "Inquiry" Notice of Restrictions

Ordinarily a landowner who purchases a lot in a restricted subdivision will have notice of restrictions in his abstract of title because the restrictions will be filed with a subdivision plat and a bill of assurance.

However, in older subdivisions landowners often had notice of restrictions only through covenants in their deeds. The problems that arise with this method of planning a subdivision stem from situations where different covenants are inserted in different deeds or where some deeds contain the restrictive covenants and others do not. Where a general scheme of development is evident from a view of the area, a landowner who has no restrictions in his chain of title would normally be placed on notice to inquire concerning covenants binding other landowners in the subdivision. If such restrictive covenants are found to exist, they create what are known as reciprocal negative easements which benefit and bind all landowners, whether or not the covenants appear in a particular chain of title. Reciprocal negative easements are imposed only where a common grantor conveyed land subject to restrictions which were intended to benefit and bind all land in the subdivision. Thus a landowner whose lot is benefited by the restrictions and who is put on inquiry notice will be bound by similar restrictions even though they do not appear in his chain of title. See Sanborn v. McLean (1925).

The term "reciprocal negative easements" does not refer to easements in a strictly legal sense because easements are created by language of grant, transfer or conveyance. Reciprocal negative easements are akin to restrictive covenants and equitable servitudes.

Retention by a developer of a power to eliminate or modify a restrictive covenant unilaterally or by subsequent agreement with one or more of his grantees will customarily be held to convert such covenants to personal covenants. In effect, the result is to vitiate or nullify a common scheme of development for all practical purposes because the covenants will not run with the land. Although there are a few cases to the contrary, this is the general rule.

On the other hand, it is not uncommon for the covenants to contain a provision allowing a majority or super-majority of landowners to modify or amend the covenants by agreeing to do so in writing and filing it of record. Usually, this provision requires the agreement of roughly sixty percent to seventy-five percent of the owners. This is distinguished from the developer retaining the right in that this is the action of the owners themselves and purchasers in the subdivision are deemed to have bought with notice of this right.

## § 10.  Restrictions as Constituting an Interest in Land

There has been some disagreement as to whether a restrictive covenant or equitable servitude creates a property interest of such a type as to make it compensable in a condemnation proceeding which vitiates the restriction. The majority view is that such an interest is compensable because it extinguishes a valuable property interest and produces loss of value to the land benefited. See Southern California Edison Co. v. Bourgerie (1973). The minority view, which is arguably based more upon considerations of public policy than upon eminent domain law, takes the position that such an interest is not compensable.

It would seem that holding a covenant to be non-compensable would be justified only if the restrictive covenant is viewed as contractual in nature. The origin of restrictive covenants emanated from contract law. However, they have since come to be regarded as interests in land requiring compensation. 2 Nichols on *Eminent Domain* Sec. 5.5(1) (Rev. ed. 1989).

## § 11.  Construction of Restrictive Covenants

Restrictive covenants are generally strictly construed by courts in the sense that a landowner may use his land for any purpose which is not specifically prohibited by the restrictive covenants or by the police power. Therefore, a land developer who wishes, for example, to restrict his subdivision to single family residences should not limit the use merely to "residential" but to "single family residential."

This rule of strict construction of covenants has caused problems where covenants must be applied to situations which were not contemplated at the time the covenants were executed. Courts have not been consistent in determining whether a covenant restricting the use of land to "residential purposes only" prohibits the erection of a condominium. A holding that a condominium (or apartment house) is prohibited goes beyond a strict construction of the wording of the covenant and is questionable. However, if in such a case there is also a restriction against subdividing lots, a condominium might be excluded on the basis that it involves a subdivision of land in the form of airspace.

Generally speaking, a residential restriction barring churches and synagogues is upheld as constitutional and not void as against public policy. This type of restriction merely prescribes certain uses and is therefore distinguishable from a racially restrictive covenant, which excludes people. Nevertheless, courts have on occasion voided restrictions against churches. As noted in the chapter on zoning, zoning ordinances excluding churches in residential districts are more vulnerable to constitutional attack.

## § 12.  The Effect of Parol Representations Regarding Covenants

If parol representations are proved, usually they can be enforced, although the grounds for such enforcement are at times less than clear because of two converging views giving effect to oral covenants. One view is that such covenants are enforceable because they create contracts relating to the use of land. This view, which disregards the Statute of Frauds, is easily applicable where the person claiming the benefit of the promise can take the position of a third party beneficiary to a contract, as where the owner of a lot in a subdivision claims the benefit of a parol restriction imposed upon a subsequent purchaser in the subdivision. Problems can arise, however, in the application of this contract theory where it becomes necessary to expand the concept of third party beneficiaries to subsequent as well as prior purchasers.

Courts have also enforced parol restrictions even while ruling that an interest in land has been created. This view would perhaps apply the Statute of Frauds but accompany it with such usual exceptions as fraud or part performance. In Bristol v. Woodward, (1929), Cardozo wrote that parol restrictions were effective since what had evolved into an interest in land retained enough of its contractual origin to overcome the bar of the Statute of Frauds. This is an interesting hybrid approach which overcomes the excess of technicalities in the interest of a just result.

Today, courts generally regard restrictive covenants as creating interests in land in the nature of an equitable servitude and thus coming within the ambit of the Statute of Frauds. However, the defendant may still be liable under principles of promissory estoppel. Remilong v. Crolla (Wyo.1978).

## § 13.  Standing to Enforce Restrictions

Since restrictive covenants, appurtenant easements, and equitable servitudes are all intended to benefit nearby or adjacent land, the rule in a majority of jurisdictions is that in order to sue to enforce one of these restrictions the plaintiff must own land which is benefited by it. See London County Council v. Allen (1914). This concept has been applied to deny standing to one who had been a developer of a subdivision and had sold all the land in the subdivision except the entrance way, but who still owned land in adjacent subdivisions. Kent v. Koch (1958).

Essentially, this rule follows a negative easement concept as to equitable servitudes.

The minority rule permits a developer who has imposed restrictions, but no longer owns land in the development, to sue to enforce the restrictions on the grounds that an interest was reserved by the conveyance which was not destroyed when the covenantee conveyed all of the land to be benefited, that the breach of the restrictions alone is enough to provide standing to sue, and that no damages resulting from the breach need be proved. Van Sant v. Rose (1913).

## § 14. Enforcement

Some cases involving enforcement deal with restrictive covenants which were written some years ago. For example, a covenant prohibiting "trailers" might be challenged by someone with a double-wide mobile home. Or, a prohibition against mobile homes might be challenged by someone wanting to place a sectional or modular home upon a permanent foundation. The general view is that removing the wheels and gear of a mobile home and placing it on a permanent foundation does not comply with the covenant. Moreover, some courts have said that a sectional or modular home fits into the "mobile home category." Brownfield Subdivision v. McKee (1975). This judicial hostility to mobile homes may be waning as the push for affordable housing becomes more and more urgent. Moreover, sectional or modular homes, when assembled on a permanent foundation, do not appear to the eye to be much different from homes constructed on the site (commonly referred to as "stick built" homes).

Some of the older covenants bar apartment houses but do not mention condominiums. Courts usually say that although ownership of a condominium is the ownership of real property in the form of a unit of airspace and common ownership of the common elements of the regime, the nature of the structure is similar to apartments and thus the covenants apply to condos also.

These cases do not conform to the oft-stated rule that restrictive covenants should be strictly construed. This is particularly true in the mobile home or sectional home cases.

There is a substantial body of case law holding that a restrictive covenant limiting property to residential use only will be enforced against churches. E.g.: McDonald v. Chaffin (Tenn.App.1975). This is usually not viewed as a violation of the First Amendment. However, zoning decisions on this subject are scrutinized to a greater degree and do not enjoy the same latitude accorded restrictive covenants.

When there has been a permanent and drastic change of conditions within the subdivision, most courts will view restrictive covenants with hostility and will not be inclined to enforce them. This is discussed under the next section.

## § 15.  Termination of Restrictive Covenants

Some developers provide that restrictive covenants in a subdivision will terminate after a specified period of time (usually 25 or 30 years) unless a majority or larger percentage of the landowners reaffirm them, or alternatively, that the covenants may be terminated at the end of such period if a majority or larger percentage of the landowners file an instrument to that effect. There are other variations on such provisions.

The reason for such provisions is that in their absence, the only way restrictive covenants can be terminated is by court decree. In such a situation, a court of equity would have to find that the character of the subdivision had changed so drastically since the covenants were imposed that it would be inequitable and without any appreciable value to the property owners to enforce them any longer. This "change of conditions" reasoning is similar to that applied in the law of waste and in zoning cases. The issue almost invariably arises in situations in which outer lots in the subdivision are affected by nearby commercial development. While courts will take such conditions into account in determining the current situation within the subdivision, they will generally not invalidate the covenants to benefit buffer or outer lots unless the residential character of the total subdivision has been impaired. Estoppel, waiver, laches and acquiescence are other doctrines which enter in where the covenants have been violated on a substantial basis without complaint.

Most courts will not invalidate restrictive covenants simply because zoning regulations permit some other use. If the covenants are more restrictive, they will normally be enforced. A rezoning, however, is some evidence that the character of the subdivision has drastically changed. In a rare situation in which the zoning was more limiting than the covenants, the stricter zoning regulations would apply if they were not arbitrary or unreasonable. As a matter of simple logic, with regard to the issue of whether a rezoning by itself could vitiate a restrictive covenant, it should be apparent that if the exercise of the police power destroyed property rights, it would amount to a taking.

Although tax forfeitures and tax deeds normally extinguish prior rights, the interests of other landowners in a subdivision, as dominant tenants, could not be extinguished by a tax sale and tax deed of one of the lots. Thus a tax deed does not terminate an equitable servitude, the benefit of which is possessed by other landowners, nor should it terminate the servitude in the lot sold for taxes since the purchaser of the tax deed should have the benefit of the restrictions as well. A condemnation action would potentially eliminate restrictive covenants on the lot, since the taking is total, but it should properly also involve compensation for loss suffered by other landowners in the subdivision due to the termination of the servitude.

## § 16.  Modification or Waiver

The general rule is that where the grantor-developer and the grantee agree that the developer reserves the right to modify or waive the covenants, there is no general scheme of development created within the subdivision. Thus, the covenants are reduced to being personal in nature and a new purchaser is not bound by them. They do not run with the land. Practically speaking, the result of doing this is to vitiate the enforcement of the covenants within the subdivision. Suttle v. Bailey (1961).

However, it is not unusual for the covenants to provide that a certain percentage of the landowners, which would be more than a majority and often as many as two-thirds or three-fourths, may agree to modify or alter the covenants by filing of record such changes as they may agree to.

Apparently, the difference in these rules stems from the fact that in the situation of the grantor-developer, he is able unilaterally to modify or waive covenants on a personal, ad hoc basis, whereas a majority or super-majority of landowners would be acting on behalf of all landowners and the alterations would apply to all the lots equally. Moreover, the landowners would have purchased with notice that such changes in the covenants could occur under those circumstances. In the second situation there is a common provision for all lot owners relating to the entire subdivision.

Modern condominium developments and planned unit developments, as well as many large scale development projects rely on covenants and designation of an association to administer and interpret the restrictions. Because these are usually large scale residential undertakings the covenants take on the role of constituting a "private government" that may have the power to regulate many details of the daily life of the residents. A body of law— usually called "community association law" or "common interest developments law"—has grown up in this area. Owners of condominium units often find themselves in disputes with neighbors or the governing association. For example, a leading California case, Nahrstedt v. Lakeside Village Condominium Association, Inc. (1994) involved an owner in a 530–unit condo development who sued the association to enjoin enforcement of a covenant against pets. Her claim was based on the fact that her three pet cats never went outside and made no noise, and in fact they were only discovered when a nosy neighbor peered through the plaintiff's curtains from outside. The court concluded that it would be unwise for courts to inject themselves into issues dealing with the reasonableness of the covenants, because a raft of lawsuits on the reasonableness of covenants would expose the other property owners to considerable legal expense. Some courts have drawn a distinction between challenges to the original covenants that are part of every owner's title and rules and regulations adopted subsequently by the governing body under the association's by-laws.

## CHAPTER IV

# THE PLANNING PROCESS, THE MASTER PLAN AND THE OFFICIAL MAP

## § 1. Background

Planning is the process which ultimately results in a comprehensive or master plan or an interrelated group of plans followed by ordinances regulating the use of land in a metropolitan area. These ordinances involve the exercise of the police power through zoning, regulation of subdivision developments, street plans, plans for public facilities, building regulations and the like. Properly, planning should precede zoning, since zoning and other regulatory ordinances merely amount to the execution of the planning process. To be effective, planning should stem from comprehensive studies of the urban area with particular reference to projected growth trends and public needs over the next ten years or more, which of course will be based largely on what has happened, what is happening, and what appears likely to happen in relation to the urban area. These studies will result in what is known as the "master plan," "comprehensive plan," "general plan," or just "the plan." This plan has been appropriately referred to by Professor Charles Haar of Harvard as an "impermanent constitution"—impermanent in the sense that it must be rewritten periodically to conform to new studies and new trends in urban development. But it is a "constitution" in the sense that the validity of zoning ordinances and rezoning will depend in large measure on whether they conform to the master plan. Contemporaneous with the master plan will come the "official map" in states having statutes providing for official maps. The map will show the location of major streets, public facilities both in existence and projected, and other such landmarks. Subdivision developers will have to plan their own developments in accordance with the official map. Some statutes provide for a number of maps— showing major street locations, parks and playgrounds, police and fire stations, and the like. All of this, plus continuing study by urban planners, forms a part of the planning process from which ultimately emanates specific ordinances enacted pursuant to such planning.

## § 2. Content of the Master Plan

Traditional master plans of urban communities take into account the location and type of activities taking place on the land and the design and type of physical structures and facilities serving these activities. Long-range projections of population and employment trends are considered. This is the approach of the Standard City Planning Enabling Act (SPEA), an early model for many states, and it serves a number of objectives, such as prediction of physical facility needs, allocation of land to desired activities, and preservation of open space for aesthetic and recreational needs. This planning process is designed to enable a locality to plan for construction of schools, streets, water and sewage facilities, fire and police protection, and other public amenities, while the private use of land is controlled by zoning and subdivision ordinances enacted in compliance with the plan.

The recent Model Land Development Code, the ultimate impact of which remains to be seen, provides for a "Local Land Development Plan" which is broader in scope than the traditional master plan, since it not only takes into account the physical development of a community but also reflects consideration of economic and social data of the area and the economic and social impact of developmental proposals. Unlike the older SPEA, the Model Land Development Code assumes that planners for a local government may or will be required to deal with state or regional planning agencies which are increasingly prevalent. The Model Code requires specification of short-term objectives so that planners will be involved in achieving goals as well as formulating them. This act further requires that the local governing body keep the plan current by adopting land development reports at regular intervals. The Code offers the potential for a major step forward in planning and development.

## § 3. Legal Effect of the Master Plan

The local governing body adopting a master plan derives its authority from a state statute or statutes which either enable or require local governments to adopt and enforce plans through local legislative enactments. A few states, such as Arkansas, Indiana, Kentucky and Minnesota, have enabling acts which require a locality to adopt a plan as a prerequisite to such land use controls as zoning and subdivision regulation. However, most states, and the Model Land Development Code, do not make planning a mandatory prerequisite to land use regulation although the planning process is given great weight in the Code.

The master plan, which is often formulated by a planning commission operating under the aegis of the local governing body, has no legal effect until it is adopted by the governing body. Cochran v. Planning Board of City of Summit (1965). After it is legally adopted, it is somewhat akin to a constitution, since subsequent land use regulation must be compatible to or in conformity with the plan.

Any master plan contemplating development over a period of years requires periodic amendments which modify it based on trends and developments which have occurred and which were not contemplated at the time the plan was adopted. Where special legislative procedures for adoption of a plan are required, it has been held that the same procedures must be followed for amendments to the plan and that the city's general powers to amend ordinances are not applicable. Dalton v. City and County of Honolulu (1969).

Although most jurisdictions continue to hold that the future land use designations shown on the master plan are merely guides for official action and not binding on the city, some recent cases have suggested that the plan may have some legal effect. This development is usually referred to as the "consistency doctrine." In its most extreme form the doctrine holds that a city that departs from the plan in its decisions on zoning or development bears the burden of proof in justifying its departure. Other states hold that although the plan should not have such an extreme rigid effect, nevertheless the plan is a major factor in determining the validity of the city's decision that is a departure from the plan.

## § 4.  The Official Map

The official map sets out in detail existing and planned streets, sewers, water lines, parks and playgrounds and other public facilities. It often establishes set-back lines for future streets and may also establish set-back lines for the widening of existing streets. There may be separate official maps—i.e., street maps, parks and playgrounds, and the like.

Historically, the official map preceded the master plan, but in the planning process the master plan ideally comes first. The drafters of New York's 1926 official map act and of a 1935 model act, Edward M. Bassett and Frank B. Williams, have distinguished the official map from the master plan as follows: the plan provides general information and includes many factors not shown on the map, while the map reflects accurate details; the plan is plastic, while the map is rigid. In some jurisdictions, such as New York and Wisconsin, the map is legally binding and the plan is not, for the plan must be adopted by the planning commission only and is thus unofficial, while the official map must be adopted by the local governing body. This procedure or policy is not universal by any means, however. Moreover, the differences in legal effect between the plan and the map should not be overemphasized because a knowledgeable landowner will generally not build in the bed of a future street even if it is included only in an unofficial document.

As in the case of most master plans, before an official map can have any legal effect it must be adopted by the local governing body, and that body must have authority to adopt and enforce it. Such authority is derived through state enabling statutes which give localities the right to adopt official maps for the purpose of reserving land for future streets, sewers, water lines, parks, schools and other public needs, and to control development in reserved areas by requiring landowners to obtain building permits as a prerequisite to building in an area reserved on the map. Failure to obtain a permit generally results in no compensation for the unauthorized structure at the time the reserved land is actually taken. Compensation should occur in circumstances in which a landowner secured official approval which was erroneously given but which he relied upon in good faith to his detriment.

As a practical matter, cities cannot afford to pay a landowner compensation at the time the land is reserved for a future public purpose, and the vast majority of states have statutes which provide for compensation at the time the land is actually taken by the locality. In the few jurisdictions which provide for compensation at the time the land is "reserved" by the filing of the official map, the right to reserve is rarely exercised.

Official map enabling statutes have been upheld constitutionally on grounds that the enactment of the map is within the police power of the state since it is for the protection of the health, safety, and welfare of the community. Where the party attacking the statute can show no injury resulting from the reservation of some of his land on the map, the map will not be stricken as an unconstitutional taking of property without compensation. Headley v. City of Rochester (1936). A probable exception would be if all of the owner's land were reserved or if the reservation served to create an incumbrance on the title. Forster v. Scott (1893). In most instances a landowner must exhaust his remedies by seeking a building permit or a variance as a prerequisite to alleging that a map ordinance constitutes a taking without compensation. Some unfavorable decisions have also been based on the court's conclusion that potential hardship will result.

To withstand constitutional attack it is essential that official map laws include savings provisions to protect individual landowners from hardship resulting from the reservation of their property on the map. Such provisions typically permit the local authority to issue a building permit in a reserved area where failure to do so would result in unnecessary hardship, such as where compliance with the map would render impossible a fair return from the property. State ex rel. Miller v. Manders (1957). The standards for what constitutes an unnecessary hardship are somewhat similar to those applied to the granting of zoning variances. As in zoning, some states allow the permit to be issued if there would be "unnecessary hardship" or "practical difficulties" involved.

## § 5. State and Regional Planning

There is an increasing tendency away from local planning and toward regional or statewide planning. Proposed federal legislation, which has not been enacted (but has come close), would spur this tendency. Some states have already enacted statutes designed to promote state or regional planning. Small states, such as Vermont and Hawaii, have adopted somewhat disparate statutes embracing the state planning concept. The Vermont statute has strong environmental overtones and contemplates the adoption by an environmental board of a rather broad state land use plan. The Hawaii statute involves a somewhat more traditional classification of lands by a state land use commission, although it too has environmental overtones in its attention to conservation of certain areas and consideration of similar factors. Hawaii reviews its situation every five years, which is desirable due to changing circumstances.

Regional planning is more conducive to the situation of states encompassing large land areas or to situations involving metropolitan areas which encompass portions of two or more states. Examples of the latter include such areas as the New York City–Newark–Philadelphia complex, the Los Angeles–Long Beach metropolitan area, and the Chicago metropolitan complex which actually extends into Northern Indiana and upward toward Wisconsin. A single metropolitan area which involves two or more states requires the use of such devices as interstate compacts and the passage by more than one state legislature of identical statutes creating agencies or "authorities" with powers over situations involving more than one state.

Some intrastate regional planning results from the recognition in progressive jurisdictions that in a metropolitan area comprehensive planning is not possible without taking into account the situation of all of the communities which comprise the metropolitan area. Every city of any size has suburban or satellite communities. To plan only for the central city, without considering the situation of the satellite communities, would make no sense. This situation exists not only in major metropolitan areas, such as those mentioned previously, but also in such medium-sized or smaller metropolitan areas as Central Arkansas (Little Rock–North Little Rock and environs), Central Oklahoma (Oklahoma City–Norman and environs), the Tri–Cities area of Northeastern Tennessee and Southwestern Virginia, the Raleigh–Durham area of Central North

Carolina, the Madison area in Wisconsin, the Phoenix–Tempe area in Arizona, and many more.

Unfortunately, most planning and land use controls are still predicated upon essentially local powers and considerations. The lack of regional planning and zoning, as indicated in the chapter on
zoning and discrimination, has caused some courts
to mandate housing requirements for all outlying
communities or townships in order to overcome
discrimination on the basis of socio-economic status
and race. If regional planning and zoning existed,
each regional planning area could disperse land uses
in a reasonable way within the area without providing for every type of housing component in every
township or community. In some states, notably
Oregon, local planning is mandated and a local
government that does not engage in a process prescribed by the legislature faces a state-level plan.
California does not go so far, but that state has
mandated several items that cities must incorporate
in their plans, e.g., provisions for low-cost housing.

An example of a state which has looked more
toward regional planning is Minnesota, which some
years ago provided by statute for regional development commissions, the result of which would permit coordinated development of the Minneapolis–St.
Paul metropolitan area including comprehensive
planning involving review of the actions of local
governmental units.

Interstate compacts today often have an environmental underlay as illustrated by the California decisions involving the Lake Tahoe area. On the other hand, many interstate compacts which affect land use simply involve such public facilities as the interconnection through bridges, tunnels and the like of the New York City–Newark area.

A useful summary of the Lake Tahoe Regional Planning Compact, the Vermont statute, and the Adirondack Park Agency Act is set out in D. Hagman, *Urban and Land Development* 117–120 (1973). The powers of the different governing bodies vary in some respects, but there are many basic similarities with regard to planning for the particular area involved.

The history of these various entities seems to be that when they are created, lawsuits usually or often result which test their constitutional validity or the scope of their powers. The outcome may be determined by how liberally a court is willing to construe its state constitution, which quite often will contain relatively antiquated provisions "freezing" the prerogatives of counties and cities into a particular mold and allowing relatively little flexibility. In Mogilner v. Metropolitan Plan Commission (1957), the Indiana Court took the liberal approach in considering a statute authorizing a single planning and zoning department for the entire county in every county containing a city of the first class. The metropolitan planning commission was to develop a plan for the entire county. The act was attacked on numerous "particulars" which included the "taking" issue, equal privileges or immunities and equal protection, procedural due process, separation of powers, vagueness, the old rule about every act embracing one subject, and violation of constitutional provisions as to where county administrative powers must be vested. Despite these and other laundry list allegations, the act was upheld.

The Lake Tahoe compact was upheld in People ex rel. Younger v. County of El Dorado (1971). This case had strong environmental overtones, and the California Court pointed out that the basic concept of the compact was to provide for the planning, conservation and resource development of the region as a whole without destroying the environment. Once again, constitutional arguments put forth the sanctity of local governmental powers. This argument took numerous forms, including tax privileges, preemption of local governmental powers, and improper delegation of powers. Equal protection was argued, as were matters pertaining to appointment rather than election of the governing body, a "one person-one vote" argument as to county representation, and some offshoots of the foregoing. The court was impressed by the goals the legislature sought to achieve, the fact that they could best be achieved on a regional basis, and the unique problems of the area due to its interstate nature.

The more progressive approach is to uphold such regional schemes wherever there is no direct conflict with state law. Not only is regional planning desirable in general, but in many situations planning is ineffective without it.

## § 6. Local Planning

Despite the trend in recent years toward recognition of the need for regional planning or state planning, most planning still takes place at the local level. This can create conflicts between counties and cities exercising overlapping jurisdiction as well as between neighboring municipalities which are part of a suburban or metropolitan area. This is illustrated by Borough of Cresskill v. Borough of Dumont (1954), which involved four adjoining boroughs and in which an amendatory ordinance of one borough changing a residential zone to a business district did not take into account the contiguous residential areas of the plaintiff boroughs. The court upheld the standing of the other boroughs to bring the suit and held that Dumont had to give consideration to the situation of its neighboring boroughs. The ordinance was invalidated as amounting to "spot zoning" and thus not in accord with the comprehensive plan. In Wrigley Properties, Inc. v. City of Ladue (Mo.1963), it was held that a proposed zoning change authorizing a shopping center was more for the benefit of other cities and towns than for Ladue. Thus, to the contrary of Dumont, the locality could not be penalized to aid its neighbors. In another case, Township of River Vale v. Town of Orangetown (2d Cir.1968), rezoning in a town in New York gave rise to an action brought by a neighboring community in New Jersey, which was held to have standing to sue.

Regardless of these cases, however, zoning decisions remain largely local in nature and usually remain unaffected by situations prevailing outside of the municipal boundaries.

In terms of the operational planning framework within a community, there will usually be a planning commission with a staff (or a planning department), or some other form of planning agency under another name. The members of the commission will customarily be appointed by the municipal governing body, and there will usually be a full-time technical staff of trained city planners (whose status will be discussed at greater length in a subsequent section). Recommendations of the commission are subject to the action of the city governing body when they propose ordinances or seek to revise existing ordinances. One unfortunate feature of the planning process is that local planning commissions are often composed to a large extent of the very people who are most affected by the decisions—building contractors, developers, real estate brokers, and architects (who often work with developers on projects). This is particularly true in smaller or medium-sized urban areas.

Federal aid, and urban renewal and redevelopment in particular, in effect demand that a community engage in comprehensive planning and develop various types of local plans. This situation tends or helps to freeze local planning into a particular mold. But whatever name is employed (such as "internal development plan" or "general plan"), statutes or regulations of government agencies are usually only referring to what is commonly called the master plan.

The Model Land Development Code also provides for a "local development plan," but its description of it is general enough to allow for more flexibility in permitting differing views of the planning process. (See §§ 3–101 and 3–106, Model Land Development Code.)

## § 7.  National Planning

Probably the closest semblance to anything that may be called national planning today is in the area of the environment stemming from such acts as the National Environmental Policy Act (NEPA). (Environmental controls are discussed in a later chapter and will not be dealt with here.) These controls, however, are somewhat negative in nature in the sense that they are directed toward protecting the environment and thereby preventing a particular harm rather than promoting a positive, comprehensive plan. Of course, there is also planning associated with national parks, national rivers, and government lands in general. But there is no comprehensive national land use program at the present time which would affect state, regional or local planning. Federal laws and policies, other than NEPA and related acts, affect what is done on a local basis—as in the case of housing, urban renewal and federal taxation. But the effects are peripheral in nature and ancillary to the basic intent of such statutes and policies.

During the great depression of the 1930's, there was a National Resources Board which advocated national planning. Moreover, during the depression and World War II, our economy in particular became one which was planned to a very large extent and remains so today. Beginning in the mid–1950's and developing extensively in the 1960's and early 1970's, urban planning was heavily influenced by massive federal aid for such programs as low-income housing and community development involving urban renewal and rehabilitation, model cities, acquisition of open space, and the construction of neighborhood and water and sewer facilities. Most of these programs were suspended or terminated in 1973, except for funding for existing projects. However, the Housing and Community Development Act of 1974, P.L. 93–383, consolidated urban renewal and several community development programs into a new approach designed to give localities more control. Federal aid in other areas affects local land use activities through funding for such projects as airports, water and sewer facilities, highways and mass transportation, public facilities of various kinds, and various conservation or environmental activities. But all of this is an ad hoc kind of approach, and there has never been an overall, cogent national land use policy. (See generally on this subject, Vestal, Planning for Urban Areas: The Fight for Coherency, 56 *Iowa L.Rev.* 19 (1970).)

Congress has in recent years developed an increased awareness of this problem, however. This was manifested in 1970 by the Urban Growth and New Community Development Act, 42 U.S.C.A. § 4501 et seq., and by the introduction of a bill intended to establish a national land use policy. The urban growth act noted the rapid and uneven growth of urban centers and related problems, observed that federal programs affect urban development and require coordination, and concluded that the federal government should develop a national urban growth policy. It set forth certain worthwhile objectives relative to wise use of physical and human resources, maintaining economic strength in all areas, reversing trends of population migration, dealing with problems of poverty and employment, encouraging good housing, improving the role of the federal government in community and urban planning, strengthening governmental institutions to contribute to balanced urban growth, and improving coordination among federal programs. It required an urban growth report from the President in every even-numbered year. This act seems to have had relatively little impact on federal activities or legislation in Congress. Federal programs which affect urban areas remain fragmented.

Despite the introduction of bills in Congress establishing a national land use policy and the backing of them on occasion by the administration, they have failed to pass both houses of Congress, although by increasingly narrow margins. Essentially, such bills would require the states to develop planning procedures, assess resources, develop certain types of data, inventory the land needed and useful for certain purposes, identify critical areas and problems, hold public hearings, and create a land use planning agency. The states would be required to develop planning and regulatory programs taking into account the various factors which planners normally consider. The federal government would establish an office and an advisory board to oversee the state programs and would make grants. Local planning obviously would be affected and, to some extent, directed in certain ways. Obviously, such a program would lead to much more land use planning on a larger scale and would take into account state, regional, and occasionally national considerations.

The Model Land Development Code "looks" in much the same direction although without the federal component. It is apparent that the trend is toward a more coordinated, public control of land use on a much wider scale.

## § 8. Publicly Owned Land

An enormous amount of land, particularly in the western states, is owned by the United States. It approximates one-third of all of our acreage. Most of this is under the jurisdiction of the Interior Department (particularly the Bureau of Land Management) or the Forest Service. Aside from the control and planning emanating from those agencies, bills have been introduced from time to time that would require the development of land use plans principally to protect and preserve public lands.

There have been some proposals which would lead to disposition of federal land to private owners, and this could eventually come to pass. Environmentalists, however, have opposed bills potentially disposing of public lands. The pressure of the energy crisis promoted the idea of selling or leasing mineral producing properties for private development. This led and will most certainly lead in the future to a clash of values. A movement, mostly in the so-called public land states, known as the "sagebrush rebellion" emerged in the 1980's. Central to that movement is the claim that under the Constitution these states are entitled to ownership of the public lands within. The claim is based on the "equal footing" clause in the Constitution specifying that new states are admitted to the Union on the same footing as the original 13. Federal courts have, so far, rejected the claim.

## § 9. New Towns

A "new town" or "new community" is the most planned of all communities since it is planned from its inception and develops according to the plan.

Under the English concept, a new town was an independent planned community which existed without interdependence on a nearby city and was large enough to permit various types of housing, economic and social opportunities, and public facilities. During the planning process, the allocation of space to various uses was determined. Such towns were started in open country and were surrounded by "green belts."

In the United States, however, new towns are customarily satellite communities lying within the orbit of or near to a substantially larger metropolitan area. They are developments on a large scale usually undertaken by a development corporation. They follow a plan providing for various kinds of housing, businesses, schools, churches and social and cultural facilities. They are carefully designed to promote the amenities of nature and eliminate or greatly minimize the undesirable attributes of urban life. They may or may not provide land for industry.

The new town concept is generally credited to Ebenezer Howard, an English stenographer and inventor, who developed a concept for "Garden City" which would alleviate overcrowding and re-establish the balance between the country and the city. He presented this idea in a book written shortly before the turn of the century. Before he died in 1928, he had seen two new towns come into being in England. The concept which he developed later became national policy there, and new towns are being built or planned in most modern nations today.

In America, even before the concept of Howard's Garden City, there were towns which were developed as "company towns" by industries wishing to locate outside of urban areas. Examples are Gary, Indiana, built by U.S. Steel, and Kohler, Wisconsin, which was the work of the Kohler Company. But these early company towns were not fully planned and did not control growth. Pullman, Illinois, however, was a company town which provided various cultural and social facilities, with housing varying according to income. Kingsport, Tennessee, was an advance beyond Pullman in that it provided for democratic local government and an early planning body, although the plan and the early zoning restrictions used were not adequate. Crossett, Arkansas, a smaller company town planned by Harland Bartholomew and Associates of St. Louis, was more of a model of planning than probably any of the others.

Somewhat different from the company towns and in some respects the forerunner of the modern suburb were the real estate communities which sought to create residential developments on the edge of cities. These communities eliminated industry and attempted to isolate themselves from urban growth through planning and through various restrictions. Although these were business ventures, these communities became self-governing, developed a sense of community, and maintained property values.

The first of the garden city new towns in America was Radburn, New Jersey, created in the late 1920's by Clarence Stein and Henry Wright. (This followed an experience by Stein of several years earlier when he developed a planned neighborhood in New York City called Sunnyside Garden Apartments.) The Radburn plan attempted to segregate roads and services from pedestrian, park and open space areas.

The federal government followed the Radburn concept during the Franklin Roosevelt administration by building three planned communities— Greenbelt, Maryland; Greenhills, Ohio; and Greendale, Wisconsin. But the two leading examples of new towns in the United States today were privately financed—Reston, Virginia, and Columbia, Maryland. Both seek to follow the garden concept enunciated by Howard, although the planning techniques which have been applied are far more advanced and sophisticated.

New communities involve a physical development which provides a full scale of urban activities but utilizes greenbelts, a variety of carefully planned uses, open space and a limited population or area, a complete range of social and public services, a development which is economically stable and will provide an adequate return on the investment, and a politically self-governing unit. They are intended to provide for a multiplicity of uses and income groups. They obviously entail a carefully conceived plan which is long-range and continuing.

The Urban Growth and New Community Development Act of 1970, supra, created a Federal Community Development Corporation which was empowered to make grants and loans to new town developers. The New Communities Act of 1968, 12 U.S.C.A. §§ 371, 1464; 42 U.S.C.A. §§ 1492, 3901 et seq., provided for guarantee of financial obligations incurred by developers of new towns. New towns have also benefited from federal housing legislation particularly when they provide for low-cost housing as a component part of the development.

As might be expected, new towns have spawned little litigation. However, in Sierra Club v. Lynn

(5th Cir.1974), the San Antonio Ranch new town, which involved a bond issue guaranteed by HUD, was attacked by environmentalists who argued that the development would pollute an underground water formation which was the sole water supply for San Antonio. Substantial efforts had been made by HUD and the developer to assure that the underground aquifer would be unaffected, and the court sustained the district court decision to permit the project. The case is perhaps most significant because the court of appeals went into the purposes behind the Urban Growth and New Community Development Act and found them commendable. In Clem v. Cooper Communities, Inc. (E.D.Ark.1972), the court was concerned with the governance of an improvement district in Cherokee Village, Arkansas, which was created for the purpose of maintaining roads, streets, and recreational facilities and providing fire protection. An Arkansas law providing for appointment of the commissioners by the circuit court was sustained against an argument that the equal protection clause required that the commissioners be elected by popular vote. It was also contended that the development company would control the district. The court upheld the statute. Generally to the contrary, however, is Burrey v. Embarcadero Municipal Improvement District (1971). The governance problem is a serious one in many planned communities. The developer wishes to control matters as long as possible in order to carry out his plan. The people are used to democratic procedures and are not used to a fashionable, well-planned equivalent of a company town. Developers err when they do not adequately provide for a transitional sharing of control.

## § 10.  The Planners

The planning function ultimately gave rise to a planning profession. In the beginning, planning was chiefly the province of architects and engineers. While they were not cast aside by any means, there gradually began to develop a specialized group, which might or might not have such backgrounds, who had devoted their education and experience solely or largely to urban planning. Moreover, universities developed schools of urban planning.

The City Beautiful Movement in the early 20th century has been referred to as the rebirth of planning. Basically, this form of planning dealt with civic centers, thoroughfares and parks. Plans for public buildings and open spaces were connected with parkways and boulevards. This emphasized the necessity of relating buildings to their sites. It made manifest the need for comprehensive city planning. It also recognized the connection between planning and socioeconomic considerations. It was limited, however, by the high costs incidental to it and the absence of public controls over private actions (such as subdivision ordinances). The movement gave rise to two permanent additions to the American scheme of planning: planning commissions and professional advisors. Architects and engineers served the latter function in the early years. Planning commissions were given an added boost by the

Standard City Planning Enabling Act promulgated
by the Department of Commerce in 1928. Lawyers,
along with engineers and architects, became increasingly involved in the process in the 1920's,
state enabling legislation became common along
with city planning, and comprehensive zoning blos-
somed.

Universities began to offer courses in city planning early in the century, beginning at Harvard.
These early courses were generally related to offer-
ings in landscape architecture, and modern schools
of city planning did not develop until later. By the
beginning of the depression of the 1930's, however,
comprehensive planning had become fairly well accepted, spurred on not only by the Commerce Department's model acts, but also by the work of such
lawyer pioneers as Edward M. Bassett and Alfred
Bettman.

The American Society of Planning Officials
(ASPO) came into being in 1934 and was the institutional vehicle of the new profession. Moreover,
thinking coalesced during the depression years to
connect physical planning with social and economic
factors as well as to recognize the need for continui-
ty in planning. The post-World War II era gave rise
to growth of planning activities by providing more
staff support and more funding. The concept of a
full-time resident staff of professionals, which had
come into fruition before the war, was implemented
in much greater measure after it. Schools of city
planning grew in number and in curricular sophisti-

cation. Planning studies increased in number and in depth, particularly with regard to transportation. Moreover, as the federal government entered the picture on a major basis, impetus to the formation of planning staffs increased. The Housing Act of 1954 was particularly significant in this respect. (See, more specifically on the foregoing discussion, the material in Wright & Gitelman, *Land Use* 753–770 (5th ed.1997).

Modern approaches to planning are often characterized by the attitudes or thought processes of the planners involved. A planner may be of the traditional school and wish to deal largely with the physical environment. At the other extreme is the social planner who wishes to utilize the planning process to further social welfare goals. In between is a physical planner who is sensitized to social needs and will take such criteria into account. On the fringes is the social policy planner who is concerned only with the social effects of physical planning and with great questions of social policy and programming. These views must be tempered somewhat by the Code of Professional Responsibility of the American Institute of Planners (AIP), which recognizes the obligation to take into consideration the needs of disadvantaged groups but also speaks of accommodating the client's or employer's interest with the public interest. The tone of the Code would seem to exclude purely social concerns if those considerations could not be accommodated without emasculating reasonable planning procedures.

## § 11.  The Legal Status of Planners

The planning profession is so new that it is still struggling to establish its acceptability and to carve out its appropriate niche. Governmental bodies and courts are at times inclined to look upon the planners with some skepticism and to view them as somewhat less recognizable as an independent profession when compared to law, architecture and engineering. (Courts perhaps forget, or are unaware, that the greatest of all English architects, Sir Christopher Wren, was actually a geometry professor at Oxford.)

This peculiar attitude is manifested in New Jersey Chapter, American Institute of Planners v. New Jersey State Board of Professional Planners (1967). The case involved a statute exempting architects, engineers and land surveyors from having to pass an examination for a planner's license. The work of the licensed planner was defined statutorily to relate largely to the development of master plans and the offering of professional planning services related to the plan and to land development in general. The AIP objected on the basis of equal protection, pointing out the requirements for planners as to substantial education and experience. (Of course, the architects, engineers and surveyors already had to take licensing examinations related directly to their fields. But the planners argued that planning was a distinct and separate profession.) Noting that modern planning had its roots in architecture and engineering, the court upheld the exemption.

Aside from recognition, a more specific problem relates to the work of planners. Practically speaking, they participate quite heavily in drafting land use ordinances of various kinds—sometimes doing the job exclusively, perhaps with some advice and assistance from the city attorney's office or from outside counsel. An ordinance involving zoning or subdivision regulations is, of course, an amalgam of the application of planning principles, requirements relating to topography and land formations, mathematical formulas and ratios, and legal requirements and considerations. It is complicated and technical, but it is also a legal document. Most attorneys and most planners do not possess the expertise to draft a comprehensive zoning or subdivision ordinance by themselves. These facts are recognized by the AIP. Therefore, when a planner participates in drafting or drafts such an ordinance or appears as an advocate before governmental bodies, is he practicing law?

The case law is sparse on this point. Generally speaking, laymen cannot appear before state agencies in a representative capacity in adversary proceedings. Moreover, in one lower court case in Illinois, a consent decree prohibited a Chicago planning firm from drafting zoning ordinances. In a lower court Pennsylvania case, a planner was held not to have the authority to practice before the board of adjustment. Consequently, it would appear that planners who are not lawyers are constricted in what they may do outside of their capacity as employees or consultants to planning boards or similar agencies.

What the planner does in his capacity as an advisor, however, unavoidably laps over into the legal arena. The planning staff must advise the planning commission on particular applications for rezoning, for example. This often involves the issue of whether this would constitute "spot zoning," which is purely a legal concept, or "strip zoning," which may have legal consequences. The staff must concern itself with whether applications for special use permits (or permits with equivalent nomenclature) fall within the provisions of the ordinance allowing such permits, or whether an application for a variance meets the legal criteria applied to it. Planners thus inevitably deal with a narrow field of law, and if they are not attorneys they should operate in cooperation with the city attorney's office or with independent counsel.

# CHAPTER V

# REGULATION OF LAND DEVELOPMENT

## § 1.  Property Rights and the Police Power

Contrary to popular adage, property rights have never been absolute in Anglo–American law. But in England after the Magna Carta private property could not be taken for public use without due process of law and later not without compensation to the owner (according to Blackstone). Similarly, the 5th Amendment to the United States Constitution, which also applies to the states through the 14th Amendment, prohibits the taking of property without just compensation as do almost all of the state constitutions. Yet the mere regulation of the use of property does not traditionally entitle the owner to compensation and is justified by the proper exercise of the police power, a concept applied as early as the case of the Charles River Bridge v. Warren Bridge (1837). The police power is generally defined as the power to legislate for the health, morals, safety, and welfare of the community, and this power can be exercised even though it imposes burdens on the use and enjoyment of private property.

Land use was regulated rather severely throughout the nineteenth century. Justice Holmes, then on the Massachusetts Supreme Court, pointed out in 1889, however, that the power of eminent domain and the police power differed only in degree and no clear line could be drawn between the two. Rideout v. Knox, (1889). In 1922, Holmes wrote that "while property may be regulated to a certain extent, if regulation goes too far it will be recognized as a taking." Pennsylvania Coal Co. v. Mahon (1922).

Some lower courts have found that regulations placing land in public "reservation" for possible future condemnation are takings if landowners are deprived of the use of their property for an unreasonably long time. Generally a one-year reservation period is considered reasonable, while a three-year period has been held to be a taking.

Ordinances controlling land development have also been attacked on grounds that they violate the due process and equal protection clauses of the 14th Amendment by depriving the owner of the most beneficial or profitable use of his land. But as long as the regulation operates to protect the health, safety or welfare of the community, as long as it is not arbitrary, capricious, or unreasonable, and as long as it operates uniformly upon all landowners similarly situated, it will be upheld. Thus where a city ordinance prohibited the operation of a livery stable within a designated area, the ordinance was upheld on grounds that it was not clearly unreasonable or arbitrary, that it operated uniformly on all landowners in the area, that the area was not arbitrarily selected, and that it is within the police power to regulate such activities within a thickly

populated area. The court pointed out that even
though the operation of such a business is not a
nuisance per se, it can be a nuisance in fact and in
law under certain circumstances. Reinman v. City
of Little Rock (1915). The burden of proving that an
ordinance is unconstitutional is on the party seeking to invalidate it, and an ordinance has been
upheld as a valid police regulation where the landowner failed to show how enforcement of the ordinance would diminish the value of the property,
even though the city had failed to show why the
ordinance was necessary or reasonable. Goldblatt v.
Town of Hempstead (1962).

A leading New York decision, Fred F. French Inv.
Co. v. City of New York (1976), held that a regulation which rendered the property unsuitable for any
reasonable productive use was violative of due process and thus void. The court refused to find that
the regulation was a "taking" on grounds that a
regulation without actual appropriation or occupation can never be a taking in eminent domain. The
decision indicates that Justice Holmes was merely
using a metaphor when he held in *Pennsylvania
Coal* that a regulation can become a taking. However, recent U.S. Supreme Court decision have accepted the statement literally.

For quite some time after the holding in *Pennsylvania Coal,* the Supreme Court did not enunciate a
clear test for determining when a land use regulation amounts to a taking. Even in the light of recent
cases, one can only surmise what principles will be
applied and in what situation a taking will be

declared. It seems clear that the fact that a regulation causes a substantial diminution in value of land is not controlling, as long as the property can still be used to the economic benefit of the owner. See, e.g., Penn Central Transportation Co. v. New York City (1978); Hadacheck v. Sebastian (1915). However, it seems equally clear today that a total deprivation of reasonable economic use will amount to a taking. Lucas v. South Carolina Coastal Council (1992); First English Evangelical Lutheran Church v. County of Los Angeles (1987). Both of these cases would permit, where appropriate, interim damages during the time from the impact of or challenge to the ordinance and the time when the ordinance was invalidated and ceased to apply. (More about that later.)

In *Penn Central,* supra, Justice Brennan listed factors which should be considered in determining whether a regulation is a taking: (1) the economic impact, with particular regard to the extent to which the regulation "has interfered with distinct investment backed expectation"; (2) the character of public activity, in the sense that a physical invasion may more readily be identified as a taking "than when interference arises from some public program adjusting the benefits and burdens of economic life to promote the common good"; and (3) the history of sustaining reasonable police power regulations "that destroyed or adversely affected recognized real property interests" and "which have been viewed as permissible governmental action even when prohibiting the most beneficial use of the property," as in zoning cases.

## § 2.  Compensation or Damages for Unconstitutional Land Use Regulation

Except for the general statement by Justice Holmes in *Pennsylvania Coal,* supra, that if regulation goes too far it will constitute a taking, and for Justice Brennan's factors in *Penn Central,* the Supreme Court did not venture into this morass in any definitive way before San Diego Gas and Electric v. City of San Diego (1981). Even then, the Court left the issue unresolved, but a strong minority joined in a dissenting opinion by Justice Brennan which required compensation under the just compensation clause of the Fifth Amendment.

This approach had been rejected in many state court decisions, including *Fred F. French Inv. Co.,* supra, and Agins v. City of Tiburon (1979).

So, at the end of the 1970's and the beginning of the 1980's, there were two opposing lines of thought: (1) the traditional view, and the view of the 19th Century, that a regulation is never a taking in eminent domain because it is enacted pursuant to the police power and the proper remedy for an unconstitutional regulation is injunctive or declaratory relief, and (2) that damages could be recovered in this situation as much as in the case of eminent domain.

The view of the state courts, almost entirely composed of adherents to the first line of thought, began to change after *San Diego Gas and Electric*. This was accelerated by *First English Evangelical Lutheran Church,* supra.

A fairly early case which was typical of the changing line of reasoning was Burrows v. City of Keene (1981), involving a denial of subdivision approval and the placement of most of plaintiff's land in a conservation zone with the balance in a rural zone. The New Hampshire Court agreed with Justice Brennan's dissent in *San Diego Gas & Electric Co.,* supra, that "it is always open to the governmental entity involved to rescind or repeal the offending regulation and thus avoid payment of damages for inverse condemnation from that point on. Until that is done, however, the owner's property has been taken during the interim period and he is entitled to compensation for that taking." Similar cases were Rippley v. City of Lincoln (N.D.1983); and Sheerr v. Township of Evesham (1982). In Corrigan v. City of Scottsdale (1986), the Arizona Court upheld the Court of Appeals in invalidating an ordinance as an unconstitutional taking without just compensation. The case was remanded to the trial court for the determination of damages. The Court followed the reasoning in S. Wright, Damages or Compensation for Unconstitutional Land Use Regulations, 37 *Ark.L.Rev.* 612, 645 (1983) stating that "limiting recovery to a landowner's actual losses where the regulatory taking is temporary should help eliminate the threat of such burdensome liability [to the local government]. This approach adequately balances the public interest against private interests by requiring compensation for regulatory takings while limiting that compensation to actual losses for temporary takings." See also, Rankin, The First Bite at the Apple: State Supreme Court Takings Jurisprudence Antedating First English, 22 *Urban Lawyer* 417 (1990). While the majority of states probably either adhere to the traditional view or are silent on the subject, there is clearly a division, and the trend in state courts would appear to be toward *First English* and *Lucas, supra.*

First English

The *First English* opinion by Chief Justice Rehnquist in 1987 made it clear that damages for a temporary taking were available by way of inverse condemnation as a remedy for a regulation which destroyed all reasonable economic use. The First English Evangelical Lutheran Church owned some land along the banks of a creek which was the natural drainage channel for a watershed area. A church camp was operated there. A forest fire denuded large amounts of acreage upstream and produced a serious flood hazard, and a heavy rain destroyed the camp. Los Angeles County adopted an ordinance prohibiting structures within the flood protection area, including the camp site. The Supreme Court held that if the ordinances had denied the church of "all use of its property" for a period of years without compensation, interim damages for a temporary taking would be an available remedy. Justice Stevens, dissenting and joined by two others, viewed the decision as a "loose cannon" that would ignite a litigation explosion. On remand, the California Court of Appeals found that the ordinance advanced a "preeminent state interest in public safety and did not deny appellant all use of its property" and was a "reasonable moratorium for a reasonable period of time." First English Evangelical Lutheran Church of Glendale v. County of Los Angeles (1989).

Since the U.S. Supreme Court in *First English* had *assumed* the validity of the taking allegation of the initial complaint, the California Court of Appeals was left free to deny that a taking had occurred. However, the precedent for recovery of interim damages for a temporary taking remained and was reinforced in *Lucas v. South Carolina Coastal Council, supra.*

*Lucas* involved a developer who had purchased coastal lots intending to construct two single-family residences. However, South Carolina enacted a statute which prohibited him from building anything except wooden walkways and wooden decks. The trial court awarded him in excess of $1.2 million in damages for a governmental taking, but this was reversed by the state supreme court which stated that the state had only kept him from building a harmful use that would cause damage to the shoreline, the public and him. Again, on appeal, the U.S. Supreme Court held that a categorical taking occurs when the owner is deprived of all economically beneficial use of his property and that the owner is entitled to compensation unless the restrictions result from restriction inherent in the title or principles of property or nuisance law. (The suggestion was that deprivation of all use could be justified only under established principles of property or nuisance law.) A "categorical" taking was explained as one that did not require a balancing of the interests as in the *Penn Central* case.

## § 3.　The Nuisance Exception as to Total Takings

The limitation on regulation imposed by the *Lucas* case is consistent with First English, supra in its reference to a deprivation of *all* economically beneficial use of the property. This casts a cloud over extensive environmental and pollution regulations and over stringent flood plain regulations. On the other hand, if *all* economic use of a valuable nature must be affected before there is a taking, the Court seems to have provided a standard which serves to protect the enforceability of most police power regulations. Even a deprivation of "reasonable" use would if anything, seem to be less than a total loss of value or deprivation of "all" use.

Deprivation of all use, or all economic use, presumably would be justified under *Lucas* only under established principles of property or nuisance law. Justification for deprivation of all economic use can be found in *Mugler v. Kansas,* supra, which had the effect of closing a brewery under the Kansas prohibition law. A more recent case, Keystone Bituminous Coal Association v. DeBenedictis (1987), may be said to be in the same line of thought in upholding a coal mining regulation aimed at preventing subsidence as against a taking argument. These and such cases as Miller v. Schoene (1928), upholding the destruction of infected trees to prevent the spread of tree disease, proceed under the idea that the economic impact must give way to public considerations. This line of cases may be compared to the prevention of a public nuisance.

The question then arises, after *Lucas* and *First English,* as to how far property or nuisance law in a particular jurisdiction might be extended to sustain a regulation which amounts to a taking of all or essentially all of the economic value. Presumably, a regulation which prevents a public harm is not sustainable *for that reason only* if there is a complete deprivation of economic use. The question would be determined by whether the result would be permitted under established principles of property and nuisance law. That is, if the established law of a State would sustain such an extreme regulation, then it would not be a compensable taking. If a severe restriction were recognized or could be justified (explicitly or implicitly) under existing state law, then it might or might not be justified in a particular case considering "the degree of harm to public lands and resources, or adjacent private property, posed by the claimant's proposed activities, the social value of the claimant's activities and their suitability to the locality in question, and the relative ease with which the alleged harm can be avoided through measures taken by the claimant and the government (or adjacent private landowners) alike." *Lucas* majority opinion.

This absolutist view of the validity of stringent police power regulation suggests that what is not currently recognized as legitimate regulation under state property or nuisance law would not pass the test. However, later parts of the opinion indicate that changed circumstances or new knowledge could justify previously unacceptable regulations. This concession by Justice Scalia for the majority is echoed in a concurring opinion by Justice Kennedy. It would seem likely that this will be recognized and accepted as an exception to the limitation of extreme regulations to existing property and nuisance law.

## § 4. Post–*Lucas* Considerations

This area of the law has to be viewed as being still in a state of flux. In *Lucas,* Justice Scalia was joined by Chief Justice Rehnquist and Justices White, Thomas and O'Connor. Justice White has since been replaced by Justice Ginsburg. Justice Kennedy's concurring opinion obviously took a broader view of what would constitute legitimate regulation resulting in deprivation of all viable use. Justice Souter rejected the reasoning of the majority. Justices Blackmun and Stevens dissented. In fact, as Justice Souter pointed out, the assumption that South Carolina had deprived Lucas of his entire economic interest was questionable since Lucas could still make use of the property for certain recreational purposes. Those purposes, though perhaps minuscule in value, would seem to keep the deprivation at under 100%, and as Justice Stevens argued that it is arbitrary to say that a deprivation of 95% of value allows no recovery, while diminu-

tion in value of 100% entitles one to recovery of the
full value of the land.

The conclusion to be drawn is that while *First
English* allowed the recovery of compensatory damages for a total taking, and while *Lucas* in the
majority opinion seeks to explain some of the older
cases with its nuisance exception, the Court remains divided as to situations in which a total
deprivation of economic use requires compensation
as opposed to being justified by recognized nuisance
considerations. What is basically at stake is a philo-
sophical difference between those who would take
great care to protect property rights against their
perception of excessive police power regulation as
opposed to those who would give extensive leeway
to governmental regulation of private property to
avert perceived harm to the public.

Federal and state cases since *Lucas* have not
added anything, although a Minnesota case is interesting in holding that a two-year moratorium on
certain development activity did not amount to a
deprivation of all economically viable use under
*Lucas,* and a New Hampshire case upholding a
limitation on development that was considered to
present dangerous health problems would be valid
under state law even if it deprived the property
owner of all economically viable use of the land and
would thus not offend the *Lucas* rationale. Woodbury Place Partners v. Woodbury (Minn.App.1992);
Smith v. Town of Wolfeboro (1992). Some state
courts have explored the application of *Lucas* in
cases of total takings that are justified under condi-

tions inherent in the title to real property. The Iowa supreme court upheld a total ban on development of land that had an ancient Indian burial mound on it and the New York Court of Appeals upheld a physical invasion of property by dumping fill dirt to shore up an adjacent street, holding that the duty of lateral support to public streets inheres in the title to land. Hunziker v. State (Iowa 1994); Kim v. New York City (1997). Also, some courts have held that a deprivation of all economic use is not a categorical taking if the landowner knew, or should have known, of the impending regulation at the time he or she acquired the land. Avenal v. United States (Fed.Cir.1996).

Some writers have suggested that the *Lucas* majority opinion is narrow enough that it may be avoided by such legislative devices as the creation of hardship variances. These would be granted to owners who could prove a total taking, and it is thought that this could avoid damages even for a temporary taking resulting from a delay in obtaining a variance. Humbach, Evolving Thresholds of Nuisance and the Takings Clause, 18 *Colum.J.Env.Law* 1, 27 (1993). Non-severance of "sensitive lands," so that they remained combined with property subject to development, is also suggested as a way of rendering the entire tract economically viable in subdivision matters.

It may well turn out to be that the impact of *Lucas* and *First English* is exaggerated in the sense that there is seldom a deprivation of all economic use in land use regulations. Where there is, it may be difficult to establish damages with any certainty. There is also the possibility of legislative loopholes through hardship variances as mentioned above. This is likely to remain for the immediate future, however, as a developing and fertile field for litigation. The approach adopted by several state courts and some federal courts has been to look first at whether the regulation in issue fits the *Lucas* definition of a categorical taking, and, if not, to apply the balancing factors of the *Penn Central* case.

## § 5.  Other Remedies—42 U.S.C.A. § 1983

Over the past twenty-five years, a number of cases have dealt with the question of the award of damages under the Civil Rights Act of 1866 to landowners aggrieved by unconstitutional regulations, and a few courts have made awards under Section 1983, which reads as follows:

> Every person who, under color of any statute, ordinance, regulation, custom or usage, of any State or Territory, subjects, or causes to be subjected, any citizen of the United States or other person within the jurisdiction thereof to the deprivation of any rights, privileges, or immunities secured by the Constitution and laws, shall be liable to the party injured in an action at law, suit in equity, or other proper proceeding for redress.

Awarding damages against cities for violations of Section 1983 is a fairly recent development. In Monell v. New York City Department of Social Services, (1978), the Court held that cities are "persons" subject to suits under Section 1983. In Owen

v. City of Independence (1980), the Court held that in Section 1983 suits cities do not enjoy qualified immunity for good faith acts. There is no exhaustion of remedies requirement to bring this type of action.

In City of Monterey v. Del Monte Dunes (1999) the Supreme Court held that the submission of the question—whether the city's rejection of five different development plans denied the owner all economically viable uses—to a jury was proper. Under the Seventh Amendment a jury trial is available even if the cause of action was not one in existence at the time of the adoption of the Constitution. Justice Kennedy wrote that while not every action under Section 1983 is one calling for a jury determination, in a land use case such as this one, a jury is fit to determine the factual issues raised and to award damages.

Lake Country Estates, Inc. v. Tahoe Regional Planning Agency (1979), was a holding by the Supreme Court that a cause of action under Section 1983 was stated against a planning agency for unconstitutional land use regulations, although it did not discuss the appropriate remedy.

Citing Brennan's dissent in *San Diego,* the Fifth Circuit Court of Appeals held that a landowner should be entitled to damages under Section 1983 for denial of a rezoning if the denial constituted a taking. Hernandez v. City of Lafayette (5th Cir. 1981).

The holdings in *Lucas* and *First English* extend to this line of cases as far as the remedy is concerned and in a proper case damages could be awarded. Section 1983 cases, however, typically involve consideration of constitutional rights violations aside from the substantive due process issue involved in a taking under the Fourteenth Amendment. Few of the decisions relate to damages, and the award of damages would appear more tenuous in dealing with such issues as procedural due process. In light of the *Del Monte Dunes* case damage suits are more likely.

Moreover, although there is clearly no exhaustion of remedies requirement for a Section 1983 suit, it is possible that a cause of action will not lie in the event that there is an adequate state procedure and thus no infringement on constitutional rights. In Parratt v. Taylor (1981), the Supreme Court found that there was no violation of due process when a prison inmate's hobby materials were lost by the negligence of prison employees because the state had provided a post-deprivation state remedy. Although some authorities contend that the *Parratt* holding applies only to alleged procedural due process violations, a similar rule has been applied in inverse condemnation actions where there is an adequate state procedure for obtaining just compensation for physical takings. E.g., Collier v. City of Springdale (8th Cir.1984). Perhaps local governments can avoid Section 1983 suits for regulatory takings by establishing procedural and remedial safeguards that insure against infringements of constitutional rights.

Occasionally, the issues may blend together in a particular case. Littlefield v. City of Afton (8th Cir.1986), involved a city conditioning a building permit on dedication of public access to benefit another parcel which was privately owned. The substantive due process issue was tied in with procedural due process and taking questions. The court concluded that denial of a building permit may be a denial of substantive due process under Section 1983, while holding that procedural due process was accorded the plaintiff and that the taking question was premature.

The type of case that could most likely produce damages is one in which the governmental unit revokes previously issued permits or changes the rules after a property owner has begun development. In Resolution Trust Corp. v. Town of Highland Beach (11th Cir.1994) the court affirmed a $30 million judgment against the town for terminating a developer's right to complete a previously approved condominium project. The court found that a vested property right was involved and the town was estopped to revoke the permits. (The decision was vacated pending a rehearing en banc).

While cases involving selective application of regulations, discrimination, or harassment of the property owner give rise to such actions, in these cases the nature of the constitutional rights that have been lost must be clearly set forth. These cases are basically non-taking cases in which the legal allegations are seldom intermingled as in *Littlefield,* supra. It may be that in some situations, however, substantive due process and procedural due process are intertwined, so that the resulting litigation involves both Section 1983 and Fourteenth Amendment allegations.

In the mid–1990's a number of state legislatures debated the adoption of statutes that would require compensation to property owners whose property value was diminished due to government regulation. Also, a similar debate took place in Congress. These so-called "property rights" statutes took various forms, either requiring governmental agencies to consider the impact of regulation on private property values, or requiring compensation if the values were reduced by a certain percentage. A few states, notably Texas and Florida adopted statutes of the latter variety. Efforts in Congress seemed to fade away in 1997 and 1998; a strong letter of opposition signed by more than 300 law professors may have had some effect. The movement toward a statutory solution to property devaluation by regulation has apparently peaked.

## § 6.  Regulation of Flood Plains, Wetlands and Open Lands

### A.  *Environmental Concerns*

The regulation of flood plains and open lands is closely related to the protection of natural resources and to environmental controls which are the subjects of later chapters. Such regulation is considered

here as it relates to the regulation of urban development on the edge of cities, lakes or rivers. But the
considerations involved cannot be entirely severed
from considerations relating to the preservation of
natural resources and environmental concerns.
Both in fact help justify flood plain regulations.

Ordinances establishing flood plains and open
lands are often attacked, as are other types of land
use ordinances, as constituting an unconstitutional
taking of property without compensation. However,
these ordinances differ from others in that the
restrictions imposed are often more severe and the
economic effects more drastic to landowners than is
true of ordinances restricting land to other types of
uses. Flood plain ordinances are usually passed with
the view of protecting surrounding areas from flooding or protecting wetlands flora and fauna, which is
also an environmental goal.

In Morris County Land Improvement Co. v.
Township of Parsippany–Troy Hills (1963), the
court struck down an ordinance which prohibited
landowners in Troy Meadows, a low, swampy area,
from filling land except with materials taken from
the zone itself and provided that special exceptions
would be allowed only in aid of a permitted use.
Permitted uses were few in number. They included
the raising of plants and fish, outdoor recreational
uses, and conservation uses. The court found that
many of the permitted uses were public or quasi-
public in nature and that the private landowner was
effectively prevented from obtaining a reasonable
return on his property. The purpose of the ordi-

nance was to use the area as a water detention
basin for flood control and to preserve the land as
open space for such public benefits as a nature
refuge established within the zone by a conservation organization. In light of the purpose of the
ordinance and of its effect upon the plaintiff-land-
owner's use of its land within the zone, the court
found the ordinance to be confiscatory.

An ordinance establishing a flood plain district
was struck down in Dooley v. Town Plan and Zoning Commission of Fairfield (1964), on grounds that
the effect of the ordinance upon plaintiff landowners was confiscatory. Uses for property affected by
the ordinance were limited to parks, playgrounds,
marinas, boat houses, landings and docks, and club-
houses. The court found that as applied to plaintiffs
these restrictions resulted in a severe depreciation
of the value of the property since potential buyers
were restricted to what amounted to public or semi-
public uses. Except when allowed by special exception, the regulations prohibited excavation, filling,
and removal of soil, earth and gravel. Although
evidence showed that much of the property was
subject to periodic flooding, much of it was on high
ground which was not even flooded in a hurricane
that had struck the area in 1938, and this land
could be used for houses. It was also noteworthy
that before the defendant had changed the zoning
classification, it had levied a sewer assessment of
over $11,000 against some of the property and that
as long as the property remained privately owned

the regulations prevented the sewer system from being utilized.

Both of these cases quoted from the opinion of Justice Holmes in Pennsylvania Coal Co. v. Mahon (1922), to the effect that where a valid police power limitation ends and a taking begins is a matter of degree, to be determined on a case by case basis. In *Dooley,* the fact that a substantial amount of the land was suitable for houses and not subject to flooding was damaging to the ordinance. In the *Parsippany-Troy Hills* case, the court suggests that the zoning is really directed toward accomplishment of public aims or goals which should be satisfied by condemnation rather than flood plain limitations. It would seem that the land described in the *Parsippany-Troy Hills* opinion should be subject to flood plain zoning if any ever could. It was a marsh. But the severity of the limitation on the landowner, joined with the apparent public purpose, led the court to conclude that the township should pay for the land if it wanted to so limit its use. By Holmes' yardstick, *Parsippany-Troy Hills* would make one wonder if one could ever create such a district.

In short span of time after these two cases however, concern mounted over the state of the environment. While there had been legislation aimed at protecting the environment prior to the late 1960's, public concern mounted to lead to more sweeping federal and state legislation. This concern and the resulting legislation in turn began to affect court decisions.

The movement toward protecting the environment resulted in legislation which, while enacted to fulfill environmental goals, provided the vehicle for regulation of wetlands and coastal areas. An example of this is seen in Just v. Marinette County (1972). Wisconsin had passed a Navigable Waters Protection Act, and a shoreland zoning ordinance promulgated under it was upheld in the *Just* case. The purpose of the ordinance was to protect navigable waters and the public's interest in them from degradation and deterioration resulting from the uncontrolled use and development of shorelands. One provision of the ordinance required a conditional use permit for the filling of more than 500 square feet of wetlands contiguous to water and the filling or grading of more than 2,000 square feet on slopes of twelve percent or less. In upholding the ordinance the court distinguished, as did the courts in *Parsippany-Troy Hills and Dooley* between a valid exercise of the police power and an unconstitutional taking without compensation. But unlike these cases, the Wisconsin Court quoted Professor Ernst Freund's analysis that property taken by eminent domain entitles the owner to compensation because the property is taken for public benefit, while property restricted by the police power entitles the owner to no compensation because the restriction is for the prevention of a public harm. Characterizing the ordinance as one preventing harm which might result from the change in the natural character of the area, the court reasoned that the regulation did not prohibit indigenous uses consistent with the nature of the land. The court recognized holdings in which ordinances establishing flood plains and open spaces were stricken as unconstitutional, but it indicated that too much stress is placed upon the right of a landowner to change commercially valueless land where the change damages the rights of the public.

Cases which hold similarly to the *Just* case include Candlestick Properties, Inc. v. San Francisco Bay Conservation and Development Commission, (1970), in which the court upheld the denial of a permit to place fill in the bay, and Potomac Sand & Gravel Co. v. Governor of Maryland (1972), which upheld wetlands legislation prohibiting dredging on plaintiff's property. And, in 1991, the New Jersey Supreme Court said that the vitality of *Parsippany-Troy Hills* "has declined with the emerging priority accorded to the ecological integrity of the environment." Gardner v. New Jersey Pinelands Comm'n (1991).

Another case in which a court attempted to formulate a test to be used is Spears v. Berle (1979), in which "Spears' Bog" had been classified as wetlands and a permit was denied to extract humus, sand and stone from it. The purpose of the wetlands statute was to balance ecological and economic considerations. The New York Court of Appeals applied the test that it had used in the *Fred F. French* case, supra, to the effect that regulation is too burdensome when the property is rendered unsuitable for any reasonable income, productive or other similar use and thereby destroys its economic value. The case was remanded for a hearing on the taking issue. It would be difficult to say in *Just* that the economic value of the property was not destroyed, except insofar as it could be used largely in its natural state. In other words, its economic value for development was almost entirely gone. Only through the argument that a public harm was being prevented and no public benefit was being gained could the court avoid the taking issue. The Wisconsin decision would thus seem to run more along the lines of 19th Century thinking that in the absence of a physical taking, reasonable police power regulations should be upheld, while the New York decision seems more in line with Holmes' thinking in *Pennsylvania Coal.*

It is noteworthy, however, that most of these cases illustrate an increased sensitivity on the part of courts when the aim is to preserve wetlands and protect the ecology as opposed to cases which seek to prevent development because the land tends to flood. The impact of the environmental movement seems apparent, and legislation of this type seems to affect judicial attitudes and the ground rules for adjudicating such cases. These statutes have led to an expansion of the police power in that when courts uphold them, they are saying that no taking is involved and that the state has legitimately exercised its police power. Thus, where the older flood plain ordinances often failed, with the courts emphasizing the severity of the limitation and speaking in terms of confiscation of property, legislation preserving wetlands has succeeded, with the courts emphasizing the public interest and the fact that the general welfare is legitimately being served. As for the older group of cases, the problem of an overly restrictive approach remains. However, some cases have upheld some rather strict flood plain regulations. An absolute prohibition of structures in a flood plain along a river was upheld in Turner v. County of Del Norte (1972). In Turnpike Realty v. Town of Dedham (1972), flood plain restrictions were upheld in a swampy area reminiscent of that involved in the *Parsippany-Troy Hills* case.

Moskow v. Commissioner of the Department of Environmental Management (1981), represented a fact situation very similar to that in the same case, but held that because 45% of the land was not in the swampy area and Moskow could still build a house on his land, there was no taking because courts should consider the entire parcel in making such determinations. Obviously, much has changed since *Morris County Land Imp. Co. v. Parsippany–Troy Hills,* supra.

While there is still a fine line to be drawn between legitimate wetlands regulation and a taking, these recent cases have tend to broaden the legitimate scope of police power controls. This may simply be a pour-over effect from the environmental cases and statutes, but it has been a significant trend. Although it does not mean that just any flood plain ordinance will be upheld, it seems to mean that reasonable controls in swampy areas or areas with a propensity toward flooding stand a much better chance of being approved today than they did thirty or more years ago.

These regulations pertaining to wetlands and flood plains, however, are affected to some degree by such cases as *First English,* supra, *Lucas,* supra, and Nollan v. California Coastal Commission (1987). Those cases, however, would seem to be distinguishable in most of the wetlands or flood plain situations. *Nollan* involved regulations of the California Coastal Commission, but the problem was created by the attempt to condition the rebuilding of a beach house on the transfer of a public easement across beachfront property. In the classification found in the *Just* case, that easement could be viewed as a public benefit to be gained and thus a taking. Although there was conflict as to whether *Lucas* actually involved a deprivation of *all* economic use, the majority opinion viewed it in that manner. Similarly, *First English* considered it to be a taking of all use when no structures could be built in a flood protection zone.

*First English* and *Lucas* seem to present a serious problem to flood plain or wetlands controls which confine the permitted uses to those which are a natural part of the existing area and which permitted uses are generally of little, if any, economic value. It has been suggested in an earlier section of this chapter that the availability of a variance procedure based upon unreasonable hardship might overcome the problem. (Such a procedure was available in *Just* and may be enough to save such severe regulation.) Another argument may be that if the area in which use is forbidden is part of a larger tract some of which may be used for development as in the *Moskow* case, an exception would be made (although Chief Justice Rehnquist seemed not to find this an acceptable argument in *Keystone Bituminous,* supra). Another possibility is that the nuisance exception expressed by Justice Scalia in *Lucas* could be applied in regard to the preventing of flooding or damage occasioned by flooding.

Some recent cases illustrate that prevention of development in environmentally sensitive areas or in wetlands areas not subject to development carries with it a presumption of validity. The landowner bears the burden of establishing that there is a deprivation of distinct, investment-backed expectations. This approach should have the effect of narrowing or diminishing the importance of this line of Supreme Court decisions.

Courts have become more sensitive to what has been called the "denominator problem," referring to the total restriction of development on a portion of the property. In wetland regulation this a common problem. The U.S. Court of Federal Appeals addressed this issue in great depth in the case of Loveladies Harbor v. United States (1994). In that case a developer who had built out most of a condominium project over several years was left with 51 undeveloped acres; the state environmental agency had an agreement with the developer to permit development on 11.5 acres and to leave the remainder undeveloped. The federal agency denied a permit to develop the 11.5 acres of wetland under the Clean Water Act. In the compensation litigation the

United States claimed that the proper denominator to determine whether a taking had occurred was the original 250 acre parcel, while the developer argued that there was a total taking of the 11.5 acres. The court held that a total taking of the 11.5 acres was established and emphasized the timing of the development, i.e., that land developed or sold prior to the application of a regulatory regime should not be included in the denominator.

Legislation to protect endangered species has prompted increasing litigation raising the taking of property issue. Land development that alters the habitat necessary for species protection can constitute a violation of the statutory language that prohibits anyone from "taking" a threatened or endangered species. Babbitt v. Sweet Home (1995). Cases are beginning to appear that present this issue, although no definitive body of law has yet emerged. One state case of interest is Department of Community Affairs v. Moorman (1995) where the court upheld an ordinance prohibiting the erection of fencing on one of the Florida Keys in order to protect the free-roaming habitat of the miniature Florida Key Deer.

## B. Flood Plains—Health and Safety Considerations

Where flood plain regulations prevented development over wide land areas, some of which involved minimal threat of flooding such as 100–year flood plains, the view of some years ago was that such extensive police power regulation was unacceptable.

Regulations which covered a less extensive area, such as the annual flood plain, were accepted as legitimate.

The National Flood Insurance Act of 1968 required local flood plain regulation as a prerequisite to flood insurance, which spurred flood plain regulation. The tendency of the courts became one of prohibiting structures from being located in the flood plain. This type of holding usually rests on the fact that a flood plain ordinance is within public safety considerations, and there is a reluctance to accept facial attacks alleging that such regulations constitute a taking. E.g.: April v. City of Broken Arrow (Okl.1989); Turner v. County of Del Norte (1972).

The leeway accorded public safety considerations in connection with flood plains may or may not be accorded regulation of steep slopes with concommitant problems of erosion, drainage and access. Cf. Sellon v. City of Manitou Springs (Colo.1987) with Corrigan v. City of Scottsdale (1986). In *Corrigan,* the plaintiff could still develop part of her land and the ordinance provided for transfer of development rights, but the Arizona Court held it to be a temporary taking entitling her to damages. This seems a state court precursor to *First English,* which along with *Lucas,* provides the basis for potential future litigation.

## C.  Open Space Preservation

Because the safety element normally is lacking, courts are less inclined to defer to regulations which provide open space. Some courts view the setting aside of substantial portions of a tract for open space, in the absence of such trade-offs as those provided by cluster development, as constituting an invalid deprivation of ownership. E.g. Allingham v. City of Seattle (1988). That case was subsequently overruled as the court realized regulation limiting the development of significant portions of land in order to conserve open space was no different from zoning ordinances prescribing the density of land coverage.

Tax incentives are sometimes employed to encourage donation of land to the city. Also, developers sometimes voluntarily designate recreational and open space areas within their projects in order to add amenities which attract homebuyers. Use of trade-offs with developers as in cluster developments is a way of gaining needed open space which is often acceptable to and desired by developers.

## § 7. Regulation of Urban Growth

With the rapid expansion of population from major urban centers into satellite cities and what were once slumbering nearby towns, some of the municipalities on the metropolitan periphery have passed subdivision ordinances providing controls leading to "phased" or "timed and sequential" growth. When a city attempts to regulate its composition and rate of growth in this manner, the validity of its ordinances are determined by a multiplicity of considerations. Where city services and facilities are in short supply in the face of a rapidly expanding population, courts have recognized a legitimate need for planned, orderly urban growth. Yet at the same time any regulation with the purpose of simply excluding additional population without providing for planned growth would likely be held unconstitutional on the ground that it impinges upon the right to travel and move freely from town to town and from state to state. See Edwards v. California (1941). In addition these ordinances must be reasonably related to promoting the health, safety, or general welfare of the community and must not be arbitrary or capricious.

In the landmark case of Golden v. Planning Board of Town of Ramapo (1972), the court upheld a zoning ordinance which had been amended to provide for timed and sequential growth on grounds that it was within the state's enabling legislation, although specific provisions for such an ordinance were not included in any statute. The court looked to the overall public purpose of subdivision regulation, which is to guide development in such a way that the community needs for housing, public services and public facilities will be met adequately and in an orderly, convenient fashion. The court found that the amendments in question were consistent with this purpose and were therefore permissible under the enabling legislation.

The town of Ramapo controlled growth by requiring the availability of certain facilities and services as a condition precedent to subdivision development. A subdivider was required to obtain a special permit which would not be issued until the proposed development had accumulated fifteen "development points." The number of points accumulated was determined by a sliding scale measuring the availability of essential facilities and services. While the city had the burden to provide these services and facilities, the developer could provide them at his own expense if he wished to hasten development. Under no circumstances would any of the affected land be restricted for a period longer than eighteen years, and the scheme contemplated that special permits would be issued as essential facilities and services became available. The provisions of the ordinance were in compliance with the town's comprehensive plan.

Noting that the ordinance under review involved a substantial restriction on the use of land for a substantial period of time, the court nonetheless found that the restrictions did not amount to an unconstitutional taking. The land was not restricted as to all uses, and any landowner could erect a single-family dwelling. Any diminution in value to land subject to restrictions might be offset by an appreciation in value when the restrictions were lifted. Even if this were not the case, the court pointed out that where land has diminished in value because of imposition of restrictions, the owner will be compelled to bear the burden where the restrictions are for the public good.

The *Ramapo* decision recognized the unconstitutionality of any ordinance aimed at exclusion, but the court found that the amendments sought "to maximize growth by the efficient use of land" through timed and sequential growth. The court found that the town was not attempting to keep population out but was realizing the need to have a well-ordered growth to prevent deterioration and blight.

A second important decision involving timed and sequential growth was Construction Industry Ass'n of Sonoma County v. City of Petaluma (9th Cir. 1975). There the City of Petaluma was faced with an accelerating rate of population expansion, most of which was in single-family dwellings. The "Petaluma Plan" constituted a group of resolutions by the city council requiring that each year only 500 "development units" could be approved for construction and establishing a "greenbelt" around the city to serve as a boundary for urban expansion for at least five years. The purpose of the plan, according to the City, was to promote orderly development of the city, to prevent sprawl, and to provide for variety in building types and densities and for a wide range in prices and rents. For purposes of the plan a "development unit" was defined as part of a project involving five or more units, so that single-family dwellings not part of a project involving five or more units were not included in the limitation and apartments of four units not a part of a larger project were likewise not included. The plan required that the 500 units be allocated equally between the eastern and western parts of the city and between single-family and multi-family units. From eight to twelve percent of the approved units were to be constructed for low and moderate income persons. A complicated point system, measuring factors such as architectural design, recreational facilities, environmental design, and availability of low and moderate income units, was developed to determine which proposed projects would be approved.

The plan was attacked on grounds that it was unconstitutional because it was exclusionary and because it violated due process by being arbitrary and capricious. Relying upon the holdings in Village of Belle Terre v. Boraas (1974), and Ybarra v. Town of Los Altos Hills (9th Cir.1974), the court upheld the plan. In *Boraas* the Supreme Court had upheld a village ordinance requiring that all residences be single-family (as narrowly defined by the ordinance) on grounds that preservation of quiet family neighborhoods serves a legitimate interest within the police power. In *Los Altos Hills* an ordinance requiring a minimum lot size of one acre was upheld on grounds that it served a legitimate governmental interest in the preservation of a rural environment. The *Petaluma* court reasoned that the plan was less exclusionary than the ordinances upheld in *Boraas* and *Los Altos Hills*, which it thought effectively prohibited future growth, and that the plan served a legitimate government interest within the concept of the public welfare because it sought to preserve the small town character, open spaces, and low density population, and to promote growth at an orderly rate. The court declined to find that the plan violated due process and viewed it as within the police power.

The Petaluma Plan was also attacked on grounds that it violated the commerce clause of the Constitution. Since the plan was a legitimate exercise of the police power, the court found it not to be violative of the commerce clause where it did not discriminate against interstate commerce nor operate to disrupt its uniformity. (The district court had viewed it as violative of Edwards v. California, supra.)

The decisions in *Ramapo* and *Petaluma* show that timed and sequential growth ordinances will be upheld as long as they are within the authority of enabling legislation, serve to promote the public welfare, possess legitimate features designed to permit orderly growth, and do not give rise to unconstitutional exclusion. Within the ambit of the public welfare are restrictions aimed at promoting orderly growth, a rural environment, a small town atmosphere, and quiet family neighborhoods. Decisions such as these give rise to the question of whether regional or state planning should be utilized to control and direct urban growth. The dissenting opinion in *Ramapo* argues that such decisions should not be left to individual localities. The *Petaluma* opinion points out that if every municipality in the region surrounding Petaluma were to adopt a plan such as the Petaluma Plan, the impact on the housing market would be substantial. This is a serious consideration and illustrates the desirability of planning on an area-wide scale. Moreover, such considerations may affect the validity of such plans under appropriate circumstances. Too much area-

wide timed and sequential growth might prove unconstitutionally exclusionary in its total regional
effect.

In Associated Home Builders of the Greater
Eastbay, Inc. v. City of Livermore (1976), the
court upheld an initiative ordinance prohibiting
the issuance of further building permits until
school, sewage and water facilities complied with
certain standards. Unlike the ordinances in *Ramapo* and *Petaluma,* this one imposed no time limitations for meeting the required standards. The
plaintiff failed to carry the burden of proving that
the ordinance did not reasonably relate to the public welfare, and the court allowed the ordinance to
stand on its presumed constitutionality. However,
the dissent pointed out the lack of a timetable and
the exclusionary effects, which could constitute violations of the state and U.S. constitutions. This
case contrasts sharply with decisions such as National Land and Investment Co. v. Kohn (1965)
and Southern Burlington County NAACP v. Township of Mount Laurel (1975), which are discussed
under the topic on exclusionary zoning. Possibly
the court in *Livermore* was giving special consideration to the fact that this was an initiative ordinance passed by the voters, a procedure commonly
employed in California.

In *Ramapo, Petaluma,* and *Livermore* the issues
involved restrictions imposed by cities in the path of
urban growth. The cities were faced with population
growth resulting from the socio-economic conditions
of the area. But where a municipality is not in the

path of urban growth and passes ordinances to
restrict the use of its land to preserve its character,
the considerations determining the validity of the
ordinances are somewhat different from the considerations in *Ramapo* and *Petaluma.* In one case rural
property owners formed a municipal water district
for a negative purpose—to retard population growth
by preventing their land from being included in
adjacent water districts which had sufficient water
to supply the rural area. The landowners who
formed the district did not want supplemental water to be available because they believed that additional water would result in urbanization. The petitioners in the case owned land within the district,
and they sought to have their land excluded from
the newly created district so that it could be annexed to one of the adjacent districts. They received
no water from the new district. The district's board
of directors denied the petition, but the trial court
held for the petitioners. On appeal the denial was
upheld and the district court was reversed on
grounds that the board of directors was serving in a
quasi-legislative rather than a quasi-judicial capacity. It was reasoned that the board was elected by
landowners in the district and was compelled to
protect their interests and could not look only to
the interest of petitioners. Even though the new
water district supplied no water, the court found
that it could exist for negative purposes, i.e., to
prevent land within it from becoming part of the
two adjacent districts. The court held that the
board's action was not arbitrary, capricious, or en-

tirely lacking in evidentiary support and that the board had followed the procedure required by law. Wilson v. Hidden Valley Municipal Water District (1967). As questionable as this may appear in a rural locale, it would seem diametrically opposed to the result to be expected in an urban setting. See, e.g., Robinson v. City of Boulder (1976), in which Boulder was held obligated as the sole public utility for the area to supply water to an adjoining rural development.

Another instance in which a court might apply standards different from those applied in *Ramapo* and *Petaluma* is where a town imposes restrictions which are intended to keep developers from building homes intended to be "second homes" or vacation homes for the urban affluent. When a six-acre minimum lot restriction was passed to keep such developers from a rural New England town, the court upheld the limitation even though it could find no reason why a six-acre limitation was imposed instead of some other. Noting that it was guided by no precedent and that the problem presented was not the same as that where restrictions are imposed in the path of a natural population expansion, the court found the six-acre limitation legitimate under the local circumstances and until further study and planning could be implemented. The avowed purpose of the limitation included preservation of the ecological balance of the area, promotion of orderly, logical growth and avoidance of population density, all of which the court found to be within the concept of the general welfare. Steel

Hill Development, Inc. v. Town of Sanbornton (1st Cir.1972). This case does not square very well with the criteria usually employed in minimum lot size cases (discussed elsewhere in this book). The usual requirement is that the minimum must have a reasonable relationship to the police power and must not be arbitrary or capricious. The limitation in *Sanbornton,* like the water district in *Hidden Valley,* when one cuts through the verbiage about preserving the ecological balance and promoting orderly growth, was intended to keep people out. The six-acre minimum related to that objective rather than to police power considerations. As is demonstrated in the discussion on minimum lot sizes, however, there is no clear-cut uniform standard, particularly when you move into a rural or semi-rural setting and courts begin taking into account such factors as ecological, historical, cultural and aesthetic considerations. The tendency to approve large minimum lot sizes is much greater in that situation than when the setting is urban, suburban, or one which lies in the path of urban growth.

*excl
zoning*

Although dealing with regulation of subdivision developments and with overall town growth, these cases interrelate with those discussed in this book under the topic of exclusionary zoning. These regulations are basically exclusionary, and that fact gives rise to constitutional problems. There is a fine line that must be drawn between plans or devices which are deemed legitimate in terms of promoting orderly growth within reasonable confines and situ-

ations in which the action of the community is
viewed as unconstitutionally exclusionary. Therefore, such cases as *Ramapo* and *Petaluma* have to
be considered in conjunction with the cases in
which the exclusionary action of the community
was invalidated. Compare, for example, *Southern
Burlington County NAACP v. Mount Laurel, supra,*
and U.S. v. Black Jack, Missouri (8th Cir.1974),
discussed in the material under exclusionary zoning. Both invalidated ordinances which had the
result of greatly limiting permissible land uses and
of keeping out most members of minority racial
groups as well as the lower income public in general. The comparison of such cases with the "timed
and sequential growth" cases leads to the conclusion that while suburban communities in the path
of growth may validly limit growth while concomi-
tantly developing municipal services, they may not
pass ordinances intended to discriminate on the
basis of race. See Village of Arlington Heights v.
Metropolitan Housing Development Corp. (1977).
New Jersey went even further in *Mount Laurel* and
held that ordinances which effectively exclude lower
economic groups are invalid under the state constitution. In *Arlington Heights,* the United States Supreme Court did not go that far, and it limited
constitutional violations to those involving racially
discriminatory intent as opposed to those having a
racially discriminatory effect, although it indicated
that under federal housing legislation, the statutory
imperative might be such that a civil rights violation would result from the effect of excluding low-

income housing from a community. In this latter situation, upon remand, the Seventh Circuit established criteria under which a community might be held to have improperly discriminated in regard to provision for low-income housing without violating the equal protection or due process provisions of the Constitution. Any future timed and sequential growth plan must take this factor into account although the decision in *Arlington Heights* generally serves to sustain plans of the type approved in *Ramapo* and *Petaluma*. See Wright, Constitutional Rights and Land Use Planning: The New and the Old Reality, 1977 *Duke L.J.* 841, 864 (1978).

Another comparison might appropriately be made in the *Sanbornton* situation with respect to such cases as Appeal of Girsh (1970). The latter case invalidated restrictions which were less severe than those in *Sanbornton*. *Girsh*, like *Sanbornton*, sought to maintain the character of the community. But unlike *Sanbornton*, the community in *Girsh* stood in the path of urban development.

The clear message to be derived is that whether a community is thinking in terms of limiting urban growth while its public facilities are developed or of maintaining the character of the community itself, there is a direct interrelationship with exclusionary practices which in some cases have been invalidated. Whether it is a zoning regulation or a subdivision regulation or a regulation of overall town development, the question of unconstitutional exclusion is relevant and should not be ignored.

## § 8. Environmental Controls and the Land Development Process

Land developers must seek approval from local governmental bodies for their subdivisions and other developments, but increasingly they must also seek approval of various other agencies of government whose purpose is environmental protection. The extent to which environmental laws and regulations apply to land development has been the focus of litigation in several respects. For example, development of land bordering a pond was held to be a "commercial" development within the meaning of the Maine Site Location Development Law, even though the development was for homesites, because the development of the property was commercially motivated in that the developer hoped to make a profit. The act required that commercial or industrial developments in excess of twenty acres be approved by an environmental improvement commission on the basis of several factors, all of which the court found to be within the police power. The court also found that the act's application only to developments in excess of twenty acres was a reasonable classification and not violative of due process. In re Spring Valley Development (Me.1973).

A similar decision extending the requirements of an environmental act to land development was Friends of Mammoth v. Board of Supervisors of Mono County (1972), involving a condominium project with over 180 units, a restaurant and specialty shops housed in six buildings of six to eight stories. Local approval had been obtained, but the court

concluded that the state environmental quality act
also applied and compliance was required. In another case, the alleged adverse impact upon the environment by a thirteen story condominium project
was alleged to be the obstruction of the view, shadow effect, excessive bulk and excessive relative
scale. Polygon Corp. v. City of Seattle (1978). It was
held that the state environmental act applied even
though the project complied with zoning requirements.

These and similar cases illustrate the problem
posed for a land developer in meeting these added
requirements and also the different interests involved. Land use planning might dictate that a
facility be located in a certain place or configuration
so as not to impact adversely on other land uses,
while an environmental agency concerned with air
quality standards might opt for some other location.
See, in general, City of Highland Park v. Train (7th
Cir.1975). It may legitimately be urged that a developer should only have to secure approval of a single
agency charged with considering all aspects of the
development including environmental concerns.

It may also be urged with some validity that
environmental legislation should not be employed
solely as a tool to defeat a proposed project. Thus,
the argument that before beginning construction of
a large housing project the Navy had to comply with
NEPA by filing an environmental impact statement,
was rejected because, to make such requirement,
the potential effect on the environment must be
"significant." Town of Groton v. Laird (D.Conn.

1972). The town was attempting to use NEPA as a device to prevent non-compliance with local setback and dwelling area requirements. "NEPA is not a sort of meta-zoning law," said the court, and was "not designed to enshrine existing zoning regulations on the theory that their violation presents a threat to environmental values."

The conflicts posed by these cases suggest that environmental requirements which are very desirable and generally work fairly well in connection with pollution of streams and waterways and air pollution caused by substantial emissions into the atmosphere are more controversial and subject to question in involving proposed land uses which do not pollute the water or air. The *Friends of Mammoth* and *Polygon* cases may be questioned on the basis that aesthetic considerations largely were at stake as opposed to pollution questions. The principal impact on the environment in *Friends of Mammoth* seems to have been on the natural beauty of the area, although other considerations were raised, such as water and sewage requirements. In *Polygon,* the impact seems to have been on the aesthetics and surroundings in the general area. While it is understandable that residents of single-family dwellings or low density condominiums would not want a high rise condominium project in the neighborhood, it would seem arguable that this is a planning and zoning question and that environmental questions of this particular nature should be addressed in that context or in the context of rezoning the property to a less intensive use.

It is apparent that how broadly particular courts tend to view environmental requirements, based on their own set of values, is an important factor. A related issue is whether aesthetic considerations alone are sufficient to justify the exercise of the police power, which is a subject taken up in a later chapter.

## § 9.  Subdivision Regulations

Subdivisions are cities at their growing points. Annexations and the development of suburban communities very much affect the appearance and configuration of a city; but within the city itself, as within peripheral, developing suburbs, the subdivision is the major point of growth. Its appearance and character, its provision or lack of it for essential facilities and services, will directly impact from a social and economic standpoint upon the life of the total community. The very permanence of subdivisions and potential problems that are avoided or created by such development are legitimate public concerns.

Governmental authority to regulate subdivision developments is not normally questioned today. Legal questions today customarily relate to the reasonableness of the requirements and whether such requirements are appropriate in a particular factual context. To the extent that the question of the power to regulate enters in, it would normally relate to whether the city had exceeded its authority under state law, under its own ordinances, or under the police power generally. The fact that this is so illustrates how far we have come since the 1920's. The older cases raised such questions as to whether a developer could be required to dedicate additional right-of-way alongside property being developed or whether this requirement amounted to a taking. The answer the courts gave was that the streets needed to be widened for public safety reasons to accommodate the development and that the city was not trying to compel a dedication but was simply imposing reasonable conditions on the developer before permitting his plat to be filed of record. Ridgefield Land Co. v. Detroit (1928). Thus, dedication was deemed to be voluntary and for the purpose of gaining the privilege of having the plat recorded.

The principle that the plat recordation is a privilege to which reasonable conditions may be attached extends not only to street dedications, but also to such requirements as the paving, curbing and guttering of streets, the width and surfacing quality of the proposed streets, sewer and water facilities in the subdivision, easements for public utilities, and similar regulations. These are subdivision exactions, which are justified on the basis that the subdivision will increase the public cost of providing services and that a developer who profits from the subdivision should bear at least a reasonable part of the burden of these increased costs and should also develop according to requirements which are aimed at reducing the cost impact on the city and at maintaining a suitable quality of life.

There are powers of cities other than the power to condition recording of plats and the general police power considerations which are involved in this process. The city has the power to condition acceptance of street dedications. In other words, if the developer wants to dedicate street easements in his subdivision to the city in return for the city agreeing to maintain them in the future, then he is required to construct the streets to meet certain specifications. The streets must also be located in accordance with the master street plan. Moreover, the community has the power to protect its right to tax real estate, and thus the accuracy of the plat and the ability of the taxing authorities to list the land correctly on the tax rolls are matters of importance. Trawalter v. Schaefer (1944).

The subdivision process, involving the division of tracts into blocks, lots, streets, open land, recreational areas, and the like, necessarily involves standards which are prerequisites for filing the plat and developing the land. This process differs from zoning in that the latter regulates the uses that are permitted and the type of building development that can take place. On the other hand, both are concerned with the orderly use of land and with the prevention of deterioration of property values and demand on community services. Some subdivision controls are directed at assisting the subdivision in comporting with the surrounding locality. This is why the street design must be such as to connect to and interact with major streets on the master street plan. The impact of the subdivision on the need for added or expanded fire and police protection, water and sewer requirements, schools, parks and recreation are also concerns which must be addressed.

Subdivision regulations are of value to the developer in providing an attractive and profitable new venture in which, in the future, the streets, water and sewer facilities, police and fire protection, will be the city's responsibility and not his. Moreover, he may sell his lots or houses by reference to a recorded plat, which is also beneficial to the city since it simplifies its record-keeping for tax purposes. As for homeowners, such regulations assure them of the orderly development of the area according to certain basic requirements for their safety and comfort. Conscientious developers are protected from fly-by-night operators as are the prospective homeowners.

Through this process, subdivisions receive many of the same planning considerations as do zoning decisions. Unlike zoning and rezoning, which theoretically at least is a purely public process, subdivision development is in some respects a joint enterprise of private developers and those who regulate on behalf of the public. The restrictive covenants unilaterally imposed by the developers on the subdivisions bear many comparisons to zoning requirements although such covenants generally go beyond zoning limitations. The point is, however, that the total process obviously has substantial public involvement through the regulatory process.

In connection with this process, one of the problems of cities relates to annexation of land in which some rural subdivisions have already been developed following either less rigid county requirements or no requirements at all. Cities sometimes refuse to accept sub-par streets or water and sewer facilities in such subdivisions as a part of the city system unless brought up to city requirements. As long as such developments can occur outside of the city's jurisdiction, the problem will remain. With respect to such rural land, a subdivider must do more than just file a plat to gain any vested rights that will not be affected by annexation. In other words, he has to institute the development process or, upon annexation, the subdivision regulations will apply to his plat. Dawe v. City of Scottsdale (1978). Generally speaking, where the developer has made substantial expenditures and has proceeded with the project based on issuance of such permits as are necessary, he cannot be prevented from proceeding by subsequent governmental action. This is based on varying theories—vested rights, equitable estoppel, detrimental reliance—but how much development must take place before a developer is free to proceed will necessarily vary with the facts. If the developer has spent substantial sums on a fairly well-developed project and acted in accord with existing regulations, subsequent ordinances cannot impose new requirements. But he must generally do more than simply file his plat or even start clearing the land. In one notable case, the court found that a developer lost his right to continue with a twelve-story apartment building on property which had been down-zoned because a vested right to continue could not be established through a four-foot footing poured to support a future column, a footing the court said occupied 9/1,000,000 of the zoned lot. Prince George's County v. Sunrise Development Limited Partnership (1993).

Another problem is the fact that the subdivision process, by definition, quite commonly relates only to dividing land into two or more lots as opposed to land development in general. If an ordinance or statute is so limited, it may be held that a non-subdividing developer does not have to comply with the regulations. City of Corpus Christi v. Unitarian Church (Tex.Civ.App.1968). Statutes and ordinances should be written to apply to development in general as well as to subdivisions.

## § 10.  Subdivision Exactions

As mentioned in the previous section, exactions result from subdivision requirements which cause the developer to have to make certain expenditures to comply with the regulations imposed upon him in return for being able to file his plat, dedicate and receive acceptance of his streets, connect his water and sewer lines to the public system, and generally gain approval of his subdivision. They are "exactions" in the sense that they exact from the developer costs which are required by the city.

Exactions raise issues which are based on the taking question. When does an exaction "go too far" and exceed what a city may reasonably require a subdivider to do in return for approval of his project? Today, such requirements as surfacing, curbing and guttering streets to prescribed standards, or constructing water and sewer facilities are commonly accepted. These are what might be called traditional exactions. Problems more commonly arise with land dedications or payment of fees in lieu of such dedications or with off-site improvements.

Jurisdictions may vary on how they construe municipal powers. Some jurisdictions regard statutes authorizing use of the police power by cities and counties as being in derogation of the common law and to be strictly construed. Some statutes, however, state that such regulations are to be construed liberally to effectuate their objectives. This question of whether the requirements of an ordinance are within the limits of the enabling statute or are ultra vires is frequently a basis for litigation. In jurisdictions with strong traditions of municipal "home rule" the courts do not strictly require the ordinances to be within the enabling acts. See, e.g., Ayres v. City Council of City of Los Angeles (1949), in which an ordinance was upheld on grounds that its requirements were consistent with the subdivision map act and were reasonable even though they were not specifically authorized by statute.

*Traditional Exactions*

Cases illustrate how much the attitude toward exactions has changed over the past thirty years or so. In Petterson v. City of Naperville (1956), the dispute concerned city requirements of curbs and gutters and storm water drainage facilities over which both the county and city exercised jurisdiction. It was held that cities may be given extraterritorial jurisdiction and that the requirements were reasonable within the intent of a statute allowing "reasonable requirements with reference to streets, alleys, and public grounds." The court rejected arguments that this was an illegal tax or a taking. As mentioned, the case also stands for the proposition that a city may be given extraterritorial authority to regulate developments and may enforce its exercise, even though the county has concurrent jurisdiction and has approved a plan with lesser requirements. Requirements of the type involved in this case are seldom contested today, but this case and the older *Ridgefield Land* case, supra, illustrate that the tradition of such exactions is not a very old one.

Exactions of this type illustrate the fact that as long as the requirements are not ultra vires with respect to the enabling act and as long as they are reasonable, their imposition will be upheld as a condition to subdivision approval. The developer may be offered the choice of installing the improvements before final plat approval, of furnishing escrow money to cover the cost of improvements as a condition to plat approval, or of furnishing a surety bond guaranteeing installment of improvements.

Other traditional improvements involve such requirements as surfacing streets of a certain width and to certain specifications, installing water and sewer lines of certain sizes and specifications, providing for public utilities to supply electricity and gas, requiring sidewalks, and in general making requirements which are directly related to the health, safety and general welfare of the people who will occupy the subdivision as well as the general public.

But even with these more traditional forms of exaction, questions as to the reasonableness of the requirement (as opposed to the nature of it) may arise. For example, what if a developer seeks approval of a water line of a certain size to connect to the city system, but the city council or planning commission requires a larger line because of the potential demand that will be created by future development outside of the subdivision? This situation combines imposition of a traditional requirement with a requirement that the developer provide for future demand generated by nearby subdivisions yet to be developed. Because the city has a responsibility for growth management, the city's action will normally stand unless its requirement is unreasonable and arbitrary or unless there is some defense such as estoppel which may be asserted. See Wright Development, Inc. v. City of Wellsville (Utah 1980). Similarly, the city can dictate the width of minor residential streets within the subdivision based on reasonable street classifications set forth in the master street plan. It can also make reasonable requirements as to the quality, composition and thickness of the street surface. Cases have held that developers can be required to pay the cost of on-site

water main extensions into new areas. The question
is whether this is reasonable or whether it is an
arbitrary or discriminatory requirement. Moreover,
cases have held that if the developer employs poor
building practices in his construction of improvements, he may be held liable by the municipality.
Town of Brookfield v. Greenridge, Inc. (1979).

As mentioned in the previous section, although
requirements may be imposed retroactively where
the plat has been approved in certain limited circumstances, courts may find the city estopped, or
that the developer has a vested right to proceed if
he has changed his position in reliance on earlier
requirements or on the fact that there were no
requirements. Compare Brous v. Smith (1952) with
Spindler Realty Corp. v. Monning (1966).

*Off-Site Improvements*

The question of what is a reasonable requirement
is more likely to be litigated where off-site improvements are involved. Requirements for off-site improvements are not presumptively invalid—the reason being that the development of a subdivision has
ripple effects on the community, and sometimes a
direct impact, beyond the physical boundaries of the
subdivision. The construction of water and sewer
lines, for example, if adequate only to serve a single
development, may retard future growth which must
depend in part on connecting to those same facilities. By then, these in-place facilities are part of the
city water and sewer system and may have to be
replaced to accommodate future growth. It is not

unreasonable to require the original developer to
install adequate lines in order to prevent such future difficulties. Similarly, reasonable requirements
may vary depending on such factors as topography,
soil conditions, population density, and whether the
subdivision is in the projected mainstream of outward growth.

The problem of allocating costs to a developer for
off-site improvements necessitated in part by his
subdivision is illustrated by some New Jersey cases.
In Divan Builders, Inc. v. Planning Board of Wayne
Township (1975), the ordinance provided that the
cost of required off-site improvements would be
allocated between the subdivider, other property
owners, or any one or more of them. The court
upheld assessment to developers of off-site improvements as being permitted under the enabling act
where such improvements were necessitated by the
effect of the development. If the improvement was a
municipally financed general improvement, the subdivider would pay the difference between the cost of
the improvement and the total amount by which all
properties serviced by it, including the subdivision,
would be specially benefited. If constructed as a
local improvement, he would in addition pay the
amount by which the subdivision property was specially benefited. A third way would be for the developer to do it at his expense with a formula providing for partial reimbursement if the improvement
specially benefited other property. The court in
*Divan* decided that there was possible discrimination in cost apportionment because no part of the

cost of this general improvement was allocated to other properties which were specially benefited. In another case, 181 Inc. v. Salem County Planning Board (1975), the plaintiff was required to dedicate land bordering a road as a condition precedent to approving its site plan for construction of a law office. The county required dedication of frontage along every county road without regard to present need or proposed use. The court found this invalid under the "rational nexus" test, holding that the developer can only be required to bear that part of the cost which bears a rational nexus to the needs created by and benefits conferred upon the subdivision. Since his limited activity did not appear at present or in the immediate future to place such burden on the road as to require its improvement, then the requirement was invalid.

The New Jersey holding in *Divan,* essentially to the effect that a developer may be required under one formula or another to pay a reasonable pro rata share of an improvement made necessary in whole or in part by his activity, seems to be equitable and justified. The theory is that since the developer is placing an additional burden on public facilities and, perhaps in concert with other developers, creating the need for new facilities, then he should bear his fair share of the cost. To do otherwise would be to place a burden on the city and on landowners in existing subdivisions to subsidize the developer by picking up the tab for the spillover costs created by his activity. (To the contrary, developers might argue that they should not be penalized for risking capital expenditures to provide homes for newcomers by having to pay for public facilities needed as a result of population growth. Further, they might argue, how can you attribute to a single development, with any degree of precision, the increased public burden?) Be that as it may, the tendency seems to be toward obtaining contribution from developers for the off-site burdens of such activity.

The rational nexus test provides a limitation on this in that the chargeable costs must reasonably relate to the activity of the developer. While this also seems fair, the problem with it is illustrated by the *181* case. It is obviously true that an office for a lawyer or even several lawyers will not alone generate such activity as to require improvement of a road. But if each small business operation along the road, as it developed, could successfully contend the same thing, then the total burden might ultimately compel its improvement or enlargement without any contribution from those along its borders. Moreover, if some businesses were required to contribute land along the road while others were not, then the result of the dedication process would be to leave periodic gaps. Complicating this problem is the practice of many cities to automatically request land dedications for future road widening in every case where a landowner seeks a development permit.

Many courts have employed the rational nexus test in these situations. The connection to the developer's activity must not only be reasonable, but also the requirement must be for presently contemplated improvements and not be for the purpose of banking the land for future use. See, e.g., Simpson v. City of North Platte (1980). A separate test is the "specifically and uniquely attributable" test, which upholds assessment for required improvements only where the need is specifically and uniquely attributable to the development. Obviously, while bearing some similarity, this is a much less flexible test than the rational nexus test, would seem to provide a greater burden for the city to meet, and would seem to eliminate in most cases the combining of the burden imposed by more than one developer and the allocation of costs accordingly. A third test is the "reasonable relation" requirement, which places the burden on the developer to establish that the required dedication bears no reasonable relation to the police power. See Wald Corp. v. Metropolitan Dade County (Fla.App.1976), where the latter two tests are rejected in favor of the rational nexus test.

If the rational nexus test could be broadened to alleviate the problem illustrated by the result in the *181* case, which is to say that it could take into account reasonably foreseeable future needs resulting from the combination of a variety of individual developments, then it would seem to be the fairer test. The "specifically and uniquely attributable" test places too great a burden on the city, and the "reasonable relation" test does the same with respect to the developer. In light of the Supreme Court opinion in *Dolan v. City of Tigard*, discussed below, requests for land dedication exactions require the municipality to have the burden of proof to show "rough proportionality" between the public need and the exaction.

*Non-Traditional Exactions*

Some cities have passed ordinances requiring dedication of land by the developer for parks, playgrounds, recreational areas, schools or other public facilities, or requiring the payment of fees in lieu of such dedications to cover the cost or part of the cost of such facilities. The amount of land to be dedicated is usually determined by the size of the subdivision or the number of lots in it or both. As in the case of ordinances requiring improvements, these ordinances have been attacked on the basis that they constitute an unconstitutional taking without just compensation. Exactions of this nature have produced mixed results in the courts, and in that and some other respects they bear a close relationship to exactions for off-site improvements.

Illinois was one of the earlier jurisdictions to grapple with these exactions. In Pioneer Trust and Savings Bank v. Village of Mount Prospect (1961), the court applied the "specifically and uniquely attributable" test to a requirement that land be dedicated for a school and playground and held that the need was not shown to be specifically and uniquely attributable to this subdivision. The court relied in part on an earlier Illinois case invalidating an attempt to allow subdividers to pay a certain sum per lot in return for not dedicating land for schools.

Having given due consideration to this decision and a similar Kansas holding, however, and having accepted application of the "specifically and uniquely attributable" test, Wisconsin reached a contrary result in Jordan v. Village of Menomonee Falls (1965). The ordinance here required dedication of land for schools, parks and recreational facilities, or in lieu of dedication, a certain fee per lot. Both the dedication and in lieu fee requirements were upheld. The fees were upheld as not constituting a taking or an unconstitutional property tax. While the results are dissimilar, both Illinois and Wisconsin adopted the same test, and Illinois presumably would reach the same result if it found the requirements of the test to be met. The Wisconsin Court reasoned that the enabling act permitted the ordinance and that the requirements were a reasonable exercise of the police power where it is shown that the development of the subdivision would increase the need for schools and parks. This rule would uphold payment of fees for public facilities which *may or may not* be located near the subdivision for which the fees were exacted, and it is essentially the rule incorporated in the Model Land Development Code for situations where dedication is not feasible. However, location away from the subdivision area, or the failure to specify in the ordinance that such facilities will be located within reasonable proximity of the subdivision, could result in a successful challenge to the ordinance predicated upon the taking argument, an allegation of an abuse of the police power, or both. It is logical to assume that if the subdivision and perhaps neighboring subdivisions create the burden, then the burden should be alleviated in the same vicinity. Otherwise, it is arguable that subdivision-produced income is being diverted to sustain existing city obligations in older areas, and the legitimacy of the exactions in such circumstances becomes suspect. Moreover, the fees in *Jordan* were to go into two special funds for school and park purposes. If instead the funds were to go directly into the general fund, that would also seem to provide a basis for challenging the ordinance.

Not all courts have passed on such exactions, but there is a clear split of authority. The more recent cases seem to show a slight trend in favor of allowing such exactions. Some cases which invalidate such dedications or in lieu fees do so on the basis that the action is ultra vires with respect to the state enabling act. A good many cases, both pro and con, are cited in R. Wright & M. Gitelman, *Cases and Materials on Land Use* 701–706 (5th ed.1997).

An economic factor to be considered in connection with this problem is the fact that subdivision exactions increase the cost of housing at a time when housing has become increasingly less affordable for large segments of our population. If the developer has to bear the costs, he will attempt to pass along to the purchasers of his lots and houses a pro rata allocation of such costs. This squeezes developers by narrowing the potential market, which may in turn depress development or diminish the quality of construction or both. On the other side of the economic coin, some potential purchasers find themselves increasingly unable to enter the market particularly in an economy of high interest rates. The contrary argument in favor of exactions, as stated previously, is that the public should not have to subsidize developers in their entrepreneurial activities by assuming exterior public burdens produced by such developments. Moreover, the public should not permit shabby developments. These are problems of substantial economic and social concern which have a way of influencing courts as well as legislative bodies.

## § 11.　The *Nollan* and *Dolan* Cases and Subdivision Exactions

Nollan v. California Coastal Commission (1987) and Dolan v. City of Tigard (1994) linked the validity of subdivision exactions to the question of a regulatory taking under the police power. The question thus arises as to what effect do these cases have or may have on subdivision exactions.

The Nollans owned a beachfront lot which was one-quarter mile away from an oceanside public park, beach and recreation area to the north, while 1800 feet south of their lot was another public beach area. They wanted to replace a small bungalow on their property with a three-bedroom house. They were permitted to do so if they surrendered a public easement to allow passage across a designated part of their property to and from the two public areas. The Supreme Court, in a 5–4 opinion by Justice Scalia, held that the requirement of the easement in the approval of the construction amounted to a taking. The majority relied on Loretto v. Teleprompter Manhattan CATV Corp. (1982), and Kaiser Aetna v. United States (1979). *Loretto* held that a permanent physical occupation of property by the government or the public would amount to a taking, and the Court regarded the permanent use of the easement by the public (even though required in connection with approval of the construction permit) as no different from the outright acquisition of an easement through eminent domain.

As the result of *Nollan,* some observers predicted that there would be a "chilling effect" on all but the more basic subdivision exactions. Most comments suggested the rational nexus test would control situations of this type. Justice Scalia stated that a regulatory condition placed on a construction permit would not constitute a taking "if the Commission attached to the permit some condition that would have protected the public's ability to see the beach notwithstanding construction of the new house—for example, a height limitation, a width restriction, or a ban on fences—so long as the Commission could have exercised its police power * * * to forbid construction of the house altogether * * * *"

In the *Dolan* case the Supreme Court addressed the questions unanswered in *Nollan.* In *Dolan* the property owner sought a permit to expand her plumbing supply business in the downtown area, where her property adjoined a creek. The city demanded a dedication of land for a portion of a proposed bikeway and for a public greenway along the creek. Justice Rehnquist, author of the majority opinion posed the issue as one requiring a determination of "whether the degree of the exactions demanded by the city's permit conditions bear the required relationship to the projected impact of petitioner's proposed development." The opinion resolved the issue by rejecting the Illinois "specific and uniquely attributable" test as too restrictive and the "any police power justification" test as too liberal. The Court then adopted the "reasonable relationship" test (the majority view in state courts), but altered the language to state the test as one of determining whether there is a "rough proportionality" between the required dedication and the impact of the proposed development. The Court also said "the city must make some sort of individualized determination that the required dedication is related both in nature and extent to the impact of the proposed development."

After *Nollan* and *Dolan*, most commentators agree that the view followed by most state courts, utilizing language like "rational nexus" or "reasonable relationship" keeps most traditional exactions immune from constitutional scrutiny. However, if challenged on an exaction, the city must show with some particularity the requisite connection. In Goss v. City of Little Rock (8th Cir.1998) a federal court said a city could not rely on automatic road-widening exactions as condition of every development permit. Lower courts have not agreed on whether the *Nollan/Dolan* principle applies equally to money exactions rather than land dedications. Some courts have upheld money exactions based on "linkage" between a developer's activity and some community needs. In one city, for example, developers of downtown office buildings were required to contribute money to a fund supporting day care facilities on the theory that the workers who be in the buildings would need such facilities. And in New Jersey the court upheld the theory of requiring commercial developers to contribute to a fund for affordable housing.

## § 12. Antitrust Issues in Development Decisions

In the 1980's some plaintiffs made antitrust assertions against cities in regard to regional shopping centers approved for development which had the effect of preventing or discouraging competing shopping center developments. The Local Government Antitrust Act, 15 U.S.C.A. § 34, et seq. greatly reduced litigation.

The typical problem is evidenced by Mason City Center Associates v. City of Mason City (8th Cir. 1982) involving a city policy of discouraging outlying shopping centers in order to preserve the central business district. The city refused to rezone some commercial/agricultural property for shopping center development on the outskirts and approved redevelopment of the downtown area by another developer. This was attacked as a restraint of trade. The federal appeals court upheld a jury trial which favored the city.

In a similar case, Juster Associates v. City of Rutland, Vermont (2d Cir.1990), the city was sued for supporting one mall developer and opposing another before state environmental agencies. The city had agreed with the favored developer whereby the developer would provide financial support for low-income housing, transportation and cultural facilities, and under which no downtown businesses would be recruited to move to the mall. The federal appeals court affirmed the trial court's dismissal of the complaint, holding that no antitrust injury was stated since consumers would not be harmed by the city's preference.

The Noerr–Pennington immunity doctrine enters into this area of the law. Basically, the doctrine provides that anti-competitive intent should give way to free speech considerations in situations in which private parties encourage the city to deny rezoning to a potential competitor. For example, in Miracle Mile Associates v. City of Rochester (2d Cir.1980), immunity applied where a developer extensively petitioned federal and state agencies to require a competitor to comply with environmental regulations. An exception to this immunity occurs where attempts to influence the public process are a sham used to interfere with the business practices of a competitor. Efforts resulting in a loss or delay to the competitor without standing to object or without grounds would be an example, as in Landmarks Holding Corp. v. Bermant (2d Cir.1981).

Closely related to Noerr–Pennington doctrine is the special situation of so-called SLAPP suits.

SLAPP denotes strategic lawsuits against public participation, and most frequently arises where corporations seek to quell protests about their land uses by threatening to sue, or actually suing, private citizens who are circulating petitions or writing letters or filing protests. Many jurisdictions have adopted legislation that seeks to address this problem by means of quickly curtailing SLAPPs or providing for sanctions against plaintiffs in such suits. State courts have taken different positions on the validity of anti-SLAPP legislation, some saying that it prevents a litigant from using the courts, while most courts have upheld the legislation. Typical of the latter is Hometown Properties v. Fleming (R.I. 1996), where a landfill operator sued a private citizen for defamation in regard to her letter-writing to the state environmental agency. The court held that, like the Noerr–Pennington doctrine, the state anti-SLAPP statute was designed to protect legitimate First Amendment speech and the right of citizens to petition government, and in the case before it, there was no evidence that Fleming's letter writing was a sham activity.

# CHAPTER VI

# EMINENT DOMAIN AND THE POLICE POWER

## § 1. Introduction

Land use controls put into effect by local governments involve the use of such tools as zoning and subdivision regulations which are based on the police power. The theory is that local governments can exercise such controls because they reasonably relate to the general welfare or to such public concerns as health, safety or morals. The police power, then, is for the benefit of all of us and supposedly does not impinge unduly on any one of us. Where it does pass the bounds of reason, becomes arbitrary or capricious, or where it is confiscatory in nature, the action is the equivalent of a taking of private property. Since no compensation has been paid in that situation for the deprivation of property rights for a public use or purpose, the use of the police power is unconstitutional.

Recent cases, such as *First English* and *Lucas* as discussed in Chapter V, have stated that damages may be recovered in an extreme situation in which police power regulation has deprived property of all economic use. These damages would be limited to losses occasioned for the period during which the challenged regulation prevents some reasonable economic use and presumably would be determined in essentially the same way that a temporary taking or damaging of property is determined in an eminent domain case.

This recent development involves a literal interpretation of Justice Holmes' statement in *Pennsylvania Coal* that if regulation goes "too far," it can constitute a taking. The Supreme Court has essentially determined in these fairly recent cases that "too far" means "all the way" in terms of deprivation of economic use. In other words, the majority of the Court as it existed in the late 1980's and early 1990's has essentially bifurcated the remedial aspect in this way: (a) a police power regulation such as zoning may be unreasonable in the sense that no one can reasonably be expected to build anything but office, commercial or multi-family residential buildings on property zoned for single-family use, and thus the remedy is to require a rezoning; but (b) if the property is so regulated that you cannot make *any* economic use of it, then the regulation amounts to a taking which is not only unreasonable and subject to invalidation but also may justify the award of damages.

Under the category of (a), the Court has isolated the overwhelming majority of police power regulation—or seems to have done so by requiring a deprivation of *all* economic use. It has been argued that landowner Lucas was left with a few little things that he could do with his property, but it was not anything of any economic significance. In *First English,* the church could not build anything on its church camp property with the result that it had been rendered useless to the church. The majority of the Court is saying—in those category (b) cases— that the regulation is the equivalent of a taking because a public benefit is gained without any compensation to the landowner and that the landowner's property is rendered just as worthless to him as if it had been acquired by condemnation for a public use. The Court seems to be saying that this form of regulation, because it is so severe, is simply a substituted form of eminent domain without the necessity of compensation. That is why it violates substantive due process.

If these cases are limited in this manner, then the qualms on the part of some land use scholars are probably unjustified. None of them would probably argue that if all the majority of the Court has done is to prohibit and compensate for a disguised form of eminent domain, then its decisions are justified. After all, regulatory bodies should not be able to do by indirection what they cannot do by direction (i.e., take property without compensation). Much of the fear of this line of cases, including the fear of these writers, centered around the possibility that allowing even interim damages would cripple the use of the police power in commonplace matters such as zoning. In other words, that even in the example given previously under category (a), the property owner could successfully claim damages for the in-

terim period from the time he challenged the existing zoning classification until he succeeded in obtaining a reasonable new classification. If the Court
had gone that far with its holdings, planning and
zoning would have been seriously undermined and
local governments could only have undertaken the
safest and most conservative of regulatory measures.

Nonetheless, it is legitimate to point out the fact
that eminent domain and the police power have
different origins and are of a different nature even
though some (arguably including Holmes) have
viewed them as little more than different aspects of
the same general instrument. This line of thought
would say that in either situation, the public acquires rights—in eminent domain, absolute title or
an easement requiring compensation; in the police
power regulation, a limitation not requiring compensation, but nonetheless the acquisition of a right
in the form of a limitation on use. Scholars would
be quick to point out that in the police power
situation, although the public benefits in the sense
of preventing a public harm through protecting
higher uses, the individual landowner benefits as to
his own property through the same protection. He
may not be able to erect a McDonald's on his single-
family property, but neither can his neighbor erect
a McDonald's and thereby greatly diminish the value of his property for single-family use. This "reci-
procity of advantage" theory is often used by courts
to justify extensive regulation of land uses.

## § 2.  Historical Antecedents

Hugo Grotius, the great philosopher of the natural law, used the term "eminent domain" to describe the power of the state over private property. Only the state could be a taker, and the state was immune from liability. J. Beuscher & R. Wright, *Land Use* 709 (1st ed.1969). But this was not the first reference to the power. While its origin is lost in obscurity, its lineage may be traced to references in the Bible and to use by the Romans. 1 Nichols, *Eminent Domain* §§ 1.2, 1.12 (Rev'd 3d ed.1993). The power originated as an inherent right of the sovereign, under a common theory. The constitutional requirement of payment of just compensation is therefore a limitation on the power rather than a grant of the power.

The just compensation requirement in Anglo–American law may be traced back to the Magna Carta, which provided that "no freeman shall be ...deprived of his freehold ...unless by the lawful judgment of his peers and by the law of the land." Art. 39, *Magna Carta* (1215). But that provision does not provide for compensation. Also, over the centuries there remained friction as to what it meant. In 1352, the King agreed that proceedings to oust a freeholder would be dealt with by his peers and outside of the King and Council. F. Bosselman, D. Callies & J. Banta, *The Taking Issue* 59 (1973). Medieval disputes involved the King's practice of designating forests for his use for hunting and the ancient prerogative of the King to use land for defense purposes which was finally abolished statu-

torily during the reign of Charles II. It has been
stated that eminent domain, as it presently exists,
apparently grew out of the common law proceeding
known as "inquest of office," by which jurors in-
quired into any matter that entitled the King to
possession of property and which became the proper
proceeding at common law to acquire land for public use. 1 Nichols, supra at § 1.21. Eminent domain
was well-recognized in England by the time of the
American Revolution and was used in the colonies
largely for roads. 1 Nichols, supra at § 1.22.

The absolute and unlimited form of the power
which had been limited in England by the Magna
Carta was limited even more by the United States
Constitution in the Fifth Amendment and in many
of the early state constitutions to require payment
of just compensation. This was an extension of the
Magna Carta, which did not refer to compensation.
The first ratified constitution in this country to
provide for reasonable compensation in the event of
a taking was that adopted in Massachusetts in
1780. Bosselman, Callies & Banta, *supra* at 95.
However, several of the first state constitutions did
not provide for compensation, and in 1868 when the
Fourteenth Amendment became effective, five of
the oldest states still lacked such a provision. Possibly the influence of Blackstone's *Commentaries,*
which were used extensively in America and in
which Blackstone advocated compensation for takings, as well as controversial situations during the
Revolutionary War and a desire to protect the prop-
ertied classes, led James Madison to insert the

provision in the Fifth Amendment. Bosselman, Callies & Banta, *supra* at 101–104. In any event, in the states which did not have such a constitutional provision until some time later, natural law was relied upon, and the courts assumed the burden of requiring a taking for a public use to be contingent upon payment of just compensation. Beuscher & Wright, *supra* at 710.

## § 3.  Public Use and Public Purpose

The basic rule is that private property can be taken only for a public use. However, only a few state constitutions specifically prohibit property from being taken for non-public uses. Early cases held that takings for private use were prohibited, first upon the ground that this was opposed to natural justice, beyond the power of the legislature and an act of spoliation, and later through interpretation of eminent domain and due process clauses of state constitutions.

There are two views of what a public use encompasses. The narrow view is that it means "use by the public," i.e., to make a use public a duty devolves to furnish the public with the intended use and the public is entitled to such use. The broad view is that it means "public advantage," and that whatever tends to enlarge the resources, industrial potential, productive power, and growth of communities contributes to the general welfare. Generally today, private purposes can be served if the public is also served. Thus, private corporations performing a public function, such as utilities and railroads, may exercise the power under statutory authorization. This is viewed, however, as involving a public use under either interpretation.

The bifurcated interpretation of "public use" is almost identical to or essentially the same as judicial considerations of "public use" and "public purpose." In a South Carolina case involving urban redevelopment of a blighted area, the court allowed part of the condemned property to go to the state university, but declined to permit part of it to pass to private parties for light industrial use. The state constitution used the term "public use," and the court did not view the seizure of slum property and its later disposition to private owners as meeting that requirement. Edens v. Columbia (1956). See similarly, Little Rock v. Raines, (1967). But in Davis v. Lubbock (1959), the Texas constitutional provision on public use was interpreted to encompass a redevelopment plan on the basis that where the property is prevented from becoming a slum again in the foreseeable future, this involves "a public right or use." The redevelopment was to be carried on by private enterprise. Perhaps the most influential case on this is Berman v. Parker (1954), in which the Court upheld a redevelopment program that would shift property to private hands and stated that public ownership is not the only way to promote public purposes.

The broad view of "public use" encompassing a public advantage or the fulfillment of a public purpose is essential to urban redevelopment projects which must necessarily either involve the private sector or ultimately lead to sales of redeveloped property to private purchasers. The weight of authority favors this interpretation.

## § 4.   Determining "Just Compensation": The Fair Market Value Rule

The measure of compensation where all of a person's land is taken is the fair market value of the property as of the time of taking. Where only a part of the land is taken, the measure may be the fair market value of the portion taken plus damages to the part not taken less any special benefits to the land not taken. This is the "value plus damages" rule. Where part of the land is taken, the measure may also be the difference between the market value of the entire tract before the taking and the market value of the remainder after the taking. This is the "before and after" rule. Jurisdictions vary as to which test they follow, although the majority probably follow "value plus damages."

The Uniform Eminent Domain Code adopts but modifies the "before and after" rule in Section 1002 by stating that where there is a partial taking, "the measure of compensation is the *greater* of (1) the value of the property taken * * * or (2) the amount by which the fair market value of the entire property immediately before the taking exceeds the fair market value of the remainder immediately after the taking." This means that where the remainder not taken is so enhanced in value as a result of the taking that there would be a zero award, the condemnor must still pay the value of the land actually taken.

The fair market value of land is the amount that the property would be reasonably worth on the market in a cash sale to a willing buyer if offered for sale by a prudent willing seller. (The situation envisioned assumes that neither is obligated to buy or sell.) This is the "willing buyer-willing seller" test. Implicit in this is that the price offered must be what a reasonable buyer would pay for the highest and best use of the land. This is the "highest and best use" rule. If the highest and best use of the land is for a subdivision, even though it is at present used for some other purpose or is open or unimproved land, then the evaluation must be based on its value for subdivision purposes. The possibility of use of the land for all purposes, both present and prospective, for which it is adapted or might be applied in the reasonably foreseeable future, must be considered. When considered, the value of the land for the use to which reasonable men of adequate means would devote the premises is the ultimate test.

The highest and best use rule is commonly accepted in the United States, although these rules pertaining to valuation are usually not found in statutes. The Uniform Eminent Domain Code defines fair market value in Section 1004 by utilizing the willing buyer-willing seller test, but also provides that the value of property for which there is no relevant market is its value determined by just and equitable methods of valuation. The highest and best use requirement is implicit in Section 1007 of the Code. In the application of the highest and best use rule, a landowner should be required to show that the property is adaptable to the other use, that it is reasonably probable that it will be put to this use within a reasonable time, and that the market value has been enhanced by this other use for which it is adaptable.

The value of the land to the taker is generally rejected as having no relevance, and the value of the land to the owner bears consideration only in the sense that the market value should represent a rough approximation of its value to the owner. The problem with permitting the value to the owner to be considered is that any compensation for sentimental value would place an unfair burden on the condemning authority and cannot be accurately measured. The Uniform Eminent Domain Code rejects both the value to the owner and value to the taker approaches and follows the fair market value test which is almost universally employed. UEDC, Comment § 1004. Value to the owner should only be a factor when the market value is practically nil. 1 Orgel, *Valuation Under Eminent Domain* § 38, at 175–177 (1953).

## § 5.  Determining Fair Market Value

Although there are many elements which enter into a determination of fair market value, the most commonly employed is the comparable sales approach. Appraisers make a determination of the price paid for similar land in the same general area sold voluntarily at a time not too distant from the time of the taking. The property sold must be comparable, and in determining that, consideration must be given to the location, size, sales price, date and character of the sale, commercial, industrial or residential advantages, the extent of improved or unimproved characteristics, and similar aspects. The comparable sales approach is the one most commonly employed by appraisers, but there are other approaches to valuation and other types of evidence. These other approaches include the capitalization of income method which is often used for industrial or commercial property and for rental property. (To be a valid approach the income must be closely related to the value of the land itself.) Another approach would be appraisal of the land value considered as vacant and available for improvement, plus the depreciated replacement cost of the improvements. These methods are resorted to only in special situations or when no comparable sales information can be produced.

The type of evidence most commonly employed is opinion testimony from experts or from persons having sufficient knowledge as to the value of the particular piece of property as well as other property in the area to offer a reliable opinion. The landowner himself is usually permitted to testify as to the market value if it is shown that he is familiar with the value of real estate in the area. Properly, all witnesses should be required to state the factors upon which their opinion is based, but some states do not require an expert witness to state the basis for his opinion.

As mentioned, a method occasionally employed to determine value is the actual rental value of the property, capitalized at the rate which local custom adopts for the purpose, if the property is then being rented for the use for which it is best suited. 4 Nichols, supra § 12.3122. Evidence of rent actually received at a time reasonably near the time of the taking should be admitted. However, it is generally held improper to consider profits from a business conducted on the property unless the profits are attributable to the character of the land. (There are some cases which admit evidence of profits from a farm.) The reason for not admitting evidence of business profits is that under the general rule the owner is not entitled to recover anticipated profits which are lost by reason of the taking. It would seem to be helpful to a court to have information on current profits which, although they are subject to change, could be considered as an element in determining value.

The cost of the property and the improvements may be admitted as an aid in determining market value where there is no readily ascertainable market value for the particular use. Evidence of the cost of improvements for restoration purposes, and evidence of relocation costs and removal costs are generally admitted.

The general rule is that the price paid by the condemnor for other land in the same area is not admissible. Such payments are not thought to be indicative of market value. While the price paid by the condemnor for similarly located lands may vary, it would seem difficult to segregate testimony of the comparable value of similarly situated property from evidence of the purchase price paid for it by the condemnor.

Unaccepted offers to purchase the property are generally excluded from evidence. Some states admit such evidence if the proponent can show that it was a bona fide offer for cash and was made by someone financially able to carry through with it. The danger of admitting unaccepted offers into evidence is that the offer might be an exorbitant offer not made in good faith. Compromise offers by the condemnor are also inadmissible. Although unaccepted offers are not admitted, the purchase price paid by the owner does have a bearing on the market value if the purchase is not too remote from the time of taking. Its usefulness must be weighed in the light of recent market fluctuations.

The Uniform Eminent Domain Code has an article which contains special rules for evidence in condemnation actions. It provides for a view of the property by the jury and judge for the purpose of understanding and weighing the valuation evidence offered. UEDC § 1102. This generally is in accord with the majority rule. It provides for opinion testimony from qualified witnesses, the landowner or shareholders, officers or employees of a corporation or partnership. UEDC § 1103. Evidence may be received on the extent of loss, the present use and highest and best use, loss of nonconforming uses, damage to crops, and zoning or other restrictions on the use and the possibility of a change in those restrictions. UEDC § 1104. Evidence as to the remainder value following a partial taking may be received on the increase or decrease in the productivity and convenience of use attributable to the taking, impairment or improvement of access to highways, benefit or detriment caused by a change in grade, enhancement or loss of appearance, view or light and air, benefit or damage from severance of the land, damage from the distance of the remainder or improvements on it to the project caused by such things as noise, fumes, vibration or the like, and cost of fencing necessary for the remainder. UEDC § 1105. Opinion evidence may be based on any nonconjectural matter ordinarily relied upon by experts whether it would be admissible in evidence or not. UEDC § 1106. A valuation witness may consider the price of any good faith sale or contract of sale regardless of when it was entered into. UEDC § 1107. The guidelines for consideration of comparable sales by opinion witnesses are in keeping with the general rule earlier expressed. UEDC § 1108. Valuation witnesses may consider the terms of leases, net rental income capitalized at a fair interest rate, reproduction or replacement costs, and the condition of property in the general vicinity. UEDC §§ 1109–1112. Witnesses may not base their opinions on the price of other property acquired by condemnation, unaccepted offers, options or listings, the assessed value for tax purposes, an opinion as to the value of other property, the terms of a trade or exchange, and in general exercises of the police power or other noncompensable damage. UEDC § 1113.

## § 6. Compensation and Compensable Interests

Generally speaking, private property may not be taken or damaged without payment of just compensation to the owner. 3 Nichols, supra § 8.1. Not all state constitutions contain the provision that compensation be paid for damaging as well as for taking property. Damages, however, are generally recoverable one way or another.

Obviously, compensation must be paid when all or part of a piece of property is taken. There are other compensable property rights, however, which may be less apparent. A person holding a vested or contingent remainder is entitled to compensation. Both the lessor and lessee are entitled to compensation for their separate interests when condemned property is subject to a lease. The holder of an easement is entitled to compensation for impairment or elimination of it. Mineral interests are compensable unless the severed mineral ownership and use remains unaffected by the condemnation. Under the better view, compensation should be paid for impairment or destruction of restrictive covenants creating equitable servitudes. All rights in property, including reversionary interests, possibilities of reverter, powers of termination, executory interests, charges upon the land, and prescriptive or adverse rights which can be established, should be compensated.

Other compensable elements are less distinct. The removal of earth from property is a compensable injury to land. Interference with an existing easement is compensable, as is interference reducing the value of property not physically taken. Loss of access or of ingress and egress or a change in the grade of a highway or street amounts to a taking of a property right, although the mere alteration of traffic flow does not go that far. Obstruction of the free flow of light and air to abutting property is an element of damage. The pollution of air and water is an interference with a property right which should be compensated. The taking or damaging of land includes interruption of the common, necessary use of the property which is so serious that it interferes with the rights of the owner to an extent greater than mere temporary inconvenience.

On the other hand, there are many "consequential damages" or side effects of condemnation actions which are not ordinarily compensable. These include loss of business income, goodwill, temporary interruption of business, temporary interference with the use of abutting property, losses resulting from relocation of a highway, and losses or inconvenience produced by noise, dust or fumes from projects. The Uniform Eminent Domain Code contains a provision allowing recovery for loss of goodwill (UEDC § 1016), but the traditional view is that this is too speculative to permit evaluation. Moreover, although state courts have traditionally not allowed compensation for moving expenses, the Code in Article XIV contains provisions allowing compensation for moving expenses, replacement housing and other relocation losses. This satisfies the provisions of Title II of the Federal Uniform Relocation Assistance and Real Property Acquisitions Policies Act of 1970 (P.L. 91–646), with which state and local agencies presently must comply in order to secure federal financial assistance.

It is difficult to catalogue compensable and non-compensable interests or elements of damage. The law is in a state of flux, tending toward a wider spectrum of compensability. The evolution of the idea that if a person's property is taken or his property rights damaged or destroyed, then he should be made whole, continues to broaden the concept of what relief should be awarded. For example, contrary to the traditional approach, the Uniform Eminent Domain Code makes provision for award of litigation expenses, including attorney's fees, upon dismissal of the action by the condemnor and under certain circumstances as part of the judgment. UEDC §§ 1205, 1303.

## § 7.  Consequential Damages

In the preceding section, mention was made of such elements as loss of goodwill, moving expenses, interruption of business, and inconveniences of various kinds. These are forms of "consequential damages" for which recovery traditionally was denied. We have seen, however, that the trend of the law is toward a broadening of permissible recovery.

There are several difficulties in awarding damages of this type. The major problem is that they cannot properly be assessed. Loss of goodwill and loss of profits due to interruption of business activity are obviously speculative. Appraisers have to pluck at rainbows to arrive at a dollar figure. Also, some of these values continue—as in the case of goodwill in the event the condemnee sets up shop at some other reasonably suitable location. Moreover, aside from a condemnation suit, some portion of loss in this regard might result in any sale.

As indicated in the last section, courts have historically not permitted recovery for inconveniences or losses occasioned by noise, dust, fumes and the like from condemnation projects. The law on this subject may be in the process of changing. Temporary inconveniences of this type would probably still not lead to a recovery in most states, but permanent changes accompanied by these side effects have led to recovery in a substantial minority of jurisdictions. Noise, dust, fumes, lights and the like have in some instances transcended the traditional nuisance doctrine and have resulted in a taking. See, e.g., United States v. Certain Parcels of Land in Kent County (W.D.Mich.1966); Thornburg v. Port of Portland (1962); Martin v. Port of Seattle (1964). In *Thornburg* these nuisance-like qualities of an adjoining airport were held to constitute a taking even though there were no overflights and thus no trespass to the plaintiff's airspace.

As stated previously, there seems to be a broadening of concepts of compensability, and this trend is nowhere more apparent than in situations involving consequential damages and inverse condemnation.

## § 8.  Inverse Condemnation

Actions brought by landowners alleging that a taking of their property has resulted from activities of public agencies or private bodies vested with authority to condemn are referred to as inverse condemnation actions. This is essentially "reverse condemnation" in that the landowner is the party bringing the suit and alleging a deprivation of property rights. No condemnation proceedings have been commenced by a condemning authority.

Inverse condemnation actions have been a fertile field for litigation in recent years. They have resulted from governmental activity which physically or indirectly invades the land or airspace of a landowner. Trespass can result, for example, from low-flying aircraft which interfere with the use of land or from the flooding of land through nearby governmental activity or, as we have seen, from excessive noise, fumes, dust and the like in some jurisdictions. Situations involving a change of grade or a loss of access in highway situations lead to such lawsuits. Extinguishment of certain private rights, such as restrictive covenants or easements, may lead to such actions. Substantial impairment of the exercise of private rights in property provide the potential for suits of this type. In addition, zoning itself, as we have seen, provides a major basis for allegations of a taking resulting from the use of the police power.

These cases, of course, result in payment by the government of the amount it would have been required to pay had there been formal condemnation proceedings if the landowner is successful. The basic arguments are about the same in every case: the defendant agency contends that it took no land and did not affect compensable property rights; and the plaintiff landowner argues that the action complained of was such an interference with or invasion of his property rights as to amount to a compensable taking. Over the past several decades, there has been a marked increase in inverse condemnation actions and a broadening of the bases for recovery which corresponds in large measure to the situation of the law of torts.

The aviation cases in particular have spawned a great many inverse condemnation actions. The *Thornburg* case mentioned in the previous section is an example, and it is a minority view only in the sense that it did not involve trespasses produced by continuous overflights. The landmark case, United States v. Causby (1946), did involve overflights which trespassed in the airspace of the plaintiff landowner and produced interference with the use of his land. Later in Griggs v. Allegheny County (1962), the Court held that flights in FAA-defined navigable airspace on landings and take-offs constituted a taking of an air easement when there was substantial interference with the rights of the landowner. An interesting "cross" between these cases and the highway loss of access cases is Bydlon v. United States (1959), in which compensation was allowed to resort operators in a national forest because a flight ceiling kept aircraft from flying in to the resorts and attempts to establish a land route were unsuccessful. Their right of access by air (which was the best means of transit) had been taken. Inverse condemnation actions involving loss of access or easements of light, air and view are related—there is no direct invasion, no physical change or improvement except on property which is already publicly owned, but in some situations the action taken is sufficient to amount to a deprivation necessitating compensation. Thus the loss of somewhat intangible property interests may form a basis for recovery.

As the Supreme Court stated in Armstrong v. United States (1960): "The Fifth Amendment's guarantee that private property shall not be taken for a public use without just compensation was designed to bar Government from forcing some people alone to bear public burdens which, in all fairness and justice, should be borne by the public as a whole."

## § 9.   Police Power or a Taking?

Whenever the use of police power is confiscatory, the result is to deprive a landowner of rights which can only be obtained by condemnation and payment of just compensation. Abuse of the police power thus becomes akin to inverse condemnation. The traditional difference in the two, up until *First English* and *Lucas*, had been that when a police power regulation was either arbitrary and unreasonable or confiscatory, the remedy was to have it invalidated, whereas in inverse condemnation, property rights had been permanently damaged or lost and the usual remedy was a suit for damages. In the traditional police power situation, the owner is normally seeking to alleviate or remove the regulation, whereas in inverse condemnation it is often too late for injunctive relief to prove to be an adequate remedy. Of course, a landowner may seek both injunctive relief and damages if it is a situation in which an injunction can be granted.

Arguably, *First English* and *Lucas* represent a tendency to ignore the historic difference between the nature of the police power and eminent domain. But they seem to be saying that regulatory deprivation of all economic use is no more than another form of inverse condemnation.

What these cases may do is draw the line to some degree between valid regulation and a police power taking. Deprivation of all economic use is a taking. Apparently, a traditional zoning classification which should be changed in favor of a less exclusive or lower use would be an unreasonable classification but not a violation of substantive due process. It is not a taking because there is an assigned economic use, although it is unreasonable to expect that use to eventuate.

This still leaves room for argument as to whether certain regulations go beyond what constitutes a reasonable versus unreasonable use. Will the line be drawn at the extreme situations involved in *First*

*English* and *Lucas* or will the Court find other situations in which the available uses are considered so minor that for all practical purposes it may be said that there has been a deprivation of all reasonable economic use? Where do you draw the line between valid regulation and a regulatory taking?

Moreover, aside from the question of the award of damages for a taking, when does a regulation exceed what is permitted?

The difficulty is that there are no rules so specific that a particular situation can always be accurately identified. These cases will normally not involve activities which are obviously arbitrary or confiscatory nor activities which have been clearly established as valid. The discussion which follows attempts to provide guidelines and insights, but with the realization that there is no litmus paper test that can be applied and no precise dividing line delineating the point at which the exercise of the police power ceases to be valid and becomes a taking. See Van Alstyne, Taking or Damaging by Police Power: The Search for Inverse Condemnation Criteria, 44 *S.Cal.L.Rev.* 1, 14 (1971). Holmes did not attempt to provide criteria when confronted with the problem and contented himself with stating that it was a matter of *degree* as to whether a regulation amounted to a taking. Pennsylvania Coal Co. v. Mahon (1922).

Commentators before and since have wrestled with the problem and have attempted to develop the general propositions which Holmes avoided. Opinions in cases have largely been of little help, with most courts being satisfied with saying that the regulation goes too far in the specific situation under consideration. How the matter is viewed is dependent in large measure on how a particular commentator or court views private property rights as opposed to rights of society as a whole. The courts have rejected the two extremes—that an individual's land may never be regulated or his rights diminished no matter what the social necessity, and to the contrary, that the state has an absolute right to regulate no matter what the effect on a particular landowner. However, the outcome in a particular case may depend upon which of these polar positions a particular court generally leans toward.

In that regard, one group of writers propounded the suggestion that the United States Supreme Court should overrule the rather general balancing test which Holmes enunciated in *Pennsylvania Coal* and declare that a land use regulation would *never constitute a taking* if it were reasonably related to a valid public purpose. F. Bosselman, D. Callies & J. Banta, *The Taking Issue* 238 (1973). They viewed Holmes' statement as historically inaccurate, unnecessary, and disastrous from an environmental standpoint. Courts will never move to such an absolutist position in view of these recent decisions allowing damages, and although state courts have generally been reluctant to award damages in police power situations, it also seems highly unlikely that state courts will move in that direction. State and federal courts have gone to great lengths over the past twenty-five years to uphold environmental regulations, but the courts have not departed from the proposition that if a regulation renders the land valueless or nearly so, the magic line has been crossed and the regulation is invalid. The flood plain cases illustrate this point.

The opposite side of the coin may be found in Blackstone's statement that the institution of private property is so greatly regarded that law "will not authorize the least violation of it; no, not even for the general good of the whole community." Blackstone, *Commentaries* 139 (1782). The same underlying philosophy is embodied in Article 2, Section 22 of the Arkansas Constitution of 1874 which states that "the right of private property is before and higher than any constitutional sanction"—a rather extreme expression which the Arkansas Court tends to quote when striking down regulatory measures.

Courts today have moved away from this latter type of thinking. But modern support for the argument that a regulation should not be a taking if related to a valid public purpose can be drawn by inference from recent environmental decisions. (Historically, probably the leading case supporting or allowing the inference of such a theory would be Harlan's opinion for the Court in Mugler v. Kansas (1887).) Just v. Marinette County (1972) is a prime example of the impact of environmentally related decisions on this subject. In upholding a shoreland zoning ordinance providing protection of wetlands, the Wisconsin Court stated that there is a taking only when the restriction is so great that the landowner should not have to bear the burden on behalf of the public and not when the damage is incidental. It reasoned that if the potential use for the prohibited purpose would produce "public harm," it could be validly banned without compensation, while if the intention was to produce a public benefit, compensation would be required. The Wisconsin Court opined that the flood plain cases place too much emphasis on the commercial value of the land if its condition is changed to make it usable. The depreciation in the *Just* case was not based on use of the land in its natural state. But the Court sought to distinguish the *Pennsylvania Coal* case by stating that the ordinance in question did not seek to improve the public condition but only to preserve the natural condition of the land based on environmental concerns. Consequently, it cannot be said that *Just* goes so far as to uphold any regulation which promotes a valid public purpose since it would be a valid public purpose to attempt to improve the public condition. Related to *Just* are such cases as In re Spring Valley Development (Me. 1973). Justice Scalia, in the *Lucas* case, severely criticized the public harm-public benefit dichotomy, stating that such a test is too dependent on rhetorical posturing; every regulation could be justified or condemned under such vague analysis.

Although environmental cases seem to go a long way toward upholding police power controls, they contain several factors which render them distinguishable: (1) The general recognition of the importance of the value sought to be protected led the courts to deal more liberally with the means employed; (2) the courts were able to rationalize that they were not preventing use of the land except in a particular way which if permitted would be harmful to the public; and (3) the "public harm" concept permitted the situation to be viewed as something related to preventing a public nuisance. While much of this may be viewed as sophistry since the end result of the *Just* case, for example, was to deny any alteration (and commercial exploitation) of the land, the fact remains that the court went to substantial lengths to avoid the appearance of changing the rule requiring compensation.

A reasonable inquiry is how valid is *Just* in light of *First English? First English* also involved environmental concerns as well as flood problems, but the end result was essentially the same—the denial of any alteration of the land. Did *First English* wipe out the rationale of *Just* or do other factors, such as pollution to Wisconsin's inland lakes and waterways, suffice to distinguish the cases?

The more common approach to the problem is to accept the general balancing test of *Pennsylvania Coal* and attempt to develop principles or propositions from the cases which provide insight into what the courts are likely to do in a particular situation. This means that diminution in value, even if substantial, does not give rise to compensation but is only a factor to be weighed. It also means that the importance of the regulation in terms of promoting the general welfare is a major consideration but not the sole determinant. In short, both of the extremes enter into the equation but both can be rejected as sole determinants in favor of considering all of the factors which lead to the result— factors which may be weighed differently under differing circumstances.

Some courts, in looking at the diminution of value of the landowner's property, follow the theory that if the owner's ability to profit from the property has been severely diminished as a result of governmental action, the landowner is entitled to compensation. The assumption is that the government regulation vests in the public certain rights which were not previously possessed at the expense, in terms of profit capacity, of the private landowner. It has been suggested by a leading scholar that this is a denial of the existence of public rights. See Sax, Takings, Private Property and Public Rights, 81 *Yale L.J.* 149, 160–162 (1971). This process, it is argued, may deter government regulation and adversely affect resource allocation because it discriminates against public rights. But we have seen from the cases that although severe diminution of value resulting from use limitations does at times lead to recovery, cases have also upheld some rather substantial diminutions of value where the public interest being preserved was viewed as very important or where the effect on other landowners in the area would have been particularly harmful. The public interest considerations can be seen in environmental litigation, and the latter situation can be seen in the spot zoning cases and in cases involving nuisance-like commercial or industrial uses. Therefore, diminution in value is tempered by public interest considerations and by the interests of other nearby landowners. If the proposed use can be viewed as a public harm requiring prevention, as opposed to some public benefit to be derived from the restriction, compensation for the limitation is much less likely to be awarded.

Consequently, while we cannot develop an equation, we can clearly identify certain factors with the recognition that their quantitative effect will differ from situation to situation: How great is the public interest in a particular restriction and how essential is it to the general welfare in terms of societal values? Is the restriction intended to procure a public benefit or to prevent a public harm? What is the overall effect on other landowners in comparison to the aggrieved landowner and as opposed to the interests of the public in general? How substantial and how severe is the loss to the landowner as a result of the restriction when compared to the public interest? Where does the particular public value involved rank on the scale of values which are being affected in the particular jurisdiction considering the issue?

The equation which cannot be developed comes out, imprecisely, like this: Public interest (weighed on the jurisdictional scale of values) + public harm (to be prevented, if any) + interest of other landowners (not the public generally)–severity of loss to complaining landowner and–public benefits unrelated to preventing harm or to neutral public interests = either a valid exercise of the police power or a taking.

Having performed this illusory exercise, one cannot help but agree with the observation of a prominent land use scholar that the search for the answer to this problem "may be the lawyer's equivalent of the physicist's hunt for the quark." C. Haar, *Land-Use Planning* 766 (3d ed. 1977).

# CHAPTER VII

# ZONING

## § 1. Background

Zoning is the principal tool employed in urban planning. Although zoning was utilized in such European countries as Germany and France in the 19th century, the first comprehensive zoning ordinance was that adopted in 1916 by New York City and upheld in a case decided in 1920. Lincoln Trust Co. v. Williams Bldg. Corp. (1920). Other states followed suit and broadened the process. Wisconsin permitted zoning outside of corporate limits in 1923 and authorized rural zoning in 1929.

The validity of zoning is predicated on the police power—the power to regulate for the advancement and protection of the health, morals, safety or general welfare of the community. Whether a particular zoning regulation will be upheld depends generally on whether it represents a valid exercise of the police power. If the application of the regulation to the property in question is unreasonable, arbitrary and capricious, it will be held invalid. If it deprives the property of all or practically all reasonable economic use, then it will be invalidated on the basis both that it is unreasonable and that it constitutes a taking of the property without just compensation. Under the test framed by Justice Holmes in Pennsylvania Coal Co. v. Mahon (1922), and followed in varying degrees since then, the extent of the police power and its valid use will depend on the particular facts of the case at hand. The same is true with respect to whether a particular type of regulation is a valid exercise of the police power.

Prior to comprehensive zoning, the police power was used for relatively simple regulatory measures relating to fire zones, building controls and limitations on certain nuisance-like uses in locations where they were not compatible. For example, Reinman v. Little Rock (1915), upheld an ordinance prohibiting a livery stable within a certain area, and Hadacheck v. Sebastian (1915), upheld an ordinance which prohibited operation of a brickyard or brick kiln within certain limits in Los Angeles. Comprehensive zoning however, has involved the creation of a variety of use, height and area restrictions in districts throughout a municipality.

After comprehensive zoning came into use, it received varied treatment at the hands of state courts. It was upheld in New York, as we have seen, and in Wisconsin shortly thereafter in State ex rel. Carter v. Harper (1923), which opinion is a rather classic statement of the rationale supporting comprehensive zoning. Maryland, however, struck down the Baltimore zoning ordinance, viewing zoning as an encroachment upon constitutionally protected property rights.

Comprehensive zoning was upheld by the Supreme Court in the landmark case of Euclid v. Ambler Realty Co. (1926), which drew upon the nuisance analogy of pre-zoning cases to uphold the basic validity of such ordinances under the police power and which decision, in particular, emphasized the need to protect single-family dwellings from commercial, industrial or multi-family encroachment. Ever since *Euclid,* such zoning has commonly been referred to as "Euclidian" or "Euclidean" zoning. A year and a half after *Euclid,* the Supreme Court invalidated a zoning provision as being unreasonable and unconstitutional as it applied to a particular tract of land. Nectow v. Cambridge, (1928). This case provided what then became the customary manner of attacking such an ordinance— i.e., the ordinance is confiscatory or is unreasonable and arbitrary in the way in which it has been applied to a specific parcel of land. (This was viewed as the logical application of *Pennsylvania Coal,* supra.) The customary remedy to the invalidity was to require rezoning in such a way as to permit the landowner to make reasonable use of his property.

## § 2.  Enabling Acts and Zoning Ordinances

The general rule is that to be valid a zoning ordinance must be authorized by enabling authority, and the validity of the provisions of the ordinance may be tested on the basis of whether they are "ultra vires" or are within the confines of the enabling authority. While such enabling authority may be found in a state constitution or a municipal

charter, it is customarily the result of a state statute authorizing local zoning ordinances, providing
the basis for the creation of planning or zoning
commissions and boards of adjustments and their
authority, and prescribing certain criteria for such
ordinances and their adoption. The original basis
for much of the zoning legislation in most states
was the Standard Zoning Enabling Act which was
prepared as a model act in the 1920's by the U.S.
Department of Commerce. This act is often referred
to simply as the "Standard Act."

State enabling legislation differs somewhat on
whether the enactment of the zoning ordinance be
preceded by a study of conditions in the community
followed by a report or reports on such conditions
and the development of the comprehensive plan on
which the zoning ordinance will be based. States
requiring such a procedure, which is considered to
be the better practice, are placing an emphasis on
planning with zoning to serve as the instrument of
planning. After a study of population trends, existing land use patterns, traffic conditions and problems, the location of major business districts and
commercial areas, drainage or sewage problems, the
location of public buildings, single-family areas, and
so forth, a master plan is developed and after public
hearings on the proposed plan following notice to
the public, the plan is ultimately adopted. The
zoning ordinance is then written based on the needs
and requirements of the master plan or comprehensive plan, and after notice and public hearings, it is
adopted. A number of cases have held that unless

such a process is followed, any zoning ordinance which is adopted is invalid. This is based on the view that zoning is not an end in itself but is a tool of planning. But, as stated, this rule is not universal. Some states do not require that a planning process precede adoption of the zoning ordinance. Also, because of the problem of controlling the development of discordant land uses until the planning process is completed, interim zoning of a temporary nature is sometimes permitted. Unless interim zoning is specifically authorized by the enabling act, however, it may be held invalid.

In all of this, the provisions of the enabling act will control the outcome. If it does not require comprehensive planning as a condition precedent to adoption of a zoning ordinance, then no such process need be followed. If it does, then the zoning ordinance must await the completion of the planning process. While planning properly should precede the zoning ordinance, it would seem desirable to permit interim zoning for a period not to exceed one year.

## § 3.  Spot Zoning

Once a zoning ordinance has been adopted and the land has been zoned, problems arise with regard to proposed amendments changing its application to specific parcels or with respect to granting relief from its provisions for certain lots. Such amendments or relief often give rise to allegations of "spot zoning."

Spot zoning, by definition, is invalid because it amounts to an arbitrary, capricious and unreasonable treatment of a limited area within a particular district. As such, it departs from the comprehensive plan. It singles out a parcel of land for special treatment or privileges not in harmony with the other use classifications in the area and without any apparent circumstances which call for different treatment. Spot zoning almost invariably involves a single parcel or at least a limited area. However, the "floating zone" device which is discussed later in this chapter was successfully attacked as constituting spot zoning even though that device normally involves substantial acreage. Eves v. Zoning Board of Adjustment (1960).

An allegation of spot zoning may arise from situations involving amendments to the ordinance, variances, special use permits or special exceptions or similar devices discussed in later sections. Any change may be subjected to such a contention except possibly for one involving comprehensive revision of a substantial area or of the master plan based on new studies and new information. Even then, some small part of the revision may come under attack.

Allegations of spot zoning are defended against with such contentions as that the change is in accord with the master plan, that conditions in the area have changed drastically since the original zoning thereby justifying the change as to the parcel or parcels involved, that the action taken by the city zoning authority was fairly debatable and entitled to be upheld unless clearly erroneous and arbitrary, that the parcel or parcels are afflicted by some condition peculiar and unique to them which justifies the change, that the change meets the criteria of the ordinance allowing a conditional use or special use permit or special exception, that the zoning would be confiscatory or an unreasonable hardship to the landowner unless the change were granted, and that (in the case of larger parcels) the change is in the public interest and promotes the general welfare.

There is some indication that where the boundaries of several communities run together, one community may rezone in such a way that it constitutes spot zoning in terms of the adverse and unreasonable effect upon adjoining communities. Borough of Cresskill v. Borough of Dumont (1954).

## § 4.  Zoning Amendments

The most obvious way to effect a zoning change is to amend the ordinance. There may be a single, major amendment as the result of new studies. The usual situation, however, involves periodic amendments resulting from applications from interested landowners. This process involves a legislative act on the part of the council or board according to the majority view.

Amendments are tested by essentially the same standards as the zoning ordinance, i.e., whether the restriction is arbitrary or whether it bears a reasonable relationship to the police power. No vested rights accrue in neighboring landowners to have land zoned the same way it has been. While a change in the character of an area is often a predicate for rezoning, it is not an essential element to rezoning if the amendment is reasonable. Moreover, a landowner seeking a rezoning amendment does not normally have to establish that denial of his request would be confiscatory as to use of his land (although he would clearly be entitled to the amendment if that could be shown). If the relative gain to the public is small when compared to the hardship to the property owner, the amendment will likely be granted. See, e.g., Duggan v. Cook County (1975).

Periodic amendments may result in allegations of spot zoning, in which the change from single-family residential to multi-family residential, for example, is essentially preferential in nature and cannot be reasonably justified. On the other hand, if the amendment in question involves rezoning in accord with a plan which has taken into account the changing circumstances inherent in or impinging upon a single-family zone, then it is more likely to survive an allegation of spot zoning. Of course, an amendment following negotiations with the owner may give rise to an allegation of contract rezoning if that course is pursued, although a rezoning with unilateral conditions attached might permit a different result, as will subsequently be discussed.

The Model Land Development Code seeks to discourage amendments involving small parcels. Section 2–205 contains rather broad provisions authorizing the revision of district boundary lines upon the making of certain findings by the land development agency.

The question of standing to attack a zoning amendment is rarely raised. It is usually the nearby neighbors who object or bring suit. Their allegations usually relate to diminution in value of their property if the proposed change is permitted and other adverse effects upon their property which would result from a different, proposed use. If the objectors include a neighborhood property owners association, again the question of standing is seldom reached; but in questioning the standing of such an association, the courts would look to its capacity to assume an adversary role, its size and composition, the potential effect on the group it represents, and whether membership is open to all property owners in its neighborhood.

## § 5.  Contract or Conditional Rezoning

These terms are sometimes used interchangeably, particularly by courts which are in the process of invalidating a rezoning on this basis. Some courts have sought to distinguish between the two, holding "contract zoning" (or rezoning, actually) to be invalid while sustaining conditional rezoning. Thus, the Maryland Court has referred to "impermissible conditional zoning," while other states have approved unilaterally imposed conditions or rezoning which is subject to revocation if certain conditions are not met. Cf.: Montgomery County v. National Capital Realty Corp. (1972), with State ex rel. Zupancic v. Schimenz (1970) and Arkenberg v. Topeka (1966).

The basis of the invalidity of contract rezoning is that a city cannot bargain away its police power. A process of negotiation between the municipal government and a private person leading to zoning reclassification of land in order to accommodate private interests has been viewed as amounting to spot zoning and thus invalid. Based on this thinking, some jurisdictions have held that rezoning on the express condition that the owner impose certain restrictions on the use of his premises is also illegal. The idea is that the conditions must be imposed, if at all, by the zoning ordinance.

Courts which have sustained conditional rezoning have segregated situations in which the city has unilaterally imposed conditions which must be met for the rezoning to take place or has rezoned the land conditionally subject to revocation of the action if the conditions are not met. Sylvania Electric Products v. Newton (1962); Church v. Islip (1960). These special restrictions are justified on the theory that they require the owner to perform some act or make some improvements which will justify a different classification and which will avoid harm to neighboring property or to the planned use of the surrounding area. Cases upholding such reclassification view the conditions as reasonable and not arbitrary and as a valid exercise of the city's police power. Perhaps implicit in those cases is the thought that to deny rezoning which would be reasonable if certain conditions existed or could be

created would, in itself, be arbitrary. Contract rezoning, on the other hand theoretically involves a
situation similar to a bilateral contract in which
both the city and the landowner enter into an
express agreement involving mutual obligations.

The distinction is obviously tenuous. Any owner
or developer seeking rezoning will undergo a period
of discussion and negotiation of sorts with the
planning staff and possibly the planning commission or even the city board. What appear to be
unilateral conditions have often been hammered
out over a period of time involving numerous discussion sessions. On the other hand, the advantage
of conditional rezoning lies in the flexibility afforded planning officials in seeking to accommodate
landowners in such a way as not to interfere with
the master plan or harm adjoining landowners. It
affords a middle ground rather than a strict "yes"
or "no." Where development of a sizeable area of
land is involved, conditional rezoning is quite common.

There is a split of authority on conditional rezoning with its validity having been accepted largely in
Midwestern and Northeastern jurisdictions. Contract rezoning is another form of spot zoning and is
invalid. The basic question is whether a given jurisdiction will "spin off" conditional rezoning into a
separate category or classify both forms as essentially the same and as illegal.

It should be noted that conditions are commonly
attached to the granting of variances and special
use or conditional use permits or special exceptions.

Therefore, why should any distinction be made between rezoning subject to conditions and administrative relief granted subject to conditions? Presumably, it goes back to the old idea that rezoning is a legislative act and (in a jurisdiction making no distinction between contract and conditional rezoning), the legislative body cannot bargain away the police power. Granting a special use permit, special exception or conditional use permit is viewed as an administrative or quasi-judicial act. Just as the distinction that many states make between illicit contract rezoning and permissible conditional rezoning is somewhat narrow, so also is the legislative-administrative distinction that is made between rezoning and the granting of a special or conditional use. In a minority of jurisdictions which regard the rezoning of small parcels as being administrative in nature, which it largely is, then there is no reason not to permit conditional rezoning. But even some of the states which make the distinction between rezoning and the administrative process view conditional rezoning as permissible.

The Indiana legislature adopted a statute which has the effect of allowing or requiring an owner to make written commitments relative to rezoning and which also has the effect of legalizing conditional rezoning by statute.

## § 6. Variances

The variance is the most controversial, most abused, and usually the most used administrative relief that can be granted in requests for zoning changes. A variance is granted when "unnecessary hardship" would result to the landowner if it were denied. Some statutes allow variances based upon either "unnecessary hardship" or "practical difficulties," but this seeming liberalization of the rule is likely illusory since cases which find "practical difficulties" to exist will be translated in other jurisdictions to mean "unnecessary hardship." "Mere" hardship is not enough to amount to unnecessary hardship, however. Devereaux Foundation Inc. Zoning Case (1945). Also, self-imposed hardship is regarded as insufficient for obtaining a variance.

These hardship conditions which lead to the granting of variances should be peculiar and unique to the land in question. If such conditions existed over a wide area, the proper remedy would be rezoning. An appropriate variance situation, however, involves a single lot or a relatively small area which suffers from peculiar, unique circumstances.

There are area variances and use variances. The former is the least controversial and least abused because it is generally granted due to some odd configuration of the lot or some peculiar natural condition which prevents normal construction in compliance with zoning restrictions. The relief is usually a simple relaxation of the requirements as to set-back or minimum floor area or the like. A use variance on the other hand involves a change in the permitted use—as from single-family residential use to multi-family use or to one of the higher classifications of commercial use. A use variance can only be sustained where unnecessary hardship (or, in some states, practical difficulties) would result, and since this must be hardship which is unique and peculiar to the lot, use variances are often attacked as constituting spot zoning. Some jurisdictions have applied the unnecessary hardship test to use variances and the practical difficulties test to area variances, which is both reasonable and descriptive of the different nature of the problem. New York has enacted a statute to that effect.

Abuses involving the use variance led one city to abolish the device, but the state supreme court ruled that the use variance could not be abolished under the state enabling act (even though the enabling act made no specific requirement along that line). Nuckolls v. City of Tulsa (Okl.1976). Since hardship cases could have been handled under other administrative devices designed to relieve hardship, and through the amendment process, the decision was unnecessary and unfortunate. Moreover, some state statutes do not permit use variances at all. Perhaps it was the desire to prevent abuse which led one court to define unnecessary hardship as a deprivation of all beneficial use amounting to confiscation. R–N–R Associates v. Zoning Board (1965). This definition perhaps requires too much, but the burden on the applicant would seem to deter the wholesale granting of variances.

The hardship which justifies granting a variance must stem from the application of the ordinance to the property in question and not from actions of the applicant which amount to self-induced hardship. Moreover, if the "unique and peculiar" circumstances of the situation actually apply to the entire area or neighborhood, the appropriate corrective device is rezoning rather than a variance.

The Pennsylvania Supreme Court quoted these requirements for a variance: "There are essentially four factors that [an applicant] must prove to be entitled to a variance....The factors are: (1) that an unnecessary hardship exists which is not created by the party seeking the variance and which is caused by unique physical circumstances of the property for which the variance is sought; (2) that a variance is needed to enable the party's reasonable use of the property; (3) that the variance will not alter the essential character of the district or neighborhood, or substantially impair the use or development of the adjacent property such that it is detrimental to the public's welfare; and (4) that the variance will afford the least intrusive solution." Larsen v. Zoning Bd. Of Adjustment (1996). If every board of adjustment and every court were more aware of these factors and applied them more rigorously in place of bending them to meet the economic aims of developers and landowners, use variances would no longer constitute a synonym for evasion of zoning restrictions. As matters stand today, zoning is as much characterized by the variances from it as by the adherence to it.

## § 7.  Special Exceptions and Special Use or Conditional Use Permits

Some writers have attempted to distinguish between special exceptions and special use permits by defining the former to involve authority by the planning board or board of adjustment to permit certain deviant uses where it can make certain findings provided for in the ordinance, and by defining special use permits as involving situations requiring particular attention and special treatment due to the neighborhood or city-wide ramifications of the special use. As a practical matter, the cases illustrate that about the only difference in special exceptions, special use permits, and conditional use permits is the term employed in a particular enabling act or ordinance. See Tullo v. Township of Millburn (1959). The ordinance will specify the conditions and findings which are required to grant such relief, and the relief will be granted only when those conditions are found to exist. Presumably, an implicit condition always would be that the relief granted must neither ravish the master plan for the neighborhood nor amount to such preferential treatment as to constitute spot zoning. One major line of attack on such actions would be that it was unreasonable and capricious for the board to find that the criteria of the ordinance was met or not met in granting or denying the special permit or special exception.

The Model Land Development Code allows special development permits based upon a finding of compatibility with surrounding areas and with developments already permitted under the general provisions of the ordinance.

It is common for boards to attach conditions to the granting of special exceptions or special use permits in order to preserve the integrity of the neighborhood. The same is true of variances. See Montgomery County v. Mossburg (1962).

The difference between variances and special exceptions or special use permits is that variances allow a prohibited use based on unnecessary hardship, while these special permit procedures are allowed in situations specified or described by the zoning ordinance in the event certain facts are found to exist.

The term "*special* exception" should not be confused with a plain *exception* in a zoning ordinance. The latter usually involves a non-discretionary determination in that the ordinance simply provides that certain types of structures or uses are excluded from the application of all or part of the ordinance.

Some cases have involved questions as to whether the special permit procedure embodied in a local ordinance is authorized by state enabling legislation. While the cases have varied, the better view is that unless the local provisions for such procedure are so loose as to involve a delegation of what is traditionally viewed as legislative authority, the issuance of special use permits should be permitted if the prescribed standards are met (including the very basic requirement that the master plan not be violated). Otherwise, municipalities are deprived of a method of alleviating the rigidity of traditional zoning regulations.

## § 8.  Floating Zones

The floating zone is described in the ordinance in such a way that its characteristics and the requirements for its establishment are defined, but its location remains undesignated. It can come into being when the board finds that a situation exists which allows the location of that type of zone in a particular area. Then, the criteria of the ordinance presumably having been met, the floating zone ceases to "float" and is located by a zoning amendment.

This device was upheld in New York and Maryland, but it was invalidated in Pennsylvania as constituting spot zoning and as not being in accord with the comprehensive plan. Rodgers v. Village of Tarrytown (1951); Huff v. Board of Zoning Appeals (1957); Eves v. Zoning Board (1960). In the *Rodgers* case, garden apartments (provided for in the "floating zone" ordinance) were permitted in a single-family residential area where the criteria of the ordinance had been met and where the court thought the action taken formed a part of a comprehensive zoning plan as opposed to spot zoning.

The floating zone is somewhat of an historical antecedent of the modern cluster zone and planned unit development. Its purpose is to provide greater flexibility to the municipality in dealing in a specified, limited way with needs which are expected to occur but cannot presently be accommodated effectively or with as much intelligence now as later.

Floating zones should normally be upheld if permitted by or not in conflict with the master plan, if the criteria and standards provided for them are adequate, and if the action taken is not arbitrary or unreasonable. The type of development should make some difference, since it would appear to be easier to "float" a multi-family residential development into a single-family residential area than to "float" an industrial area or a high density commercial area into disparate zones. But this did not form the basis for the ruling in Pennsylvania. Nor, for that matter, did it form the basis for the favorable ruling in Maryland. The keys to the question of whether a floating zone provision will be upheld probably relate to the interpretation courts are willing to accord to the enabling statute, the criteria employed in the ordinance, and the general attitude of the court toward the issue of the appropriate amount of flexibility to be accorded local authorities.

By way of example, in one case a proposed rezoning involved a floating zone which was upheld against allegations that it amounted to an improper delegation of legislative authority, was lacking in uniform regulations, failed to define standards for project approval, and constituted spot zoning. The court stated that there were uniform restrictions within the type of zone involved, general standards to be considered, and that the fact that spot zoning might occur in a particular circumstance would not invalidate the zoning. Treme v. St. Louis County (Mo.App.1980).

## § 9. Planned Unit Developments and Cluster Zones

These are relatively recent devices intended to ameliorate the rigidity of Euclidian zoning. Their applicability and importance is best understood by reference to subsequent sections in this chapter relating to setback lines, side-lot lines, minimum lot sizes, and the like. Traditional zoning located structures on similarly sized lots in similar locations much as Washington's head might be similarly located on each dollar bill.

Cluster zoning permits residential uses to be "clustered" more closely together than normally permitted, leaving substantial area to be devoted to open space in the form of parks, playgrounds, woods, and the like. The population density in the cluster zone remains essentially the same, and the only advantage to the developer may be the saving of some money on street construction. See Chrinko v. South Brunswick Township Planning Board (1963). The advantage to homeowners and to the public is the creation of an area which preserves many of the amenities of rural living within an urban environment. Property values are maintained (—and, in good developments, promoted—), and thus a basic aim of residential zoning is carried out in a nontraditional context.

The planned unit development (PUD) is broader in scope. It not only involves the clustering of residential uses but also permits commercial uses which are compatible and perhaps even light industry. Height variations may also be involved. See

Orinda Homeowners Committee v. Board of Supervisors (1970). Once again, the relative population and use density of the total area is intended to remain stable while the amount of open space is increased. Implicit in the PUD is the requirement that varying uses blend harmoniously within the area and create an attractive, interrelating unit which should maintain both property values and the aesthetics of the area. The PUD obviously presents a greater potential for abuse than a cluster plan because it involves mixed uses. If it were utilized as a sham to permit commercial or industrial incursion into an area zoned residential, thereby failing to fulfill the underlying rationale for permitting a PUD, it would amount to an arbitrary and capricious abuse of the police power.

A PUD or a cluster zone which is in accord with the criteria previously described should also meet the requirement of being in accord with the master plan (or, if not, the master plan should be amended to permit such developments). *Euclid* sustained zoning at least partly on the basis that this exercise of the police power resulted in maintaining property values. A properly planned PUD or cluster zone does that and with considerably less monotony than the scheme approved in *Euclid*. Moreover, the PUD has the planning value of allowing people to live closer to shopping areas and perhaps closer to where they work, which is a substantial factor in a time when the energy problem is important. The only danger in the PUD would be its potential abuse by greedy developers who were able to overcome the planners politically and create a monstrosity in the name of the PUD.

The PUD concept obviously goes beyond that of the floating zone in that it involves the harmonious integration of multiple uses. It is somewhat comparable to the new town concept on a smaller scale and is attached to an already developed urban area. Proper utilization of the PUD, however, readily lends itself to a comparison with new towns in the sense that both should have similar objectives. PUD ordinance provisions must be carefully drawn to require adequate open space and to achieve the objective of a successful blending of uses. In this regard it is important that adequate acreage be involved in a development, since otherwise the utilization of the PUD concept could result in a peculiar hodge-podge which could adversely affect property values both in the PUD area and in the surrounding area. Most PUD ordinance provisions require public approval of a set of covenants to enforce the PUD plan, including public enforcement of the covenants. If utilized properly, however, the PUD provides a new dimension particularly for suburban or fringe area development. It offers the potential for creating the equivalent of small, model towns around an urban core.

When employed properly, the PUD also offers considerable potential for alleviating the problems of commercial strip zoning and the unfortunate traffic situation which it usually creates.

In judicially evaluating challenges to local actions approving PUDs, the most important role of the courts is to determine whether they are dealing with a device which conforms to the intent behind and the criteria for a PUD or whether the particular action taken allows a large-scale developer to achieve indirectly what he could not achieve directly. Entering into this determination are questions as to population density, the architectural and engineering considerations involved in arranging and locating different uses within the PUD, the interrelationship or successful blending of the various uses, traffic patterns, and provisions for open space and recreational areas.

Similarly, in evaluating PUD ordinances, courts should be primarily concerned with whether the provisions of the ordinance are designed to achieve the purpose of the PUD (or of a cluster zone, if it is that type of ordinance).

## § 10. Buffer or Transition Zones

An older device which was also intended to provide for compatibility of nearby disparate uses was the buffer or transition zone. Such a zone was employed, for example, to assure that in the area between a single-family residential zone and a commercial zone, a multi-family residential zone would smooth the transition or, more appropriately, provide a "buffer" for the single-family residential zone. Open space in the form of a park or playground area could provide for a similar transition

and amount to a buffer. See, generally, Evanston
Best & Co. v. Goodman (1938).

Of course, the use of buffer zoning cannot destroy
the value of the property thereby zoned. The use of
the device must be reasonable and not confiscatory.

The interrelationship of the buffer zone with the
PUD or cluster zone, both of which are of later
lineage, is that these devices attempt to blend harmoniously the uses within an urban area, maintain
property values, and on occasion provide open space
which adds to the amenities of the urban environment. Transition zoning, or a buffer zone, may but
does not necessarily involve open space and is an
earlier recognition of the problem of reconciling
different uses. The PUD is a more recent, more
sophisticated device. Both have been upheld in situations not involving unreasonable or arbitrary classifications or applications.

## § 11.  Judicial Review of Zoning

Some courts in fairly recent years have wrestled
occasionally with the problem of the nature of the
zoning process and the standards for review of
zoning decisions. Traditionally, the process was
viewed as legislative in nature, and this remains the
predominant view today. Under this approach, the
exercise of judgment by a zoning authority is not
overturned unless it is shown to be arbitrary, capricious and unreasonable.

While courts seldom go beyond that statement,
some have attempted to distinguish the original

legislative enactment of the ordinance from situations in which an owner is petitioning for reclassification of his land or for administrative relief. See South Gwinnett Venture v. Pruitt (5th Cir.1973). This case refers to the "adjudicative decision inherent in tract rezoning" which "requires the decision maker to adhere to concepts of minimal due process." In Kropf v. Sterling Heights (1974), the Michigan Court stated that it could not "second guess the local governing bodies" unless the action taken was arbitrary or capricious, but the concurring opinion argued that zoning "represents particularized applications of administrative power, reflecting choices made over an extended period of time * * * *ad hoc, ad hominen*." It argued that such actions were administrative and quasi-judicial in nature. Following this latter line of thought, the Oregon Court rejected the idea that review of zoning decisions by local governing bodies is limited to the question of whether the action was arbitrary or capricious. Fasano v. Board of County Commissioners (1973). The court recognized that most jurisdictions regard a zoning ordinance to be a legislative act and entitled to presumptive validity. But it held that zoning changes involve judicial rather than legislative actions. The opinion states that while it may be argued that planning authorities should be vested with the ability to change classifications due to changed conditions, account must also be taken of "the almost irresistible pressures that can be asserted by the private economic interests on local government."

This approach would allow a court to overturn a zoning change without having to find the action taken to be arbitrary, capricious and unreasonable. In affecting the presumption of validity, it would conceivably affect the result in cases in which the court finds that "reasonable minds might differ" and that the action taken would thus have to be sustained. The reason why some courts have challenged the old premise is expressed in part by one court's concern that in most of the rezoning cases "there actually has been spot zoning and the courts have upheld or invalidated the change according to how flagrant the violation of true zoning principles has been." Fritts v. Ashland (Ky.App.1961).

It may be said in opposition to eliminating the presumption in situations involving zoning amendments or administrative relief that courts should not become super boards of adjustment actively involved in the zoning process. To the contrary, however, it is the widespread abuse of the process on the local level which has encouraged courts to rethink the traditional rule. The minority jurisdictions are correct in that it is too much of an ad hoc process and that zoning changes actually involve more of an administrative, quasi-judicial type of activity than a legislative one.

The reconsideration of what is actually taking place in the rezoning process is a recognition of the fact that a rezoning ordinance is not normally the end product of a comprehensive study by planners over a period of time culminating in proposed amendments. It is normally an ad hoc process

which zeroes in on a relatively small parcel of land
and which is heavily influenced by developers and
other real estate interests of the type that are often
predominant on planning commissions. The effect
of the zoning request on the neighborhood involved
is often submerged by the desire to let the project
proceed and thereby satisfy the developer. The project may be approved at the commission or city
council level over the opposition of the professional
staff. Why then should such a basically administrative, and sometimes politically tainted, process be
clothed with the finery of the legislative presumption of validity? It is not surprising to find courts,
having become aware of what is actually happening,
looking at this "legislation" with increased cynicism
and recognizing it for what it actually is. Although
most jurisdictions continue to follow the conven-
tional rule of considering rezonings as legislative
acts, presumptively valid, some courts are injecting
into the judicial review process an assessment of
whether the city is adhering to or departing from its
comprehensive plan. These courts emphasize that
the plan is an important factor in looking at rezonings. Nova Horizon, Inc. v. City of Reno (1989).

Finally, another phenomenon which was discussed in an earlier chapter is the increasing tendency of plaintiffs to resort to federal court relief
for alleged violations of their constitutional rights.
These cases include due process and equal protection allegations and suits involving alleged antitrust violations. Moreover, the use of 42 U.S.C.A.
§ 1983 to question zoning decisions has increased

dramatically since Monell v. Department of Social Services (1978) held that cities are subject to suit under that provision. The complaint must allege that a constitutional right has been infringed upon, but in zoning cases, the federal courts (unlike the state courts) have shown an increasing willingness to permit damages for "taking" property which accrue in between the time the city refuses to change an improper zoning classification and the time that the zoning classification is changed (after it has been declared invalid). This remedy of damages and the injection of the federal courts into what has traditionally been largely an area of state adjudication has been an area of substantial concern to many scholars but is in keeping with federal judicial activism over the past thirty years or more. Federal courts have upheld causes of action under RICO (Racketeer Influenced and Corrupt Organizations) where cities have engaged in solicitation of bribes or extortion in connection with zoning requests.

## § 12. Nonconforming Uses

While zoning traditionally intended to exclude disparate "lower" uses within a zone, it could not eliminate structures which were already in existence. Thus, when zoning came in, and when an area was zoned residential, the corner grocery store and neighborhood service station became nonconforming uses. The same problem reoccurs today with regard to municipal annexations. Zoning deals with these largely through a "control" approach, i.e., a different form of nonconforming use cannot be permitted, the location cannot be changed, the use cannot be expanded, and a new product or service cannot be allowed. This approach has not been too successful. Interpretive problems arise in regard to repair of a structure as opposed to expansion or extension, in regard to whether new equipment or machinery is an extension or only a replacement, in regard to whether a new product is such an addition as to amount to an extension, and in regard to whether an increase in the use or volume of business is a violation. Generally speaking, significant changes which involve substantial alterations in the nature of the business, or equipment which is not a replacement but a subterfuge to expand the use, or new structures, amount to illegal expansion or extension.

Another problem arises in regard to the destruction or partial destruction of the nonconforming use by fire or similar occurrences. Can it be rebuilt? Ordinances generally provide that if it is destroyed beyond a certain percentage of the nonconforming structure (usually half or more), it cannot be rebuilt or repaired. These ordinances are valid, but in the absence of such a provision, the building could be repaired and the use resumed. Moreover, the ordinance could not be unduly restrictive—i.e., it could not provide for discontinuance based upon minor fires.

There is a problem also with discontinuance of use not resulting from natural causes. Some courts have held that statutory provisions stating that a discontinuance for a specified period (such as a year) will terminate the nonconforming use refer to a purely mechanical interpretation of discontinuance (i.e., it is the non-use that matters, not the intent of the user). But the general view is that the word "discontinuance" implies also an intent to abandon the use. Discontinuance due to repairs, acts of war or nature, government controls, foreclosure, condemnation, or injunctions are not regarded as manifesting an intent to abandon where the situation is beyond the control of the user, or even a discontinuance under statutes relating to a specific period of non-use. The underlying assumption is that the use would continue but for the outside interference.

The most active tool in dealing with nonconforming use situations is the amortization device. The idea is that the useful economic life of nonconforming structures can be estimated to the point that the use must cease within a district after a given number of years. Unless the time span is too short or the classification is arbitrary or discriminatory or the regulation is deemed unreasonable, such ordinances are normally upheld. However, such ordinances are usually limited to certain uses. Since it is difficult to justify the amortization period for fixed structures, and since the time span involved is usually too long to prove useful, this device is used most often in connection with billboards, junkyards or similar uses. See, e.g., Grant v. Mayor & Council of Baltimore (1957). Even then, the device may on occasion be declared to be an unreasonable exercise of the police power. See, e.g., Akron v. Chapman (1953). Obviously, in attacking an ordinance, the plaintiff will allege that it is confiscatory and amounts to a taking without just compensation, in addition to some of the allegations previously mentioned. Although the *Grant* case upholding such ordinances represents the majority view, and although many ordinances contain amortization provisions, the device has not proved very effective in eliminating nonconforming uses due to its rare application to buildings or structures representing a substantial capital investment. (But see City of Los Angeles v. Gage (1954), which upheld a five-year amortization period causing the defendants to discontinue using property for a plumbing business in a situation in which they had had eight years to move and the property was suitable for residential purposes.)

While nonconforming uses could be eliminated through use of nuisance doctrines or through eminent domain, nuisance rules seldom can be successfully applied and condemnation costs normally exceed available funds.

Nuisance doctrines could be employed if the court followed the thinking of such cases as Hadacheck v. Sebastian (1915), in which an ordinance forced a nonconforming brick kiln to cease operations and move. This approach, however, would be useful only in a situation in which the nonconforming use was noxious in some respect when compared to surrounding land uses.

Finally, one argument that can sometimes be asserted successfully against a nonconforming use is that it was not established or in place at the time of zoning. Often, the question of a good faith change of position by the landowner in making substantial expenditures on the improvement of the site will be dispositive. Had construction begun and how much of the work had been done are questions relating to this proposition.

The result of the foregoing is that most nonconforming uses remain in existence until the landowner finds it economically desirable to terminate them. This situation illustrates the need for regional planning and zoning.

## § 13. Popular Involvement: The Initiative and the Referendum and Consent by the Neighbors

Ordinances allowing property owners to establish zoning regulations are unlawful in the absence of a referendum submitted to public vote. Cases have, however, permitted modification or waiver of restrictions by concerned landowners. The former is regarded as a legislative delegation of authority to private persons, and thus unlawful, while the latter is viewed as valid if the police power is not abused and if there is no reasonable basis for denying the modification or waiver.

A case illustrating this distinction is Valkanet v. Chicago (1958). The court upheld a consent provision in a situation involving location of a home for the aged in an apartment district but ruled that consent was not needed since no valid distinction could be made between an old folks' home and apartments or boarding houses. *Valkanet* applied the rules mentioned in the first paragraph of this subsection predicating its decision on Eubank v. Richmond (1912), and Thomas Cusack Co. v. Chicago (1916).

If zoning restrictions can be waived or modified by homeowners in the affected area, then may a city condition the granting of a variance on consent of abutting property owners? This was answered in the negative in Lugar v. City of Burnsville (Minn. 1980). There was no specific statutory authority permitting this, and unlike a referendum, this was not an exercise of power reserved to the people by themselves.

Referendums have been treated almost with holiness by the United States Supreme Court. James v. Valtierra (1971), sustained a provision in the California Constitution which required approval by referendum within the community of any proposed low-rent public housing project. The thought that such an election might have racial overtones or involve economic discrimination did not appeal to the Court. A later case reversed the Ohio Supreme Court's conclusion that use of the referendum process, provided for in a city charter, in submitting zoning amendments to the voters constituted a delegation of power violative of federal constitutional guarantees and a violation of due process because the voters were given no standards to guide their decisions. Eastlake v. Forest City Enterprises, Inc.

(1976). Relying on *James v. Valtierra,* supra, the hallowed town meeting concept, and its reverence for populistic democracy, the majority of the Court refused to recognize the chaos that such procedure would create in land use planning and the fact that such process is the antithesis of what the court approved in *Euclid v. Ambler Realty Co.,* supra (although the dissent does recognize the problem).

One theory in sustaining such referendums is that the referral to the voters only "stays the effect of the action * * * until the electorate has had an opportunity to approve or reject it" and "does not change zoning as an initiative would." Queen Creek Land & Cattle Corp. v. Yavapai County Board of Supervisors (1972). Such reasoning is nonsense. The submission of technical, planned decisions to a popular, generally uninformed, vote may be good populistic politics, but it is the antithesis of the use of zoning as a tool of comprehensive planning.

In the aftermath of *Eastlake*, some state courts have utilized the theory that rezonings are not legislative in character and thus not subject to the referendum. Those state courts that adhere to the theory that all zoning decisions are legislative recognize the applicability of the referendum. The states are almost equally divided on this issue.

## § 14.  Intergovernmental Zoning Conflicts

This problem arises in conflicts between city and county planning and zoning authority, or between cities and neighboring local governments, or between state and local instrumentalities of government.

City versus county problems are usually resolved on the basis of what the courts regard to be the prerogative of each under the applicable state statutes if it is simply a matter of conflicting jurisdiction. But it is not all that simple. What if a city wants to take some action inside the borders of a neighboring instrumentality of local government? Fargo v. Harwood Township (N.D.1977) held that in seeking a site for a sanitary landfill, a city had to comply with a neighboring township's zoning ordinance. But in Kirkwood v. Sunset Hills (Mo.App. 1979), it was held that a city acquiring a municipal swimming pool by eminent domain in a neighboring town was not bound by the zoning ordinance. The courts thus seem to be in conflict on what is required. The latter case seems to reflect the eminent domain test for intergovernmental immunity, which is subsequently discussed.

With regard to whether state agencies are required to comply with local zoning regulations, various doctrines have been applied. One which a good many states still adhere to is the "superior sovereign" test, which provides a presumption of state immunity in the absence of statutory provisions to the contrary. Another is the "governmental versus proprietary" test, which provides immunity if the agency is performing a governmental function. Finally, there is the "eminent domain" test, where immunity is presumed if the agency possesses that power. Brown v. Kansas Forestry, Fish and Game

(1978). *Brown,* after reviewing and rejecting these tests, tended toward the "balancing of the interests" test applied in Rutgers v. Piluso (1972), Pittsburgh v. Commonwealth (1976), Oronoco v. Rochester (1972), and other cases. Under this test, which seems to represent the trend, the "superior sovereign" test does not apply and the "eminent domain" test and "governmental versus proprietary" test are not conclusive of the issue. Instead, credence is given to the local zoning regulations, to the extent merited, and the court looks at various factors suggested as relevant by the *Rutgers* case, *supra,* and by *Brown,* which include (a) according deference to the needs and goals of the state agency, (b) examining the importance of the function to be performed by the agency when compared with public interest in maintaining the local zoning intact, (c) considering the interests and needs of the public with regard to the proposed project as compared to the impact on the locality by overturning its zoning to permit the project, (d) the convenience or inconvenience of relocating the project elsewhere, and (e) the impact on the land use plan and on the affected neighborhood if the project should be carried out. Obviously, these considerations are somewhat overlapping, but they illustrate the major considerations involved. Under the "balancing of interests" test, obviously, considerable credence and importance is attached to local zoning and while the state may prevail, it must make its case. It does not win automatically as in the "superior sovereign" test or by flexing its power of eminent domain or by demonstrating that it is performing a governmental function.

These cases might be compared with Matter of Suntide Inn Motel (Okl.1977), in which the court stated that as a general rule a state agency is not subject to local zoning, but that state agencies must establish that (a) the project is for a public use, (b) the public purpose is an essential governmental function, (c) the public need for it is urgent, (d) the public goal would be thwarted by local intervention, and (e) the statute is devoid of legislative intent that such a facility should be restricted by local zoning. These, in essence, are the same or similar considerations to those listed previously. This seems to be the trend in the case law, but some courts still accord to the state superiority and immunity from local zoning on the basis that to do otherwise would hamper the state unduly and would thwart state policy. E.g.: Dearden v. Detroit (1978); New Orleans v. State (La.1978).

As for the federal government, the "superior sovereign" rule still applies in the absence of congressional actions to the contrary. E.g., see: United States v. Chester (3d Cir.1944); and Groton v. Laird (D.Conn.1972).

An additional problem is that of standing to sue. What are the rights of neighboring units of local government with regard to actions taken by an adjacent governmental unit? In the leading case of Borough of Cresskill v. Borough of Dumont (1954) some Dumont landowners who joined neighboring boroughs in attacking zoning amendment clearly had standing to sue, but the court stated that Dumont owed a duty to her adjoining boroughs and nearby residents and consider their objections. In River Vale v. Orangetown (2d Cir.1968), an allegation of depreciation of property values without due process and violation of its constitutional rights were sufficient to keep a New Jersey township in court against a New York town. A number of cases reach essentially the same result. However, in Rohnert Park v. Harris (9th Cir.1979), it was held that Rohnert Park lacked standing to assert a violation of the federal antitrust laws by a developer and a neighboring city because it had to show a threatened loss or injury cognizable in equity as the proximate result of the alleged violation. It also lacked standing to allege violations by HUD of federal housing statutes in approving the sale.

The state of the law on standing to sue seems directed toward the principle that if injury or deprivation of constitutional rights can be shown by the neighboring governmental unit, then it has standing to sue. Another issue, not fully explored however, is whether a unit of local government may act as parens patriae for its citizens. The *Rohnert Park* court answered in the negative and stated that the city's own proprietary interests were speculative. That case, however, involved a different issue than the adverse impact of nearby rezoning, as in *Cresskill*. If proposed land use controls in one community adversely affect land use controls in a neighboring community, then clearly its governmental interest is affected. In that situation, standing to sue should be granted.

In recent years more cases have raised the question of whether local zoning regulations are preempted by federal statutes and regulations. Courts have found such preemption in rules regulating the siting of wireless communication towers, federal environmental regulation under CERCLA (Comprehensive Environmental Response, Compensation and Liability Act), and federal regulations regarding the construction of manufactured homes.

# CHAPTER VIII

# ZONING AND DISCRIMINATION

## § 1. Exclusionary Zoning

Zoning ordinances segregate uses and make differentiations even within the use classifications. By their very nature they are exclusionary. "Exclusionary zoning" thus appears to be a somewhat redundant term. What is intended by the use of it, however, is to describe a form of economic segregation, with perhaps occasional racial overtones, which has the effect of keeping out lower income groups. If large-lot minimums are prescribed, if a house must contain a certain minimum amount of square feet, or if no apartment houses or mobile homes or low-cost, government-sponsored apartments are permitted in an area or in a community, the result is to exclude what is often a substantial segment of the population. In recent years the issue has arisen in a variety of situations as to whether this form of exclusion is a valid exercise of the police power. How exclusive can a community be without raising constitutional problems relating to equal protection, due process, the right to travel from place to place, and similar issues?

Other issues relate to other types of land uses. Can certain types of commercial or industrial uses be excluded by local governments? To the contrary, must every type of land use be permitted within a particular township or unit of local government or can some be turned away?

We will attempt to develop this problem and the answers to it by proceeding through a variety of land uses, beginning with the most protected—the single-family home. In all of this, it must be kept in mind that just because an ordinance is exclusionary does not necessarily mean that it is invalid. We have to look for what is invalid in a particular context, keeping in mind that there is considerable disagreement among jurisdictions with respect to many of these issues.

## A. The "Single–Family" Classification

Zoning, in its original form and before innovations such as the PUD, created a hierarchy of districts with the most protected being the single-family residential district. This district was protected from all other uses. In fact, Euclid v. Ambler Realty Co. (1926), the landmark case which approved comprehensive zoning, clearly has as its foundation the desire to protect single-family dwellings from incursions into the district by apartments. Justice Sutherland's opinion denounces apartments as being "mere parasites."

Zoning originally was cumulative in the sense that higher uses could exist in lower use districts— thus permitting someone to build a single-family house in an apartment or duplex zoning district. Today, most zoning ordinances are non-cumulative and make an effort to keep disparate land uses apart except in a carefully planned arrangement such as a cluster zone or planned unit development. This change, however, serves only to heighten the apparent importance placed on protecting single-family dwellings.

In more recent years, there have been attacks on the legitimacy of the single-family classification itself. In Des Plaines v. Trottner (1966), the court struck down a definition of family as one or more persons each related to the other by blood, adoption, or marriage, together with the relatives' spouses, including domestic servants and not more than one gratuitous guest, living together in a single dwelling and constituting a common household. The court found the ordinance objectionable because it was not based on a specific type of use but sought to inquire into the relationship of the occupants.

But the United States Supreme Court in Belle Terre v. Boraas (1974), upheld a definition which limited the application to persons related by blood, adoption or marriage (excluding servants) or to two unmarried and unrelated people. This case upheld the exclusion of a number of unrelated people living together in a communal arrangement over allegations that the ordinance interfered with the right to travel, with persons traveling in interstate commerce, with social preferences, with the right of privacy, and with our open and egalitarian society. Justice Douglas, speaking for the majority, regarded a "quiet place where yards are wide, people few, and motor vehicles restricted" as "legitimate guidelines in a land use project addressed to family needs."

*Belle Terre v. Boraas* was in effect reinforced by the difficulty the Supreme Court had in striking down a patently ridiculous ordinance in Moore v. East Cleveland (1977). The people involved were all related by blood and yet it had the effect of making the occupancy of a dwelling by a mother, her son, and her two grandsons (who were first cousins) illegal. The Court distinguished *Boraas* as involving only unrelated persons and regarded this ordinance as an intrusive regulation of the family which violated the due process clause.

Despite the emphasis placed on protection of the single-family classification by the Supreme Court, state courts are free to disagree based on their own interpretations of their state constitutions. This was the result in Santa Barbara v. Adamson (1980), in which an ordinance's definition of family included groups of no more than five unrelated people. The court relied in part on the right of privacy but also said that the city's goals could be met by the use of less restrictive means. Other cases involving foster homes, nuns, and similar non-traditional families also illustrate situations in which either the ordinance has been invalidated or the courts have considered such unrelated individuals to be the equivalent of a single family. See, *e.g.*, State v. Baker (1979).

Although most state courts probably have no quarrel with the traditional single-family definition, the trend seems to be to liberalize it to include certain non-traditional living arrangements and to place emphasis on the type of structure, its appearance, its surroundings, its basic use and the way the "family" operates—*i.e.,* if they act like a family with a common kitchen and dining facilities and if the house looks like a traditional single-family dwelling and functions largely in that way, then it is a single-family dwelling. Courts thus have tended in these recent cases to look to whether there is "a legitimate aim of maintaining a family style of living" or whether the "group bears the generic character of a family unit as a relatively permanent household" or whether the unit involves "a reasonable number of persons who constitute a bona fide single housekeeping unit."

Without belaboring the point, this continuing difference of opinion is illustrated by such cases as McMinn v. Town of Oyster Bay (1985), involving a house leased to four unrelated young men whose families lived in the general area. The attack on the ordinance was based on state constitutional and statutory provisions, and New York's highest court invalidated the ordinance on the basis that biological or relational definitions of family bear no relationship to the objects of zoning. This was rejected by the Missouri Court of Appeals in City of Ladue v. Horn (1986), in a case involving an unmarried couple living together in a large house with their teen-age children from earlier marriages. The court rejected the federal constitutional arguments, relying on *Belle Terre v. Boraas,* and also rejected the arguments as to state law, finding "a governmental interest in marriage and in preserving the integrity of the biological or legal family." A similar case is Zavala v. City of Denver (Colo.1988); but to the contrary is Borough of Glassboro v. Vallorosi (1990), striking down a single-family definition applied to ten college students leasing a house who shared housekeeping duties and were regarded as the functional equivalent of a family.

This bifurcated attitude will likely continue, since on the national level *Belle Terre* provides a safe refuge for courts following the traditional definition of family. It is thus left to the question of judicial interpretation of the law of each state.

## B.   Large Lot Zoning Requirements

Provisions in the ordinance specifying a minimum area for a particular use have health, fire control and traffic control benefits, but also may affect tax revenues, promote aesthetics, and preserve property values. These provisions are most controversial where they are applied so as to require large residential lots. A leading case from Massachusetts, upholding a one-acre minimum, held that a city is justified in asserting the police power for such purposes where the public interest is involved and the devices and means employed are reasonable. Simon v. Needham (1942). That case also stated, however, that such a regulation cannot be used to exclude respectable people who want to come in and build on lots of fair and reasonable size.

What is reasonable and not exclusionary in nature cannot be defined with mathematical precision. Five-acre, four-acre, and three-acre lot sizes have been upheld. See, *e.g.*, County Comm'rs. of Queen Anne's County v. Miles (1967); Flora Realty & Inv. Co. v. Ladue (1952). Lot sizes of four acres and 100,000 square feet have been invalidated. National Land & Inv. Co. v. Kohn (1965); Aronson v. Sharon (1964).

In order to understand these decisions, consideration must be given to the factors which courts utilize. Factors which courts use to support the upholding of large-lot zoning include overcrowding and undue concentration of people, the burden on public facilities (including schools, fire and police stations, streets, water and sewer systems), the fact that there are other zones with smaller minima, the rural and occasionally historic character of the area, the desire to promote tourism, and compatibility with the socio-economic situation and existing uses prevailing in the community. Factors which courts cite in invalidating large-lot zoning include the lack of reasonable relationship to the police power, a size which is so large and reduces the overall value of the land so much that the court regards it as confiscatory, a tendency for the lot sizes to be exclusionary and to serve private interests, the fact that the town is in the onward path of suburban development, and the fact that the result would be to exclude low-income people from living there.

These latter factors, relating to exclusion, were the primary factors in the leading *National Land* case, *supra.* See also Appeal of Kit–Mar Builders (1970).

This problem of exclusion is the basic concern relating to large lot zoning today. The rule expressed by the Pennsylvania Court in *National Land* that Easttown Township could not "stand in the way of natural forces which send out growing population into hitherto undeveloped areas in search of a comfortable place to live" is essentially the same as the thinking of the New Jersey Court in the oft-heralded, sometimes criticized and much discussed case of Southern Burlington County NAACP v. Mount Laurel (1975), *Mount Laurel I* discussed infra, in which a zoning regulation was invalidated on the basis that low and moderate income families were unlawfully excluded by it. Unlike *Mount Laurel*, in which the concern over exclusion was involved with low income people, *National Land* involved a suit by a developer concerned with the diminution in the value of his property as a result of the regulation. The thrust of the *National Land* opinion, however, as in *Mount Laurel,* is that the police power cannot be employed to keep people out.

A key point in *National Land* is the fact that the township was in the path of population expansion outward from an urban area. The result might have been different (and some cases have produced different results) except for that circumstance.

. Not every court, by any means, has shown a tendency to invalidate ordinances of this type on the basis that they discriminate against poor people. *Mount Laurel* was based on the New Jersey Constitution. *National Land* was based on the idea that people in general were being excluded. But in Ybarra v. Los Altos Hills (9th Cir.1974), an ordinance was upheld which zoned only for single-family housing built on one-acre lots against an attack by Mexican–Americans alleging that it prevented construction of a multi-family housing project. The court held that the ordinance did discriminate against poor people, but found that to be valid because there was no showing that the plaintiffs were deprived of an opportunity to live in such housing elsewhere in the county.

Consequently, the validity of large-lot zoning is likely to vary depending on the size of the lot, the circumstances of the community or area involved, and the hostility or lack of it to large-lot zoning in a particular jurisdiction.

Large-lot zoning is obviously discriminatory from an economic standpoint. But unless a court regards it as requiring such large lots that there can be no justification under the police power, it is generally upheld as being constitutionally legitimate if small lots and low cost housing are permitted elsewhere within the general area. This, however, may lead to arguments as to the possible racial effect of economic discrimination. *Mount Laurel I* held economic discrimination itself to be unlawful under the New Jersey Constitution. The notion that lower cost

housing opportunities elsewhere in the region legiti-
mizes more restrictive zoning in other parts of the
region is coming under increased scrutiny in communities that allow "gated" subdivisions and other
physical devices of insularity. Subsequent discussion will consider federal cases relating to the economic and racial impact of zoning limitations on
housing for low income persons.

## C.  Minimum Building Size

This type of regulation has its counterpart in
subdivision regulations. However, the requirement
of a certain minimum square footage has been
upheld in many cases, particularly in older ones. In
recent years, particularly since the initial *Mount
Laurel* decision, such regulations have increasingly
been attacked as promoting economic segregation.
However, the general rule remains in most jurisdictions that a minimum size requirement which can
be reasonably related to health considerations is
valid. Modern courts have shown a tendency to look
with skepticism at such requirements, however, because substantial variations in the size of the family
make such requirements less meaningful in terms
of mental health considerations and because some
ordinances provide for different minimum requirements in different districts.

Some courts have found regulations prescribing
cubic foot content to be invalid (when all a person
would have to do to comply would be to enlarge the
attic). Frischkorn Construction Co. v. Lambert
(1946). Others have invalidated sliding scales as to

floorspace requirements on the theory that what amounts to minimum requirements for one district ought to be the minimum for all districts if it is a reasonable use of the police power. Appeal of Medinger (1954).

The fluctuation in the attitude of courts with respect to such requirements is somewhat illustrated by the New Jersey cases of Lionshead Lake, Inc. v. Township of Wayne (1952), and Home Builders League, Inc. v. Township of Berlin (1979). *Lionshead Lake* was a leading case for the proposition that minimum square footage could be required. The case was debated pro and con at the time, and some scholars periodically returned to the attack. That ordinance only provided for a 768 square foot minimum. In *Home Builders League,* the court took another look at *Lionshead Lake* and agreed with its critics. How big an area is required for the mental well-being of a house's inhabitants will depend on how many occupants there are, said the court. Another problem in *Home Builders* was that the minimum floor area varied for similar housing in different zones. *Lionshead Lake* was thought to have rested its conclusion on the protection of land values and the character of the community. The ordinance in Berlin Township was thought to be directed toward economic segregation and not related to a valid police power concern. Although the court did not reverse *Lionshead Lake,* it severely reduced its value as precedent. *Lionshead Lake* related to preserving the character of the area as against small vacation homes and might remain as a precedent in that limited situation. Moreover, the court stated that the earlier case had been erroneously characterized by scholars as based on "public health grounds" (presumably because it would have to overturn it if that were so), but the decision in *Lionshead* is by its own words based in part on such grounds.

These New Jersey decisions should not mislead those who live and work in other jurisdictions, however. Despite these recent questions about the validity of such requirements, most jurisdictions have upheld regulations as to minimum size. Also, unlike New Jersey, most jurisdictions do not hold (as New Jersey did in *Mount Laurel* ) that economic discrimination is invalid. It is fair to say, however, that the rational relationship of such a regulation to health considerations is increasingly being questioned because how much space is required is based on how many occupants there will be.

If public health is a legitimate concern of the police power, which it is, then reasonable minimums as to living space are and should be valid. Arguments as to exclusion should only form a basis for invalidating the unreasonable. Moreover, courts should uphold reasonable variations within a city from district to district. Cities and their inhabitants are not monolithic, and reasonable variations should be permitted even within prescribed minima. The contrary theory potentially diminishes health considerations without diminishing the exclusionary effects of minimums.

In a few recent cases occupancy-based minimums have been examined by courts. These cases usually involve cities facing overcrowding problems in rental houses near colleges and universities. In one such case, College Area Renters and Landlord Association v. City of San Diego (1996) the court found a regulation relating number of occupants to square footage, bathrooms, and parking to be invalid because it treated owner-occupied houses differently than rented houses.

## D. *Exclusion of Commerce and Industry*

The area of zoning law involving exclusion of apartments, commerce and industry is still developing, and the cases present conflicts. Cases have held that a suburb may restrict the use of all land to single-family dwellings, thereby excluding all other residential uses and all office, commercial and industrial uses. McDermott v. Calverton Park (Mo. 1970). But other courts have held to the contrary. Gundersen v. Bingham Farms (1964). The theory of courts which uphold one-use zoning is that some suburban or "bedroom" communities are best suited for such uses considering the character of the area and the police power is not abused by such a limitation. Decisions to the contrary vary from those concerned with the exclusion of other residential uses, such as apartments, to those concerned with exclusion of non-residential uses. The cases dealing with multi-family uses hold that these cannot be entirely excluded because suburbs which are logical areas for development and population growth cannot close their doors to people who seek or can only afford this type of housing. Appeal of Girsh (1970). These cases will be considered at greater length, *infra*.

Other cases, particularly Pennsylvania cases, hold in effect that a unit of local government must provide adequately for all types of uses within its confines. Thus, each community must accept its "fair share" of commercial growth. *E.g.:* Beaver Gasoline Co. v. Zoning Hearing Board (1971); Sullivan v. Board of Supervisors (1975). Where some land is allocated for commercial use, the burden is on the developer to show that the allocation is inadequate in relation to the needs of the citizens. A total ban on otherwise legitimate commercial uses places the burden on the municipality to justify the ban. The Pennsylvania cases have carried this to an extreme—even to the point of forcing townships to permit waste disposal facilities and quarrying operations. Exton Quarries v. Zoning Board of Adjustment (1967); General Battery Corp. v. Zoning Hearing Board (1977).

Most jurisdictions that are concerned about single use zoning at all are not concerned about exclusion of certain commercial and industrial activities. These cases usually focus on housing and hold such zoning invalid on the basis that it excludes housing for people of low and moderate incomes. Such zoning usually also excludes a disproportionate number of non-whites. But most jurisdictions would not deny municipalities the ability to exclude all or certain types of industrial activities or limit commercial acreage. However, some types of exclusion raise constitutional concerns, e.g., exclusion of all sex-oriented businesses, or abortion clinics.

The argument to the contrary is based in part on the idea that since zoning is local, rather than area-wide, in most jurisdictions, the exclusion of such uses by one body of local government could lead to exclusion of such uses from the entire area. Thus, each governmental unit (Pennsylvania says) must absorb its "fair share."

But most courts that are concerned about exclusionary zoning have limited their concerns to housing considerations and "keeping people out" as opposed to keeping out commercial or industrial operations. Regional or area-wide planning and zoning obviously could relieve most of these problems and concerns.

## E.  *Exclusion of Apartments and Condominiums*

As stated, the concerns of the courts are largely with exclusion of various forms of residential use. Thus, zoning which excludes apartments and condominums, although it has been approved in some jurisdictions, is looked upon with disfavor in others. *Appeal of Girsh, supra.* Courts that disapprove of such exclusion commonly state that zoning cannot be used to keep people out or to stand as a barrier to outward population expansion from a central metropolitan area. These cases follow the same theory as *National Land, supra,* which invalidated a large-lot zoning requirement because of such considerations. Moreover, in the *Mount Laurel I* case, to be discussed *infra,* and other cases, we see instances in which courts have taken an affirmative action approach to force communities to create a situation which will encourage development of housing for people of low and moderate incomes.

Clearly, the attitude of the courts has shifted since the 1920's when Justice Sutherland, writing for the majority in *Euclid v. Ambler Realty Co., supra,* sought to protect single-family uses at the expense of all others and referred to apartment houses as mere parasites.

As we have seen in *McDermott v. Calverton Park, supra,* all courts do not agree that exclusionary residential zoning is a matter of concern. There is a split of authority on this in the state courts. In the federal courts, as we shall see, local zoning regulations cannot operate so as to exclude federally subsidized housing for low and moderate income people. With that exception, however, unless there is proof of an intent to discriminate racially, single use zoning is an issue to be decided by each particular jurisdiction. The trend of recent years would seem in the long run to augur against ordinances which exclude multi-family and other residential uses.

As to the requiring of multi-family classification, however, it should be apparent that a required zoning classification of that type will not alone be sufficient to spur housing for low and moderate income families. The result may simply be a proliferation of apartments or condominiums for wealthy or middle-to-upper income people. In some cases in both state and federal courts, we see instances in which courts have required communities to provide for or encourage subsidized housing for people of low and moderate income. These approaches amount to affirmative action in housing.

Condominiums, although involving ownership of real property as opposed to a rental agreements, have received much the same treatment as apartments from the standpoint of zoning. At the same time, they have received the same protection in situations in which the existing zoning is regarded as too restrictive. Thus, in McHenry State Bank v. City of McHenry (1983), a zoning ordinance was held invalid in allowing new condominiums in only two zones which were limited to condominiums and precluded conversion of existing apartments in apartment zones into condominiums. The Illinois Appeals Court refused to permit differentiation between the two based solely on the form of ownership—which is the majority view. Condo conversions of tax-depreciated apartments became commonplace in the 1970's and early 1980's. However, resistance to condos by single-family neighborhoods has equalled resistance to apartments. This attitude has manifested itself in the courts and in ordinances in which the density of occupancy of an area is the defining factor as opposed to the form of ownership.

Time-share condominium developments usually receive the same zoning treatment in urban areas as ordinary condominiums. Efforts by cities to control time-share developments through moratoriums, where the considerations were valid under the police power, have been upheld. Jackson Court Condominiums v. City of New Orleans (5th Cir.1989). Many time-share developments are not in urban areas and thus subject to few if any controls.

## F.  Exclusion of Mobile Homes

If Justice Sutherland viewed apartment houses as mere parasites, as he stated in *Euclid,* then mobile homes have taken the place of apartment houses in recent years with respect to how they are viewed by many courts. Thus, the Supreme Court of New Jersey in the 1960's could uphold an ordinance which permitted a rural township to exclude mobile homes entirely from its 23 square miles. Vickers v. Township Committee of Gloucester Township (1962). The dissenting judge argued that localities should not be able to erect exclusionary walls around their borders and keep people out. He later wrote the majority opinion in *Mount Laurel I, infra,* which effectively overruled *Vickers* in that it required local governments to accept their "fair share" of population growth and make accommodation for low and moderate income housing.

But this attitude has begun to change. Limitations on mobile homes which are regarded as unreasonable have been struck down as unconstitutional, and courts are increasingly recognizing the need by many people for housing of this type. Glocester v. Olivo's Mobile Home Court, Inc. (1973). Most efforts to exclude mobile homes totally from a multiuse community have been held unconstitutional;

but courts generally permit the separate classification of mobile homes and the restriction of them to certain zones because of their adverse impact on neighborhood development and property values, their minimum storage capacity for items of personal property, and the fact that aesthetically they are less pleasing. See, *e.g.,* Duckworth v. Bonney Lake (1978).

There was an increasing pressure in the United States during the 1980's for affordable housing. Spiraling interest rates placed much of traditional housing, whether single-family homes or condominiums, beyond the financial reach of many citizens. This led to a reassessment of attitudes toward the mobile home market in general and particularly toward prefabricated or modular housing which is manufactured off of the site and is assembled on the site from the component units. These manufactured houses look much the same as on-site or "stick built" single-family homes. The same change in attitudes, to a lesser degree, is true with regard to "double wide" mobile homes which look more like a traditional house than an elongated, narrow trailer. Probably, we will see an increase in ordinances which permit prefabricated homes to be trucked to the site in segments and assembled on the site, at least in some residential classifications. But as far as the mobile home, including the "double wide," is concerned, substantial public resistance remains because of the ill effect on property values and neighborhood development and because of aesthetic considerations. Mobile homes will likely continue to have separate zoning classifications or be permitted as conditional uses in some, not highly restricted, residential zones.

Numerous cases address the issue of whether a mobile home can be disassembled by removal of the wheels, axles and the like, planted on a permanent foundation on a lot, hooked up to the utilities, and then qualify as a single-family home. The cases still generally say no, holding that mobile homes can be limited to certain specified districts because of their adverse effect on the neighborhood, their stunting of development, their minimum storage capacity (leading to an overflow of tools, toys and other things into the yard), and their lack of aesthetic qualities. The result is that cities segregate mobile homes from traditional housing. See e.g., Duckworth v. City of Bonney Lake (1978). In California, a state statute preempts local zoning restrictions on manufactured homes in single-family districts.

Even with regard to manufactured or prefabricated homes, a separate zoning district may still be required and upheld by the courts. However, this type of home, manufactured off the site in units or segments assembled on the premises, seems most likely to crack the single-family barrier. This is illustrated by some recent cases, such as Cannon v. Coweta County (1990), in which a per se exclusion of manufactured homes from single-family districts was held unconstitutional. The argument that manufactured homes adversely affect the tax base or the value of nearby site-built homes was questioned by the court. Also, in Hansman v. Oneida County

(1985), a modular or manufactured home permanently attached to a foundation was held not to be a mobile home. These cases, however, remain sufficiently limited in number that they cannot be represented as constituting a definite trend, although it would seem increasingly difficult to classify separately a home manufactured off the site from one built on the site if the appearance is essentially the same.

Obviously, neither a mobile home nor a manufactured home can escape the ban of a properly worded restrictive covenant excluding them from a subdivision.

## G. *Institutional Uses and Group Homes*

The problem here normally arises from the question of whether an institutional or "group" home constitutes a single-family residence under the terms of the zoning ordinance. When such homes are operated in essentially the same manner as a single-family home, they can quite often avoid exclusion. Thus, a home for foster children who live with a married couple in a family atmosphere or type of arrangement has been held to be a family for purposes of the single family classification. White Plains v. Ferraioli (1974).

The same holding would probably result in most cases involving restrictive covenants which limit the use to "single family," although the definition of family could be written in such a way as to exclude group or institutional homes. If it were so written, courts would have to enforce the restrictive covenant since these private rights would outweigh the general public policy favoring such facilities and there is no constitutional violation with respect to race, religion or the like. Where there is no definition of "family," then if the group home functions as a family does, courts will usually permit the use to continue. Thus, the result in interpreting restrictive covenants has, in the absence of specific words of exclusion, been much the same as in most of the zoning cases. There are, of course, cases to the contrary.

Some of the cases involving group homes for mental patients, the mentally retarded or wayward children have arisen in the context of homeowners seeking an injunction against them based on nuisance allegations. An injunction generally will not be granted in such circumstances based on fear of anticipated injury. Moreover, some of these cases involve state-operated facilities which raises the issue of whether the state is immune from local zoning. On this latter point, most courts today do not hold the state totally immune but apply a balancing of the interests test. In zoning cases, however, some courts will give priority to state policy.

A different definition of the single family requirement may be employed if the group home is supervised by a professional staff as opposed to a live-in couple operating the house as a family would. This may be said to be the operation of an institution in a non-family setting as opposed to the family situation provided by a resident married couple. See, *e.g.*, Culp v. Seattle (1979).

The more controversial group homes involve "halfway houses" for convicted felons or parolees whom the state is gradually attempting to return to society or institutional homes for delinquents. Such rehabilitation facilities are often excluded from single family districts. The decisions upholding this are predicated on the reasonableness of such classifications, although the root of the matter is the fear of the nearby populace. Similar issues arise in connection with group homes for AIDS patients and recovering addicts.

As in some other zoning considerations, an analogy can be drawn to nuisance doctrine. In fact, courts have held that the operation of a halfway house for parolees and prisoners constitutes a nuisance in fact. See, *e.g.*, Arkansas Release Guidance Foundation v. Needler (1972); but compare Nicholson v. Connecticut Half–Way House (1966), which arrived at a different result where suit was instituted prior to the beginning of operations by the halfway house.

The Supreme Court considered a group home in the context of equal protection rights of the mentally handicapped in City of Cleburne, Texas v. Cleburne Living Center (1985), with the majority rejecting classification of mental retardation as a suspect class entitled to heightened scrutiny. The Court's majority, however, wrote at such length on mental retardation and heightened scrutiny that the result was to afford that examination even though the majority decided that it was not required. Ultimately, the Court held that the irrational distinction of the ordinance between group homes and other similar uses was unjustified and that requiring a special permit under these facts rested "on an irrational prejudice against the mentally retarded."

The *Cleburne* case would seem to provide some caution to local communities and state courts seeking to classify such specialized group homes differently from fraternity houses, boarding houses or the like. Presumably, the nuisance argument and the assertion as to a reduction in property values remain unaffected.

The group home concept is intended to normalize as much as possible the return to society or membership in society of people suffering from homelessness, neglect, orphan status, mental handicaps, or criminal behavior. As crime has grown in scope and media attention, the public backlash against such homes has increased. The great majority of states, however, have statutes which attempt to advance these efforts at normalization as against zoning exclusions. Many of these statutes numerically limit the residents of a single home. Others apply to designated types of homes. Some courts have been quite sympathetic, and some have ruled that the state policy in this regard takes precedence over zoning limitations. Others have strictly construed the law in a manner favorable to exclusion or have found some technicality to justify exclusion.

There are obviously conflicting values and viewpoints at work here. Some of the cases utilize the
theories relevant to intergovernmental zoning conflicts to resolve the issues, as most group homes are
licensed under the state or sponsored by state agencies.

## H.  *Religious Institutions and Private Schools*

Opinions of courts vary as to the exclusion of
churches from areas zoned single-family. Some decisions   have   invalidated   ordinances   excluding
churches entirely from single-family districts on the
basis that this does not relate to the police power or
that it is an infringement on religion. Other courts,
however, have said that the question should be
whether it is an *undue* infringement—*i.e.*, whether
exclusion of the church will promote the general
welfare or whether the exclusion is a burden which
is not commensurate with the general welfare. See,
e.g., State ex rel. Lake Drive Baptist Church v.
Bayside Bd. of Trustees (1961). If there are other
available sites, as was held in *Bayside,* then the
zoning would not be invalid (although the church
won in that case for other reasons).

In many zoning ordinances, churches are permitted as special or conditional uses in single-family
districts. This would seem not to be unconstitutional because modern churches usually meet or have
functions during the week and sometimes have a
recreational or educational component. If a church
could locate anywhere in a residential district as a
matter of right, it might choose a site which from a

traffic and safety standpoint was wholly unsuited and harmful to the neighborhood. There *are*, therefore, police power considerations which apply to churches, and courts which hold that such regulation is a per se violation of freedom of worship are not taking such factors into account. It is likely, however, that the conditional use procedure could be successfully defended in most courts (except those which permit no regulation of churches at all). But when this procedure is employed, the criteria for granting or denying the permit must be specified, or the ordinance may be invalidated on that ground.

A number of modern cases involve the issue of ancillary uses that churches sponsor within their buildings, such as homeless shelters, counseling facilities, schools, athletic fields, and the like. Obviously, some of these ancillary uses are considered to be nuisance-like by neighbors and the courts must consider whether those uses can be prohibited under the zoning ordinance. The cases are in conflict. Most courts have held that church-sponsored schools are ancillary uses that require special permits. On the other hand, homeless shelters in churches have been upheld as "religious activity akin to worship."

It is well to observe, in connection with churches, that some courts appear to reverse the usual presumption in favor of police power regulations and to place the burden upon the municipality of showing a lack of impairment or insubstantial impairment of religious freedom.

This separate standard manifests itself in connection with ancillary religious institutions such as convents, monasteries or use of a dwelling by members of a religious society. Some cases have held that unrelated members of a religious society living together as a single housekeeping unit constitutes a "family" within the meaning of the ordinance. But this is not applied to college fraternities, sororities or clubs even where they have kitchen and dining facilities and operate as something similar to a large "family." An extreme example of this is a holding which considered sixty student members of a religious order to constitute a single-family group. Laporte v. New Rochelle (1957). A fraternity or sorority house would have lost. Thus, the true nature of the "use" is ignored. This is clearly a double standard because it is the nature of the use that is at issue under the police power and not the nature of the organization.

The fact that it is the use that should be at issue is also illustrated by an occasional double standard as between public schools and private schools. Sometimes a distinction is made between public schools, which are permitted, and private schools, which are prohibited, on the basis that public education is a governmental function. Private schools, it is argued, discriminate and impose all of the burdens of a public school without the same benefit to the public. State ex rel. Wisconsin Lutheran High School Conference v. Sinar (1954). But in terms of land use controls, it can hardly matter to the people around the school as to whether it is public or private since the impact on the neighborhood is the same in terms of noise, traffic and congestion. Moreover, if the contention of the court in the above case were relevant, it might be pointed out that private or parochial schools do serve the public indirectly by relieving the public schools of the burden that would be added if they were non-existent. Since the tax base remains the same, it might be said that the public is indirectly subsidized by private and parochial schools. See Roman Catholic Welfare Corp. v. Piedmont (1955).

A sounder approach from a land use standpoint is illustrated by cases which require that classifications in zoning ordinances must bear a reasonable relationship to the police power. Thus, governmental attempts to distinguish between a permitted grade school or high school and a non-permitted prekindergarten or nursery school have been invalidated on the basis that the latter is no more of an impact on land use in the neighborhood than the former. Chicago v. Sachs (1953). There must be reasonable distinctions made between classes of uses, and like uses should not be excluded from a particular class. Many cases involve the problem of defining a school. A Montessori school for infants and toddlers was held not to be a grade school under an ordinance that permitted educational institutions equivalent to public elementary schools. City of Little Rock v. Infant–Toddler Montessori School, Inc. (1980). A national organization, Visionquest that operates ranches where juvenile offenders go to classes half the day and work on the ranch

the other half has been found to be a school in
Arizona, but not so in Pennsylvania.

## *I. Housing Discrimination*

### (1) *Racial Exclusion*

The Civil Rights Act of 1866, passed pursuant to
congressional authority under the Thirteenth
Amendment to eliminate the badges and incidents
of slavery, was followed over a century later by the
Civil Rights Act of 1968 which included provisions
designed to assure fair housing practices in the
United States. 42 U.S.C.A. § 3601 et seq. In that
same year, in Jones v. Alfred H. Mayer Co. (1968),
the Supreme Court held that private persons could
not discriminate on the basis of race in the sale of
houses.

The Fair Housing Act of 1968, however, gave rise
in the 1970's to cases which focused on the legality
of zoning practices in the light of the requirements
of this act and of equal protection and due process
in general. This development extended the "badge
of slavery" basis of *Jones, supra,* into the area of
exclusion by zoning of certain types of housing.

A prime example of this litigation is United
States v. Black Jack (8th Cir.1974), in which the
prohibition of multi-family housing by a suburb of
St. Louis was invalidated under Title VIII of the
1968 Civil Rights Act. Black Jack is one of the
suburbs which ring St. Louis on its western border.
Statistics were employed by the court to show that
such zoning had the effect of locking in the large

black population in the central city by preventing erection of public housing for low and moderate income families. Thus, the ordinance was deemed to have a discriminatory effect in that it denied availability of housing on the basis of race and could not be justified by any compelling governmental interest. (This case was followed by a $450,000 award of damages under a consent decree in the district court and, some years later, by a holding that the city was under a continuing duty to take affirmative action to promote the development of moderately priced, interracial housing. Park View Heights Corp. v. City of Black Jack (8th Cir.1979).)

Other cases, however, held that a negative zoning decision on such housing could be defended by the city's demonstration of its adherence to a good faith use of basic zoning principles and an absence of discriminatory intent coupled with other nearby opportunities for housing for low income families. Ybarra v. Los Altos Hills (9th Cir.1974).

The question of "discriminatory effect" as opposed to "discriminatory intent" was addressed by the Supreme Court in Arlington Heights v. Metropolitan Housing Development Corp. (1977). This case was interrelated with Hills v. Gautreaux (1976), which required the Chicago Housing Authority and HUD to utilize the entire Chicago metropolitan area, including the suburbs, to disperse publicly financed housing throughout the area. Arlington Heights is a Chicago suburb, and considered in a racial context, the result of *Gautreaux* was somewhat similar to the desegregation cases mandating the busing of school children. In fact, the Seventh Circuit opinion in *Gautreaux* was largely predicated upon such cases.

*Arlington Heights* held that a "discriminatory effect" was insufficient under the Fourteenth Amendment to invalidate a zoning regulation and that, under normal circumstances, a "discriminatory purpose" or intent would be required. As far as due process and equal protection were concerned, an exclusionary zoning ordinance of a suburban community would be permitted. However, the case was remanded to determine whether the requirements of the Fair Housing Act might necessitate a different standard as to public housing. That was answered in the affirmative by the Seventh Circuit upon remand. The circuit court addressed four critical factors to be considered and stated, in essence: (1) "Discriminatory effect" is relevant when it has a greater adverse impact on one racial group than on another or when it serves to perpetuate racial segregation in a community; (2) while of lesser importance, the question of discriminatory intent is relevant if there is some evidence of such intent, even though inconclusive; (3) the interest of the defendant in taking such action as produces a discriminatory impact is pertinent if it is a governmental body acting within the scope of legitimate authority; and (4) courts should be more reluctant to grant relief when affirmative action to compel construction of integrated housing is requested than when a plaintiff simply seeks relief from being prevented by a defendant from building integrated housing. Applying the foregoing to Arlington Heights, the court held that it had a statutory obligation under the Fair Housing Act to refrain from zoning policies which effectively foreclosed construction of publicly financed housing for low income families within its borders. Metropolitan Housing Development Corp. v. Village of Arlington Heights (7th Cir.1977).

These cases need to be distinguished from Southern Burlington County NAACP v. Mount Laurel (1975), discussed *infra,* which was based on the New Jersey Constitution and which invalidated zoning regulations that had the effect of excluding low and moderate income families. That decision, decided on economic rather than racial grounds, was based on state law rather than on the federal Constitution or federal statutes.

The upshot of these cases would seem to be: (1) states remain free, as in *Mount Laurel, supra,* to override exclusionary zoning based upon state law, or as in *Calverton Park, supra,* to uphold exclusionary zoning based upon state law, except insofar as such practices are racially motivated or would violate the Fair Housing Act; (2) absent a discriminatory purpose or intent, cities do not violate the federal Constitution through exclusionary zoning practices as a general rule; (3) but, in the case of the Fair Housing Act and public housing, a more extensive examination may result and such factors as those delineated by the Seventh Circuit upon remand of *Arlington Heights* will quite possibly be considered. (See generally, Wright, Constitutional Rights and Land Use Planning: The New and the

Old Reality, 1977 *Duke L.J.* 841 (1978).) It would be an over-simplification, however, to say that the developer of racially integrated housing for low and moderate income people has clear sailing under the Fair Housing Act and the more stringent requirements suggested by the Seventh Circuit. Not every denial of a building permit or refusal to rezone can be shown to be racially exclusionary, particularly in cities with many different types of zoning classifications including high density multi-family.

## (2) *The Problem of Standing*

Those seeking to challenge allegedly exclusionary zoning ordinances must comply with the procedural limitations imposed by Warth v. Seldin (1975), which held that certain individual taxpayers and organizations interested in providing housing for low and moderate income persons lacked standing to sue. The petitioners lived in Rochester, N.Y., and the suit was against Penfield, a suburb. The Supreme Court affirmed the Second Circuit's decision that they lacked standing to press a claim that Penfield excluded low income persons from living there. The petitioners would have to show that they purported to represent a class. It was held that the associations in the suit had no standing because the interests of their members were not directly affected.

This decision was a severe deterrent to suits by organizations representing racial minorities or poor people. Plaintiffs must be able to establish a connection between the zoning and the denial of their constitutional or statutory rights. An owner of property who could not develop it for low-cost housing would have standing. A housing authority thwarted by such regulations would normally have standing. Someone with a property interest such as an option to buy affected land, contingent on rezoning, would have standing. Someone prevented by the zoning from buying land for a public housing project would presumably have standing. But outsiders who could not show some deprivation to themselves would not have standing.

Some state courts have shown a tendency not to be so strict. Some have permitted a showing that the zoning practices excluded them from residing in the city in question. See *e.g.,* Home Builders League v. Township of Berlin (1979).

### (3) *Age Discrimination*

The Fair Housing Amendment Act of 1988 made it generally unlawful to discriminate in the sale or rental of housing or to make a dwelling otherwise unavailable on the basis of "familial status," as well as on the previous grounds of race, color, religion, sex or national origin. 42 U.S.C.A. § 3604. However, an exception was created for "housing for older persons" in which discrimination on the basis of family status (i.e., families with children under 18) is not prohibited. Housing for older persons was defined to include housing intended for or solely occupied by persons of 62 or older, or intended for occupancy by at least one person 55 years of age or older per unit. 42 U.S.C.A. § 3607(b)(2)(B), (C).

Based on this federal legislation, the California Court of Appeal held that the federal statute clearly exempted housing specifically built for the elderly. Colony Cove Associates v. Brown (1990). That particular case involved a mobile home park rule restricting residency to persons 55 or older, and the effect of the application of the rule was to evict tenants who had children who were born after the park's enactment of its age restriction and were not grandfathered in against the restriction as were their parents.

The attitude of the court in *Colony Cove* runs counter to that of the California Supreme Court in Marina Point, Ltd. v. Wolfson (1982), in which the court struck down a landlord's limitation on rentals to families with a minor child. The case was decided under California law and predated the federal housing amendments mentioned above. The California Supreme Court stated that a "society that sanctions wholesale discrimination against its children in obtaining housing engages in a suspect activity" and that even "the most primitive society fosters the protection of its young."

But the Fair Housing Act Amendment of 1988 did not ignore the problem of minor children and adopted a rule against discrimination in the rental of apartment housing on the basis of familial status (i.e., children under 18). This provision is more controversial than the one pertaining to older people since the result is to prohibit adults-only apartment rentals, which was a widespread practice predicated on the belief (asserted by the landlord in

*Marina Point* ) that children are more destructive or damaging to rental property. This does not affect housing designated for the elderly because Congress expressly exempted housing designated for older persons from the application of the familial status amendments. Seniors Civil Liberties Association v. Kemp (11th Cir.1992); 42 U.S.C.A. § 3607(b)(1).

A much-noted case which preceded this activity was Taxpayers Association v. Weymouth Township (1976), involving a mobile home park classification which limited occupants to those of 52 years of age or above and which was upheld based on the special housing needs of the elderly. A leading case to the contrary, decided on the basis that creating such a category would be ultra vires under the enabling act, was Hinman v. Planning and Zoning Commission (1965).

In *Weymouth Township,* the community had a general ban on mobile homes, but this exception in favor of older people was deemed to be reasonable. (Of course, the *Mount Laurel cases* would have an impact on general bans of this type today in jurisdictions which adhere to that concept.)

Unless the area had other land zoned for mobile homes, without age restrictions, it would seem difficult to say that this was not exclusionary. Also, it seems arbitrary to say someone is "old" at 52 if he or she were not considered "old" at 51. With regard to the federal statute, where is the magic in 55, as opposed to 54? Could one underlying reason for such limitations be to eliminate people most likely to have minor children who might thereby create additional burdens for more schools and more public facilities, financed by more taxes? In other words, is this concern for the "special needs of the elderly" a genuine police power consideration or is it an excuse for the elimination of the presence of children?

One important factor that should be kept in mind in connection of these federal provisions as to older persons is that regulations must be adopted by HUD defining requirements for legitimate senior citizen housing. These regulations must include at least a requirement that there be significant facilities provided to meet the physical and social needs of older persons or "provide important housing opportunities" for the elderly. Developments for the elderly which do not meet such requirements may have to open up to younger residents. See, e.g., Park Place Home Brokers v. P-K Mobile Home Park (N.D.Ohio 1991). In 1995 Congress removed this requirement from the statute. P.L. 104–76, § 2.

In the absence of the ultra vires question, and assuming compliance with federal law, the key to the legitimacy of such zoning would seem to be whether zoning based on age allows substantial housing opportunities in the community or immediate area for people of all ages.

## § 2.  Inclusionary Zoning

### A.  *Providing Low–Cost Housing Opportunities*

The leading case on this is Southern Burlington County NAACP v. Township of Mount Laurel

(1975), otherwise known as *Mount Laurel* (or as *Mount Laurel I,* to distinguish it from later opinions). In this case, the New Jersey Supreme Court held that townships must absorb their "fair share" of the housing needs of their particular geographical areas. A township could not be wholly or largely single-family and would have to provide for all types of housing. Mount Laurel was held to be unlawfully exclusionary by not making it possible to provide for housing for low and moderate income persons. This economic exclusion was held unconstitutional under the state constitution. The court indicated that if zoning and planning were conducted on a regional basis, the situation would be different; but since zoning and planning are local, then each local unit must absorb its fair share.

*Mount Laurel I* did not require affirmative action by the township. The township was only required to provide the opportunity for such low income housing developments through its zoning regulations. It was suggested, however, that the township might be required to take further action in the future.

This decision left a number of unanswered questions, such as what is the "fair share" of a particular township, what is a township's particular area or region, and how much zoning for multi-family units is required to meet the "fair share" requirements. Further litigation was bound to ensue, and it did. In Oakwood at Madison, Inc. v. Township of Madison (1977), it was stated that a lower court need not define the region and set the number of low-cost housing units to be allowed as a township's fair share; it required zoning for "least cost" housing but did not require precise formulae for estimating the fair share and did not require governmental aid to private developers of such housing; it did provide certain minimal criteria which had to be met to provide for the township's fair share.

Eventually, in Southern Burlington County NAACP v. Township of Mount Laurel (1983), a very long opus, the court developed new burdens of proof, procedures and standards intended to lead to faster and more effective remedies. The test would not be whether good faith attempts had been made by a community to meet such needs, but whether a real opportunity had been provided for "least cost" housing. Plaintiffs would not have to prove what a "fair share" amounted to in a locality, but only would have to show that the zoning is substantially affected by restrictive devices—which would apparently then create a rebuttable presumption that such zoning was unfair. Exclusionary zoning cases would be assigned to one of three judges, each of whom would have responsibility for a certain area of the state, and who could make use of masters. Implementation of new policies would be phased in. Local governments found in compliance would be protected from such suits for six years thereafter.

In summary, *Mount Laurel II* did two important things: (1) strongly suggested that the legislature do something to provide a way to eliminate local exclusivity in zoning, and (2) indicated that the courts would provide some real remedies for exclusionary zoning. The suggestion was made that courts could order a community to seek state and federal housing subsidies and provide incentives for private developers to set aside units for low and moderate income persons. Mandatory set asides, incentive zoning, and mobile homes could be used to meet the fair share requirement. The designation of special courts reflected discontent with extended litigation over these situations.

After *Mount Laurel II,* the New Jersey legislature passed a fair housing act that created an administrative agency with the power to define housing regions and the regional needs for low and moderate income housing. This agency also was given rule-making power to establish criteria for determination of what constitutes the "fair share" of a community. This act was challenged and upheld in Hills Development Co. v. Township of Bernards (1986), a case generally referred to as *Mount Laurel III,* although it involved a different township. The New Jersey Court praised the approach of the legislature and thought it would provide more consistency. Newspaper reports of that time period suggested that the result of the legislation was to attract mostly young, first-time suburbanite home buyers, retired people, divorced persons and renters. Only a distinct minority of people were said to have migrated to the suburbs from urban centers.

Subsequent to this litigation, in Holmdel Builders Association v. Township of Holmdel (1990), the New Jersey Supreme Court upheld the concept of development exactions on non-residential development as a device for supporting affordable housing, accepting the principle that there was a linkage between commercial and office development and the housing needs of a municipality. These particular exactions were invalidated because of the need for uniform development of such regulations by the state agency on affordable housing.

The judicial activism manifested by *Mount Laurel I* and its progeny has caused some concern among scholars. For one thing, it is dubious that low and moderate income people have benefited from judicial activity directed toward assisting them in their housing problems. Certainly, what facts are available suggest that they have not benefited to any appreciable degree. An underlying assumption of this line of cases and the legislative actions is that it is economically feasible to build new housing for low and moderate income families, but that may be questioned in light of the funds available over the past fifteen years or so. *Mount Laurel* was a judicial attempt to solve a problem that was heavily rooted in economics.

The *Mount Laurel* decision had an impact primarily on other northeastern jurisdictions, and it met with a somewhat mixed acceptance. Berenson v. New Castle (1975) held that zoning ordinances must give consideration to regional housing needs. After the trial court, upon remand, ordered the town to provide for 3,500 units of multi-family housing over approximately the next decade, the Appellate Division held that this order went too far and simply directed the town board to remedy its zoning deficiency and to rezone the plaintiff's property multi-family. Berenson v. New Castle (1979). In Pennsylvania, Surrick v. Zoning Hearing Board (1977), provided that state's version of the adoption of the "fair share" concept. A concurring opinion disagreed with the "fair share" approach, stating that it would impose an unnecessary burden on the courts and should not be imposed on localities or regions.

In Fernley v. Board of Supervisors of Schuylkill Township (1985), there were varied opinions which agreed that the ordinance's exclusion of apartments was invalid. The majority ruled that the township was not in the path of anticipated growth and that the fair share analysis was thus inapplicable. But the township was directed to permit the development project involving apartments on the basis that total exclusion was not shown to serve a public purpose. There were differences of opinion about the applicability of Pennsylvania's fair share test and whether the township was in the path of growth. As compared to New Jersey, Pennsylvania has continue to play a limited role in changing the status of exclusionary zoning.

Judicially mandated inclusionary zoning has also been employed in some federal courts in such a way that the orders issued parallel the desegregation cases mandating school busing. Such a case is United States v. Parma, Ohio (N.D.Ohio 1980), subsequently affirmed, which went so far as to mandate numerous affirmative acts which had to be undertaken by the city governing body. The New Jersey experience and the experience of the federal courts in school desegregation cases would seem to suggest that this process would engage the courts in a constant case-by-case approval and general review process, in which, aside from new cases, the old cases would continually go from the trial courts to the appellate courts and back again. This is no doubt the reason why such judges as the concurring judge in *Surrick* are hesitant about venturing into such a milieu. Perhaps this is also the reason why, despite the applause which originally greeted *Mount Laurel,* there numerous second thoughts about it and more critical observations. *E.g.:* Rose, The Mount Laurel II Decision: Is It Based on Wishful Thinking?, 12 Real Estate L.J. 115 (1983).

*Mount Laurel* differs from *Arlington Heights* in that it holds that the state constitution prohibits economic discrimination while the U.S. Supreme Court opinion holds that the Fourteenth Amendment only prohibits discrimination based on race or religion. Most state courts have not gone beyond *Arlington Heights,* and it seems doubtful that many will.

The answer to the problem lies in regional planning and zoning of a type that would adequately provide for the various types of housing within a reasonable geographical area.

## B.   Legislative Approaches

Some states have passed statutes which confer on boards of appeals or agencies concerned with urban development the power to override local zoning, generally for the purpose of promoting housing for low and moderate income families. These laws have withstood objections that such legislation violated the home rule amendment to the state constitution, amounted to spot zoning, and were void for vagueness of standards. *E.g.:* Board of Appeals of Hanover v. Housing Appeals Committee (1973). Such decisions view special efforts to provide housing for low and moderate income people as promoting the general welfare.

There are non-judicial approaches which seem preferable to the judicial process. The latter almost inevitably lapses into some form of court-supervised affirmative action. Such legislation may be politically unrealistic in most jurisdictions because local control of zoning is highly entrenched, and there is usually legislative opposition to state control or to special agencies fulfilling a social function and exercising a veto power over local actions.

## C.  Inclusionary Zoning Ordinances

What then of local ordinances themselves? In Board of Supervisors v. DeGroff Enterprises, Inc. (1973), a zoning amendment requiring a developer of fifty or more dwelling units to agree to build at least fifteen percent of such units as low and moderate income housing was invalidated as being ultra vires with respect to the power granted local governments by the enabling act. The county viewed the ordinance as attempting to promote a public purpose, but the court viewed it as "socio-economic zoning" which attempted to control the compensation for the use of the land. It was also held to be a taking in that it compelled the sale or rental of property to low or moderate income persons at prices not fixed by the market.

It should be noted, however, that a dissenting opinion in *Oakwood at Madison* spoke approvingly of mandatory inclusionary ordinances as remedial measures, pointing out that ordinances similar to that invalidated in *DeGroff Enterprises* have been implemented in several parts of the country. The opinion criticizes *DeGroff* for its "excessively narrow" view of the zoning power, and asserts that the taking argument can be avoided by making certain that developers receive a fair and reasonable return on their investment.

However, perhaps because of the ultra vires and taking arguments and perhaps also due to the opposition from developers, these inclusionary ordinances do not appear to have been adopted on a widespread basis.

# CHAPTER IX

# AESTHETICS AND PRESERVATION OF HISTORICAL AND CULTURAL RESOURCES

## § 1. Introduction

Zoning, as previously discussed, is predicated on the police power. This relates to such tangibles as health and safety, but it also relates to the general welfare. Is it within the "general welfare" to regulate land use based upon aesthetic considerations alone? Can you measure what is aesthetically acceptable when beauty, in the old cliche, lies in the eyes of the beholder? Is it valid to regulate land use for the purpose of preserving our historical and cultural heritage? This brief chapter deals with these issues.

## § 2. Sign and Billboard Regulations

The amortization device is often employed in regard to signs. However, some ordinances limiting the size of signs, without utilizing amortization provisions, have been upheld. State v. Diamond Motors (1967), predicated such a decision on the acceptance of "beauty as a proper community objective, attainable through the use of the police power." But the majority of courts have found it necessary to uphold such ordinances on the basis of traditional considerations such as health, safety or morals, to accept aesthetic considerations only as a side benefit, and to strike down ordinances which solely achieve aesthetic objectives. See, *e.g.,* Thomas Cusack Co. v. Chicago (1917); Baltimore v. Mano Swartz, Inc. (1973). The trend, however, seems to be in favor of viewing aesthetics alone as a valid basis for exercising the police power to preserve the appearance of the community. (See, *e.g.,* People v. Goodman (1972); Fayetteville v. McIlroy Bank (1983).)

The *Goodman* case upheld an ordinance limiting the size of signs on buildings (although allowing nonconforming signs to exist for a period of two years unless destroyed or changed). The court pointed out that the state and local governments could regulate outdoor advertising under the police power and that communities had statutory power to regulate various kinds of signs. Although this ordinance was predicated upon aesthetic considerations, promotion of the appearance of the community was viewed as a valid police power objective. An ordinance regulating "off-site" signs or billboards was upheld in California with regard to signs which had been fully amortized; but as to a few signs not fully amortized, the court ruled that a reasonable amortization period would have to be allowed. National Advertising Co. v. County of Monterey (1970). This decision obviously depended upon the amortization approach. This is more common, and sign regulation ordinances without some traditional police power considerations and without reasonable amortization periods will normally fail.

The principal argument against the "aesthetics alone" rule, as suggested in the introduction, is that since beauty is in large measure in the eye of the beholder, then decisions based on aesthetic considerations would be subjective determinations governed by personal feelings and attitudes. The answer to that may be that if such attitudes result in capricious use of the police power, such decisions can be invalidated in the same manner as arbitrary zoning classifications. The problem is the lack of objective criteria and, in that respect, it might be compared to the obscenity cases.

An important United States Supreme Court decision which bears upon this problem was Metromedia, Inc. v. San Diego (1981), which involved a ban on off-site billboards while permitting on-site signs. The ordinance was challenged on the basis that it prohibited noncommercial speech and violated the First Amendment. Political campaign signs had been specifically exempted from the ordinance's application. The plurality of four justices stated that the ordinance's purpose of promoting aesthetics and traffic safety were valid goals, but it did not regard the ban on off-site, noncommercial advertising as valid because such speech is afforded greater protection than commercial speech, and the city could not choose permissible subjects of noncommercial discourse. The ordinance was thought to reach "too far into the realm of protected speech." A concurring opinion of two justices stated that the city had failed to justify its substantial restriction on protected activity and had also, due to the partial ban, failed to show a sufficient governmental interest in promoting aesthetics in this manner.

Much subsequent litigation followed on the heels of *Metromedia* with unclear and sometimes confusing results. Cities today generally take the position that on-site signs should not or cannot be banned, but they can be regulated through setbacks, size, lighting, placement and the requiring of permits and through use of variances, conditional use permits and amortization. Limitations on (usually off-site) political signs run the risk of being struck down under the First Amendment even though such restrictions sometimes are upheld. Thus, content neutral" sign ordinances which do not distinguish between commercial and non-commercial speech may still encounter this difficulty. In Village of Schaumburg v. Jeep Eagle Sales Corp. (1996) the Illinois Court of Appeals held that an ordinance prohibiting display of more than three official flags violated the First Amendment rights of an automobile dealer whose lot was ringed by an array of oversize American flags. Other cases use a First Amendment analysis in regard to political campaign signs and "For Sale" signs in racially troubled neighborhoods. The Supreme Court held invalid a prohibition of signs in single-family districts as applied to a homeowner who displayed an anti-Gulf War sign in her bedroom window. City of Ladue v. Gilleo (1994).

Federal and state efforts to beautify the highways by controlling billboards originally relied on the state police power to control outdoor advertising. State legislation was generally upheld as being within the general welfare in promoting natural beauty. However, the 1965 Highway Beautification Act required that states pay just compensation to landowners and billboard owners when signs lawfully placed there prior to the establishment of controls were removed. The 1978 amendments to the Act were very specific in requiring compensation for the removal of certain signs.

## § 3.    The Appearance of Structures: Architectural Considerations

Cases have upheld ordinances which regulate architectural "appeal" and functions on the theory that protection of property values is a legitimate concern of the police power in that such regulations promote the general welfare. State ex rel. Saveland Park Holding Corp. v. Wieland (1955). That case stated that it was immaterial whether the sole objective was to protect property values. Such decisions are not predicated upon aesthetics alone, although Berman v. Parker (1954), contained dictum suggesting that aesthetic considerations alone were a sufficient basis for the exercise of zoning powers. *Berman v. Parker* stated that the public welfare concept was broad enough to include aesthetics. In a Missouri case involving the much-protected St. Louis suburb of Ladue, an ordinance required that a board approve plans and specifications for structures in order to promote conformity to "minimal architectural standards" and prevent "unsightly, grotesque and unsuitable structures." When the ordinance was challenged by someone whose proposed residence was described by the city as "a monstrosity of grotesque design," on the basis that the state statutes did not authorize such an ordinance, the ordinance was upheld as being within the general welfare and promoting property values. State ex rel. Stoyanoff v. Berkeley (Mo.1970). But other cases have overturned such ordinances on the basis of lack of authorization under state enabling legislation, vagueness of provisions contained in the ordinance, and disapproval of the function of the architectural review board. *E.g.:* Piscitelli v. Township Committee of Scotch Plains (1968); West Palm Beach v. State ex rel. Duffey (1947); Pacesetter Homes v. Olympia Fields (1968).

One of the leading cases sustaining land use controls based on aesthetic considerations alone is People v. Stover (1963), in which an ordinance prohibiting clotheslines in front or side yards was sustained in a situation in which the Stovers erected and continually added to clotheslines of rags and unsightly apparel in their front yard to protest against high taxes. Nonetheless, the majority of courts sustain these ordinances, if at all, based on some more traditional ground in addition to aesthetic considerations.

A case subsequent to *Stover,* Cromwell v. Ferrier (1967), made it clear that ordinances enacted for aesthetic reasons alone were permissible in New

York (if there was any doubt about it). It cited *Stover* as "now the leading case" on the "aesthetics only" rule and rejected prior holdings that required some other valid police power objective.

## § 4.  Junkyards

Before leaving amortization of signs and billboards, it should be pointed out that junkyards can sometimes be the target of valid amortization ordinances also—and indeed, amortization ordinances are usually aimed either at signs and billboards or at junkyards. Ordinances excluding junkyards or wrecking yards from the city have been upheld as a valid police power exercise based solely upon aesthetics. Oregon City v. Hartke (1965). Again, this is the minority view, as the majority of courts require the more traditional police power basis which, when established, may be combined with aesthetic considerations.

## § 5.  Historic Districts

Akin to and yet apart from aesthetics is the preservation of historic districts. Purchase or condemnation by the government for historic preservation purposes is valid. More importantly, acts establishing historic districts have been upheld as promoting the public welfare. See, *e.g.*, Opinion of the Justices (1955). And zoning to preserve historic architectural patterns has been upheld. Sante Fe v. Gamble–Skogmo (1964). The only problem seems to be one of proof with regard to the historic or cultural nature of the area.

The reasoning of courts in these situations is illustrated by the thinking of the Massachusetts Court in approving preservation of Beacon Hill in Boston. The court noted the historic nature of the area, the uniformity in design and structure, and held that the prevention of inappropriate forms of construction from coming into this area was for the educational, cultural, and economic advantage of the public and was within the general welfare. Opinion of the Justices (1955). Obviously, there are some aesthetic considerations involved in such cases, but the courts generally view these as secondary to the main object of preserving the historic and cultural structures of the past and, in so doing by preventing commercial intrusion, maintain the property values of the area.

In addition to Boston and the New Mexico decision preserving "Old Santa Fe Style" architecture, Louisiana has a long history of attempting to preserve the character of the French Quarter. New Orleans' "Vieux Carre Ordinance" was based on constitutional authorization and was upheld as not being just for sentimental purposes but for preserving the commercial value of the area. In Williamsburg, Virginia, zoning was employed to preserve a restored area rather than an existing historic area. In Illinois, a historic district regulation was upheld which served to protect only one historic structure within the district—Lincoln's home. Rebman v. Springfield (1969).

Such ordinances have come into widespread use and have generally been accepted by the courts.

They exemplify the blending of aesthetic, historic and cultural concerns. They have been bolstered by such legislation as the National Historic Preservation Act of 1966 and by statutes in such states as Arkansas and New Mexico designating or creating commissions or committees with functions and duties on the subject.

## § 6.   Landmark Preservation

Landmark preservation interrelates with historic preservation except that it normally involves a structure rather than an area. Landmark preservation ordinances, such as that in New York City, prevent demolition of buildings designated by a commission as landmarks. Such ordinances have, at times, run into the difficulty of being declared confiscatory as to the particular situation. See Lutheran Church v. City of New York (1974). Solutions include authorizing acquisition of an easement in the facade of the structure rather than the entire fee and transfer of development rights permitting more intense development than allowed by zoning regulations as compensation to the landmark owner for not demolishing it. Fee title acquisition, through condemnation, presents the problem of acquiring property in prohibitively expensive locations. One particular difficulty is that many of the architectural treasures in the United States are churches, and efforts to landmark church buildings are often attacked as interfering with the free exercise of religion. The Second Circuit held in St. Bartholomew's Church v. City of New York (1990) that the church could be denied the right to sell airspace rights over its vestry building on Park Avenue for $50 million, the money to be used to further the church's social mission. The Supreme Court was faced with this issue in the case of City of Boerne v. Flores (1997). In this case the Catholic Church in Boerne challenged the inclusion of portions of the structure in the historic district citing the Religious Freedom Restoration Act (an Act of Congress specifying that any regulation impacting religion must be justified by a compelling governmental interest). The Court held that the Act exceeded the powers of Congress under the Fourteenth Amendment. Afterwards, the church and the city negotiated an agreement allowing construction of new facilities while preserving the façade.

The National Historic Preservation Act of 1966, 16 U.S.C.A. § 470 et seq., established a national register of historic sites. It was aimed at federal agencies and imposed no duties on state or local governments. It provided for protection and restoration of historic sites and districts. Any federal agency must take into account the effect of any project which might demolish an historic site, but preservation is not guaranteed even if the site is listed in the National Register. The standing of citizens to sue under this act to protect historic landmarks has presented a hurdle to relief in some cases. See Kent County Council v. Romney (W.D.Mich.1969).

## § 7.  Transfer of Development Rights

As mentioned, this device has been proposed for use in connection with landmark preservation, as

well as open space acquisition. Referred to occasionally as "TDR," it is a relatively recent land use
control device. The device has even been advanced
as a substitute for zoning.

What TDR essentially involves is separation of
the right to develop property from other property
rights. A landowner may have his property limited to open space or may agree not to demolish a
landmark in return for issuance of certificates of
development rights which will allow him to develop elsewhere. He may also be allowed a tax reduction. The question arises as to whether this
satisfies the just compensation requirement for a
taking under the power of eminent domain. The
owners may contend that the designation amounts
to inverse condemnation and that the development rights certificates represent only a potential
for future development elsewhere and do not
amount to just compensation. The contrary argument is that by transferring development rights
the landowner had received his equivalent elsewhere.

In Fred F. French Investing Co., Inc. v. City of
New York (1976), the New York Court of Appeals
held that "floating development rights" which could
be used elsewhere within a certain area of Manhattan could not be evaluated until such rights were
applied to a specific piece of property. The award of
such rights as compensation for rezoning two private parks as public parks was held to amount to a
deprivation of substantive due process because such
rights were an "abstraction," the value of which

could not be determined until some uncertain later date.

But in Penn Central Transportation Co. v. City of New York (1977), the court sustained the city's landmark preservation provisions and a denial of Penn Central's request to develop the airspace over the Grand Central terminal—one of the main reasons being that Penn Central would be allowed transferable development rights at some other location. These rights were viewed in that case as "valuable" and as providing "significant, perhaps 'fair' compensation." The court went to some lengths to distinguish a contrary holding involving ownership of an historic structure by the Lutheran Church, in which the ordinance had been declared unconstitutional because economic conditions did not permit the building to be maintained in its present form and the church was a charitable institution which did not reap the same pecuniary benefits of massive governmental investment enjoyed by the railroads and Grand Central Terminal.

*French* and *Penn Central* appear to be in conflict, but a factor in *Penn Central* that was not present in *French* was the landmark preservation provisions of the city code. Since landmark preservation generally has received favorable treatment in the courts and since the Penn Central railroad could continue to be benefited by use of the landmark terminal, then the transfer of development rights sweetened the pot, so to speak, with regard to the action taken. Moreover, these rights could be attached to specific parcels of property, some of which were already owned by Penn Central or its affiliates. In this context, the rights were viewed as being of value.

The Supreme Court avoided an opportunity to decide the question of whether TDRs could be considered just compensation in the case of Suitum v. Tahoe Regional Planning Agency (1997). The owner of a small parcel in an environmentally protected area was denied development permission and awarded a single TDR of some 18,000 square feet. The agency resisted her lawsuit on the ground she had failed to exhaust her remedies and the case was not ripe for adjudication. The Supreme Court held that the case was ripe and remanded. Justice Scalia, in a concurring opinion, stated that he thought TDRs might be regarded as partial just compensation. That issue remains to be decided.

# CHAPTER X

# NATURAL RESOURCES

## § 1. Introduction

The preservation of natural resources interrelates with preservation of historic and cultural districts and sites; and both bear a relationship to the preservation of aesthetics and of the environment. The interlocking effect of such problems and activities should be kept in mind.

## § 2. Restrictions on Removal of Earth

Many cases have upheld zoning ordinances which prohibit the removal of natural resources from property lying in specified zones. Problems arise when the question is whether it is reasonable and not arbitrary to do so under certain circumstances. In one case, it was demonstrated that the plaintiff's property had no real economic value for anything other than excavation of rock, sand and gravel, but an ordinance restricting the land to agricultural and residential uses was upheld. (Nearby communities housed people suffering from respiratory ailments.) Consolidated Rock Products v. Los Angeles (1962). While the court found that many other uses might be made of the land, it was conceded that the value of these other uses was small in comparison to excavation of natural resources. But the court rea-

soned that if the classification was reasonably justified, it would be the antithesis of zoning theory to
permit private benefits to override public welfare
considerations. On the other hand, such ordinances
may be declared to be unreasonable and confiscatory in situations in which adjacent lands are being
used in a similar manner or in which there are no
standards to govern determination of the grant or
denial of a permit to excavate. Lyon Sand & Gravel
v. Township of Oakland (1971). The nuisance cases,
such as *Hadacheck v. Sebastian*, illustrate the importance of surrounding uses in upholding or overturning such regulations.

Restriction on excavation in Pennsylvania might
run afoul of that state's rule that all lawful uses
must, in general, be accommodated within each
township. Thus, a complete ban on quarrying was
invalidated in Exton Quarries, Inc. v. Zoning Board
of Adjustment (1967), which stated that a total ban
must receive greater scrutiny than regulations con-
fining such use to a particular location. The court
rejected contentions that quarrying operations interfere with the public welfare due to dust, noise,
vibration and excessive truck traffic, interfere with
the water supply, and create conditions which
would endanger children.

## § 3.  Agriculture

Zoning sometimes classifies land lying outside of
urban areas as agricultural and limits the use either
to pure agricultural uses or a variety of rural uses
bearing some similarity or interrelationship. As the

urban fringe extends outward and subdividers appear on the scene, the ordinance is amended to accommodate residential development within the agricultural zone.

Agricultural zoning has real estate tax implications. Those whose land is zoned exclusively for agriculture (with farm-related structures permitted) receive a tax break. This usually extends until reclassification of the land as residential.

Some problems have arisen from loosely drafted ordinances involving the urban fringe, in which farming has been treated as a permitted use. Expansion or development of operations involving animals, such as cattle, pigs or chickens, has led to litigation based on whether such operations or the expansion of same are permissible. The result often hinges (in the absence of specific wording in the ordinance) on whether the court views the large scale raising of animals as farming or industry.

Many states have adopted "right to farm" statutes that purport to protect agricultural operations at the expanding urban fringes from nuisance suits by subdivision dwellers. Although these statutes are usually held valid, often they use a restrictive definition of farming. Wellington Farms, Inc. v. Township of Silver Spring (Pa.Cmwlth. 1996). In the absence of statutory definitions, some courts have confronted ordinances that define agricultural uses so broadly that use of farms for such commercial activities as hayrides and shooting ranges are called into question. Columbia Twp. Bd. Of Zoning Appeals v. Otis (Ohio App. 1995); Little v. Winborn (Iowa 1994).

Occasional agricultural designations have limited land uses over a substantial area. This is usually for the purpose of preventing nonconforming uses of land which may shortly become urban or semi-urban in nature. Courts have to be alert to prevent abuse of the ordinance through the establishment of "pre-existing" nonconforming uses which are not really pre-existing. Mang v. County of Santa Barbara (1960).

## § 4. Forests

Regulations restricting or prohibiting the wasteful or unnecessary cutting of timber have been upheld as falling within the police power and as not constituting a taking. Opinion of the Justices (1908). Similarly, statutes requiring private forest landowners to patrol their woods during dry seasons or pay for such patrols have been upheld. Destruction of trees to eliminate Dutch elm disease, cedar rust in cedar trees, orchard pests or other types of diseases has been upheld. Preservation of timber and the food supply is considered to be a valid objective of the police power. Thus, it is valid either to enact legislation to conserve trees or to destroy diseased ones.

Some subdivision exactions require landscaping in the form of tree planting as a condition to approval. In England, tree planting is required in connection with land development.

## § 5.  Coastlines and Beaches

The Coastal Zone Management Act of 1972, 16
U.S.C.A. § 1451 et seq., arose from concern about
industrial complexes (particularly oil refineries) in
coastal waters, rapid shoreline urbanization, the
threat to the wildly beautiful Pacific coastline produced by residential growth, commercial fishing activities, waste disposal and related problems. This
act did not involve direct federal regulation of coastal areas but provided encouragement and money for
the states to develop coastal management plans. All
affected states and territories have moved toward
development and implementation of coastal zone
plans. California voters by initiative adopted a commission possessing the power to require on an interim basis a development permit for land extending
1000 yards inward from the mean high tide line.
The Commission was charged with submitting a
coastal zone plan to the legislature for its adoption
and implementation. The validity of the California
act was upheld when challenged as a violation of
substantive and procedural due process, a taking, a
violation of the right to travel, an invalid delegation
of legislative power, and the like. See CEEED v.
California Coastal Zone Conservation Commission
(1974).

Regulation of beaches has been upheld on two
theories: custom and prescriptive rights. The issue
may arise as to the power of the state to prevent
landowners from enclosing the dry sand area of
ocean-front property. This power to regulate use
was upheld in Oregon, Florida and Hawaii under

the custom doctrine, *i.e.,* the custom of the public to use the beaches for recreational purposes joined with the relative inadequacy of such areas for erection of permanent facilities. State ex rel. Thornton v. Hay (1969); *Daytona Beach v. Tona–Rama* (Fla. 1974); In re Ashford (1968). In the Oregon case, the state had passed a statute maintaining state sovereignty over ocean beaches. While it was admitted that the legislation could not divest a landowner of his rights, the court (without rejecting the doctrine of prescriptive rights) held that long-standing customary use of the beach by the public as a recreational area resulted in vesting in the public a right to use the beaches. Relying on Blackstone, the court found that all requirements of the custom doctrine had been met—antiquity of use, without interruption, reasonable and peaceable use, certainty as to the boundaries, obligatory upon all landowners, and not inconsistent with other customs or other law.

Since use by the public of the dry sand area of beaches based upon custom does not create any rights in the beach, Florida upheld the right of a landowner to construct a tower in an area near a pier because this did not interfere with customary use. *Daytona Beach v. Tona–Rama, supra.*

Obviously, the custom doctrine bears some relationship to the prescriptive rights doctrine, which involves prescriptive use by the public for the statutory period of time. The problem with that doctrine is that it must be proved in each case, whereas a decision which follows the custom doctrine easily applies to all the beaches. But two states with long shorelines, California and Texas, have adopted the prescriptive rights approach. See, *e.g.,* Gion v. Santa Cruz (1970).

Controls relating to beach or shorefront areas have presented other problems. Michigan rejected the argument that public rights in Lake Michigan created an implied easement of access to the lake across private lands. Pigorsh v. Fahner (1972). A New Jersey decision involved whether a city could charge nonresidents higher fees than residents for use of the beach. The court construed the public trust doctrine (which derives from the English principle that the land covered by tidal waters is held by the sovereign for the common use of all the people) as extending to recreational uses and as permitting municipalities to charge reasonable fees for use of their beaches but as not permitting discrimination between residents and nonresidents. Neptune City v. Avon–By–The–Sea (1972). Wisconsin has held that the public trust doctrine extends to all public uses of water. Hixon v. Public Service Commission (1966).

While the above doctrines and statutes based on them are more common forms of regulating beaches, zoning has been used to prevent beachfront development. McCarthy v. Manhattan Beach (1953).

Certain asserted rights of public use have been held to be outweighed by other considerations as where the Secretary of the Interior successfully banned public nude bathing due to environmental harm being caused due to increase of people and traffic in the area. Williams v. Hathaway (D.Mass. 1975).

## § 6.  Rivers and Streams

Generally speaking, the state is the owner of the bed of a navigable river or stream, and the owners of land along its banks own only to the high water mark (or low water mark, depending on the jurisdiction). In the case of a non-navigable stream, adjoining landowners own the stream itself out to the center or thread of the stream. But this ownership relates to the definition of navigability. Traditionally, a stream is viewed as non-navigable if it is not subject to commercial use. Some recent cases, however, have extended the definition to encompass recreational use. *E.g.,* State v. McIlroy (1980). A better approach would seem to be the passage of a statute creating a public easement for recreation in all waters of the state, subject to the right of the state and local governments to enact reasonable police power regulations and subject to other statutory and common law rights of landowners. Otherwise, it would seem that by changing the definition, riparian landowners are deprived of a valuable property right. Support for this contention may be found in Kaiser Aetna v. United States (1979), in which the water was found to have been made navigable by its private owners, and the public was held to be excluded until just compensation had been paid to the owners.

Another way to acquire the right to navigate non-navigable waters is through prescriptive use by the public for the period of time necessary to establish prescriptive rights.

## § 7.  Other Regulatory Activities

The situation with regard to regulation of agriculture, forests, coastal areas and the like extends to similar subjects of regulation. Requirements that farmers dip cattle or sheep to destroy ticks or disease, statutes requiring destruction of weeds, regulation aimed at preserving fish and wildlife, legislation to assure drainage of farmlands, statutes prohibiting the waste of natural gas and crude oil, acts aimed at conserving the water supply, and the establishment of conservancy districts to prevent floods, have all been upheld under the police power. The courts have over the years shown a strong tendency to approve reasonable legislation intended to preserve and protect our natural resources.

# CHAPTER XI

# ENVIRONMENTAL CONTROLS

## § 1.  Introduction

As earlier mentioned, there is an interrelationship between regulation of aesthetics, historic preservation, controls on exploitation of natural resources, and environmental concerns. When the environment is regulated, or when historic and cultural districts or landmarks are preserved, aesthetics enters in. It is aesthetically pleasing to have clean air in a city or clean water in a lake or stream. Similarly, it is aesthetically pleasing to preserve our coastlines and beaches for public use and protect them against unsightly exploitation. All of these activities involve aesthetic considerations and all of them have environmental ramifications.

Environmental law and regulations, stemming particularly from the federal government, have become so pervasive over the past quarter-century that it is impossible to cover this subject effectively as only a small part of a Nutshell. It is a law unto its own, taught separately in law schools and engaging the attention of a substantial number of lawyers who do little else.

Consequently, we can only touch upon a few of the salient features which affect land use. Suffice it to say that most environmental regulations, by their very nature, affect land development, sales of land, and the use of land.

## § 2.  National Environmental Policy Act

Whatever may have gone before, and much did, the National Environmental Policy Act of 1969 (NEPA), 42 U.S.C.A. § 4321 et seq., made both the public and private sector conform to certain environmental standards and involved the federal courts in the review process. The interrelationship of the objectives of NEPA and more traditional forms of land use control under the police power are illustrated by its stated objectives, which relate not only to the environment, but also to assuring aesthetically pleasing surroundings, protecting health and safety, preserving our historic and cultural heritage, and preserving our national resources.

Probably the most significant effect of NEPA pertained to federal agencies. Not only were they required to undertake certain specific acts related to environmental policy and make information available on the subject, but they also had to include a detailed statement on the environmental impact of any proposal involving major federal activity. There were requirements as to consultation on the statement with federal agencies having expertise on the subject as well as to circulation of the statement to interested agencies of government at all levels. Agencies were also required to propose

policies and measures to bring themselves into conformity with NEPA. NEPA was intended to supple-
ment and not supersede the mission of the federal
agencies. Nonetheless, it clearly placed an additional burden upon the various agencies as well as
supplementing their powers.

The goals or objectives of NEPA are fulfilled
principally through the Council on Environmental
Quality (CEQ), which was created under Title II of
the Act, and through the work of the Environmental Protection Agency (EPA). The Council was given
powers relating to examination of the quality of the
environment, review of federal programs and activities, and preparation of environmental quality reports. Subsequent acts or orders added functions
permitting the Council to gather information and
coordinate the activities of different agencies. The
Council advises the President, but its greatest impact is probably felt in the guidelines it prepares for
environmental impact statements. Its studies on
various topics have influenced national policies affecting the environment.

The CEQ guidelines are treated somewhat like
agency regulations by the courts. These guidelines
are influential and are employed by the courts, but
they are not invariably followed. Cases have varied
on whether the guidelines should be viewed as
advisory or should be applied in all or practically all
instances. *Cf.:* Greene County Planning Board v.
Federal Power Commission (2d Cir.1972); Trout
Unlimited v. Morton (9th Cir.1974); and Environ-

mental Defense Fund, Inc. v. Corps of Engineers (E.D.Ark.1971).

CEQ does not control or veto procedure or policies of agencies or pass upon impact statements. But the Environmental Protection Agency (EPA) is more active. Under one section of the Clean Air Act, 42 U.S.C.A. § 1857h–7, EPA is directed to review and comment in writing on the environmental impact of matters relating to the subject of that act contained in any federally proposed legislation, newly authorized Federal project, major federal agency action, and proposed agency regulations. This gives EPA a powerful check on other agencies of the federal government. Moreover, criticism by EPA of federal projects or proposed regulations has a substantial effect on the courts.

NEPA amounted to a policy decision that federal agencies would have to conform to environmental standards and that their actions would be subjected to careful scrutiny. After a great deal of litigation and the enforcement of environmental standards by the courts, the agencies seemed to realize that environmental concerns would have to be met. Judicial admonition along that line no doubt led to this realization. See, *e.g.*, Calvert Cliffs' Coordinating Comm. v. U.S. Atomic Energy Commission (D.C.Cir. 1971).

*Calvert Cliffs* was the first court of appeals case to apply NEPA, and it was a strong affirmation of the congressional intention that federal agencies comply with the requirements of the act. In this case the Atomic Energy Commission had adopted rules on environmental matters which were held not to comply. The AEC was compelled to adopt rules which took environmental concerns into account and which would lead to a "systematic balancing analysis" in evaluating projects and activities of the agency. Looking specifically at the AEC rules, the court found them to be a "crabbed interpretation of NEPA" that "makes a mockery of the Act." The court viewed the agency as reluctant to meet its obligations, and it refused to condone such footdragging.

## § 3. Judicial Review

Judicial review of agency actions has been a careful and thorough process involving rather close scrutiny. This is in line with the decision in Citizens to Preserve Overton Park, Inc. v. Volpe (1971), which required that judicial review involve "substantial inquiry" and be searching, probing, and complete. Thus, administrative decisions must be carefully contrived and subject to reasonable explanation.

In the *Overton Park* case, the agency had attempted to rely upon a provision in the Administrative Procedure Act, 5 U.S.C.A. § 701(a)(2), which eliminated judicial review where action by the agency was by law made dependent upon agency discretion. But the Supreme Court held that this was true only where there was no applicable law affecting the situation. Although courts were held not empowered to substitute their views for those of the agency, the inquiry should be searching and careful and the reviewing court should determine whether relevant factors were considered and whether there was a clear error of judgment.

In this process, agencies may be called upon to explain how decisions were arrived at and what formed the basis for such decisions. See Kennecott Copper Corp. v. Environmental Protection Agency (D.C.Cir.1972). The matter may also be remanded for further hearings on questions not considered.

## § 4.  Federal Pollution Legislation

Although there were federal laws pertaining to air pollution prior to the 1970's, the present law on air pollution largely stems from the Clean Air Act. See 42 U.S.C.A. § 1857 et seq. This act deals with fixed sources of air pollution, emissions from motor vehicles and airplanes, as well as provisions pertaining to administrative and judicial review. Among other things, this Act contemplates a national program to prevent and control air pollution, establishes air quality control regions and criteria, and makes provision for ambient air quality standards, standards of performance by manufacturing plants and similar sources, and national emission standards for hazardous pollutants.

The counterpart to the Clean Air Act is the Federal Water Pollution Control Act, 33 U.S.C.A. § 1251 et seq. It too was preceded by other federal laws dealing with the subject. After providing in two titles for research and demonstration projects and grants for sewage treatment plants, it provides for imposition of standards and for rules relating to enforcement. It also provides for permits and creates the National Pollutant Discharge Elimination System.

Of less importance than the air and water pollution legislation in terms of its scope and the volume of cases it produces is the Noise Control Act of 1972, 42 U.S.C.A. § 4901 et seq. Noise pollution is simply excessive noise, and this act attempts to control noise on a federal basis. The act emulates many of the provisions of the earlier pollution control laws. EPA is authorized to conduct or contract for research on the subject. Technical assistance to local governments and studies are provided for. Most importantly, however, federal regulations are authorized in the establishment of noise emission standards for various sources and aircraft noise can be regulated. The enforcement provisions of the act, however, are relatively weak. Although the act gave EPA important duties, substantial power was retained in the Federal Aviation Administration and the Civil Aeronautics Board. This included authority over noise emitted by jet aircraft.

Other federal legislation includes the Federal Environmental Pesticide Control Act of 1972, 7 U.S.C.A. § 135 et seq., which involves various registration provisions prior to sale of pesticides. A pesticide can be classified for restricted use, which means that the environmental or personal risk in using it is substantial.

## § 5. Hazardous Waste

Recent legislative and judicial activity has centered in large measure around hazardous waste, which in turn has generated a substantial amount of litigation. An EPA study in 1981 concluded that five to six times more hazardous waste was being generated than the agency had believed to be true even a year before. The Resource Conservation and Recovery Act, 42 U.S.C.A. § 6901 et seq. provided for granting permits for 8,500 waste facilities sites. Cleaning up known hazardous sites was the objective of the creation of the "Superfund" or Comprehensive Environmental Response, Compensation and Liability Act, 42 U.S.C.A. § 9601 et seq., adopted in 1980. This Act is known as "CERCLA," and activities and litigation related to it will continue into the indefinite future.

Basically, CERCLA requires the clean-up of hazardous waste sites. The basic provisions as to removal and remedial action are found in 42 U.S.C.A. § 9604(a)(1). A parent corporation is potentially liable for the actions of a subsidiary. A subsequent purchaser who was not the polluter may be held responsible for the action of the previous owner-polluter. The statutory provisions hold liable, among others, the owner, the operator, a disposal or treatment contractor or one who arranged for transport for disposal or treatment, and the transporter. There are defenses available for acts of God, acts of war, or (subject to strict limitations) acts of third parties.

This legislation has been upheld as against numerous challenges in numerous federal courts. In fact, it has been held that the Act can be applied retroactively to pre-enactment costs incurred by government in cleaning up hazardous waste sites. O'Neil v. Picillo (1st Cir.1989). It is a strict liability statute with only a limited number of available defenses. General Electric Co. v. Litton Indus. Automation Systems (8th Cir.1990). Landowners who lease the land to a company which stores hazardous wastes can be held liable for costs for partial removal even though they claimed to be innocent absentee landlords. United States v. Monsanto Co. (4th Cir. 1988). There is absolute liability except for the limited defenses mentioned previously and such defenses as lack of foreseeability, contributory or comparative negligence by the government, and exercise of due care are irrelevant. Moreover, there may be joint and several liability. *O'Neil v. Picillo,* supra.

CERCLA also provides for retroactive revival of state claims previously barred under state statutes of limitation. 42 U.S.C.A. § 9658; Light, New Federalism, Old Due Process, and Retroactive Revival: Constitutional Problems with CERCLA's Amendment of State Law, 40 *U.Kan.L.Rev.* 365 (1992). A catch-all case holding that retroactive application of CERCLA does not violate due process, applying it to preenactment response costs, applying liability to past off-site generators and transporters (42 U.S.C.A. § 6973(a)), imposing liability without proof of negligence to present conditions resulting from past activities, and imposing liability upon individual corporate officers and employees as well as the corporation is United States v. Northeastern Pharmaceutical & Chemical Co. (8th Cir.1986). In United States v. Denver (1996) the Tenth Circuit Court of Appeals held that CERCLA preempts conflicting state or local regulation of hazardous waste. In this case a local regulation required removal of certain radioactive waste while the EPA order required on-site solidification of the soils.

## § 6.  Endangered Species

The Endangered Species Act of 1973 impacts to a much greater degree on both private and public land development than is generally realized. It is given little attention in land use casebook and thus is only of passing concern to law students focusing on exams. Its severe limitations should merit more attention than it has received legally, although considerable newspaper space has been devoted to the effects of preserving the Tennessee snail darter, the Northern spotted owl, and various birds and bugs.

An "endangered species" is any species in danger of extinction "throughout all or a significant portion of its range" other than an insect determined administratively to be a pest. 16 U.S.C.A. § 1532(6). The federal government is impacted by 16 U.S.C.A. § 1536(a)(2), which requires federal agencies to insure that federally authorized and funded projects do not jeopardize endangered or threatened species or destroy or adversely modify their habitat. However, it is also extended to private persons through 16 U.S.C.A. § 1538(a)(1). A "taking" of a member of a designated endangered species, which includes harming or harassing it, is prohibited. Within the Act, provision is made for incidental taking permits to be obtained if certain stringent migration measures are observed. This would entail submission of a habitat conservation plan. 16 U.S.C.A. § 1539(a)(2)(A). In Babbitt v. Sweet Home (1995) The Supreme Court held that the word "take" in the statute could be interpreted to include damage to the habitat in addition to direct physical force. Thus, land development can be severely impacted by the Act.

The seriousness with which the Act is applied is illustrated by Tennessee Valley Authority v. Hill (1978), in which the Supreme Court considered the fate of the three-inch fish known as the Tennessee snail darter. The Court opined:

> "It may seem curious to some that the survival of a relatively small number of three-inch fish among all the countless millions of species extant would require the permanent halting of a virtually completed dam for which Congress has expended more than $100 million. The paradox is not minimized by the fact that Congress continued to appropriate large sums of public money for the project, even after congressional Appropriations Committees were apprised of its apparent impact upon the survival of the snail darter. We conclude, however, that the explicit provisions of the Endangered Species Act require precisely that result."

The Court concluded that the Act was intended to be accorded the highest priority no matter what the cost.

The result is that land use activities that might adversely affect endangered species have involved the expenditure of substantial time and money to discover the impact and to formulate and obtain approval of their plans. Both public and private land use projects have either been limited or prohibited. Numerous cases or problems have involved species of various kinds including butterflies, mice, rats, birds, whales, lizards, snakes, beetles, et al. See generally, Arnold, Conserving Habitats and Building Habitats: The Emerging Impact of the Endangered Species Act on Land Use Development, 10 *Stan.Envtl.L.J.* 1 (1991).

For land use purposes, we cannot ignore the effect of this legislation and cases involving it on both public and private projects. The difficulty in considering the subject objectively is the polarized nature of the argument. Environmentalists or species preservationists regard the law as a finite good to be achieved no matter what the cost, how rigid the regulation, or how damaging to persons or agencies affected by it. Developers generally regard the other side as zealous crazies. Disinterested commentators, such as Justice Powell dissenting in the snail darter case, refer at times as he did to the "absurd result."

Without question, the Act impacts upon the ability of public agencies to construct essential facilities and on private landowners who may be seriously

harmed financially, suffer severe land use limitations, or even deprived of all use of their land. See
generally, Arnold, supra; and Kmiec, Environmental Inequities—Observations on Mandelker's "Environment and Equity—A Regulatory Challenge," 57
*Notre Dame Lawyer* 313, 303–336 (1981).

This naturally leads to questions as to whether
this Act under certain circumstances may be said to
constitute a taking. (The Act itself talks about a
"taking" in relation to a taking of the endangered
or threatened species, but we are concerned here
with whether the Act itself as applied under certain
circumstances may amount to a taking of private
property without just compensation.) It would appear that if the landowner is deprived of all economic use of his land, then under the *Lucas* and *First
English* decisions, a case could be made that there
has been a regulatory taking. The defense, of
course, would assert that the landowner has not
been deprived of *all* economic use if he is free to use
the land for something that does not interfere with
the species in question. Based on the severe constraints of the Supreme Court imposed in those
cases, that defense would probably suffice in many
or most situations. To the contrary, if any development activity on the plaintiff's land will adversely
affect the designated species so that no activity will
be permitted at all, it would seem to amount to a
taking under *Lucas* and *First English*. In one "man
bites dog" type of case, Moerman v. State (Cal.App.
1995), a rancher brought an inverse condemnation
suit against the state after it had relocated a herd of

endangered tule elk near the ranch. The elk destroyed the rancher's fences and ate the forage intended for his livestock. The court dismissed the suit ruling that the elk were not under the control of the state nor were they instrumentalities of the state.

Presumably, a taking under the Fifth Amendment of the property of American citizens still takes precedence over the taking of a bird's habitat under the Endangered Species Act.

Another factor, of course, is the economic consequence of the Act. The cost of public projects, including the Tellico Dam in the snail darter case, have sometimes increased dramatically as a result. Some no longer are feasible. Similar costs may be incurred by private developers or landowners, and such private projects may also be lost as a result. The answer of the Congress, as correctly interpreted by the federal courts, is that cost is no object.

Courts have therefore approached this subject without considering the economic consequences and with only the issue of whether the law applies. In Sierra Club v. Lyng (E.D.Tex.1988), the subject was the occupancy of the piney woods of East Texas by the red-cockaded woodpecker, "a small undistinguished woodpecker indigenous to the southern United States" and an even-aged forest harvesting management program in the national forests. The Texas federal judge issued a permanent injunction against the Forest Service after observing:

"This woodpecker makes no great or even necessary contribution to ecological balance, his song is unremarkable, and his plumage causes no heads to turn. However, these apparent short-comings do not enter into the equation of the task assigned to this Court. The red-cockaded woodpecker's chief claim to fame is the fact that it succeeded in having its name inscribed on the endangered species list."

The court observed in a footnote that this put the woodpecker in the ranks of such flora and fauna as "the Santa Cruz long-toed salamander, the Dismal Swamp southeastern shrew, the purple-spined hedgehog cactus, and the Appalachian monkeyface pearly mussel." Ibid.

Whether these concerns be viewed as deadly serious national concerns, as by the environmentalists, or as absurd laws provoking unjust economic harm, as by developers and landowners, the fact remains that they are extremely strong limitations upon land use and constraints upon development in any situation to which they apply.

And as the Supreme Court stated in the snail darter case, " ...in our constitutional system the commitment to the separation of powers is too fundamental for us to pre-empt congressional action by judicially decreeing what accords with 'common sense and the public weal.' Our Constitution vests such responsibilities in the political branches."

## § 7.  Other Recent Federal Concerns

Other recent concerns which may ultimately be the subject of new federal legislation include acid rain, groundwater loss and pollution, and what is sometimes referred to as cross-media pollution. Although the problem is still being studied, somewhat incessantly, industrial air pollutants which produce acid rain many hundreds of miles from the source appear to be damaging American forests in addition to polluting the atmosphere and offering water pollution problems. This is an example of cross-media pollution, as is the apparent fact that most metal deposits in the Great Lakes come from air pollution rather than water pollution, according to one report.

With respect to groundwater, there are already serious problem areas of the United States because of the exhaustion of underground aquifers by excessive agricultural or industrial use requiring large quantities of water. This is rapidly becoming an acute problem, for example, in the fertile high plains area of West Texas. Competition for groundwater in the West is an increasing problem, and the decision in Sporhase v. Nebraska ex rel. Douglas (1982), holding unconstitutional state restrictions on the transfer of interstate groundwater, could lead to new conflicts and increasing litigation over groundwater, including suits between states. The *Sporhase* decision, joined with increasing groundwater shortages and pollution problems, would seem to call for a national initiative. But the Water Resources Council was disbanded in the early 1980's, and water resource policy or management from the federal level is largely absent.

## § 8. State Legislation

The states have adopted various and sundry statutes which emulate the federal legislation. These laws are usually more general in nature and less powerful in terms of enforcement. They create state and sometimes local air and water pollution control agencies.

Enforcement of state laws is generally weak and less consistent than at the federal level. Many or most states have probably come to depend upon federal control over the abuse of the environment. Whatever the cause, the center for imposition and enforcement of standards has largely resided in the federal courts and with EPA.

There are state and local environmental policy acts (SEPA's) which provide some assistance. Most of the states now have requirements relative to environmental impact statements, and a number of states have comprehensive legislation. An example of a rather extensive law is the California Environmental Quality Act of 1970. Cal.Public Resources Code § 21000 et seq.

## § 9. The Impact of Environmental Considerations

The impact on federal activities of environmental impact considerations has been quite substantial. In Hanly v. Kleindienst (2d Cir.1972), by way of illustration, the situation involved construction of a jail and related facilities by the General Services Administration. The case had twice been before the district court, and this was its second trip to the court of appeals. The case was again remanded due to the failure of the GSA to make certain required findings. Earlier, the court of appeals had found GSA's environmental impact statement to be insufficient in that it did not take into account the effect of the detention center on its neighbors with respect to noise, the danger of crime from the outpatient treatment center, certain traffic problems, and the need for parking. This time, the court was concerned with the standard of review to be applied and the determination of whether there would be a "significantly" adverse environmental impact as a result of the project. After adopting the "arbitrary, capricious" standard of the Administrative Procedure Act, the court decided that every major federal action had some adverse effect on the environment. But in considering whether a specific activity affected it "significantly," the proposed action would have to be considered in the light of the extent to which the adverse environmental effects exceed those created by existing uses and the quantitative adverse environmental effects of the action including resulting cumulative harm. Although the GSA had submitted a new 25–page environmental assessment, the court of appeals did not feel that it had dealt adequately with the question of the effect of a drug maintenance program and whether crime in the area would be increased, and it also felt that GSA had failed to comply with certain procedural requirements. For one thing, it had not given notice to the public of its proposed action and allowed relevant facts to be presented prior to making its "threshold decision." The GSA was directed to consider the two questions and permit further evidence to be submitted by those opposing the project.

The thought of the Second Circuit that every major activity affects the environment in some way is illustrated by Aberdeen & Rockfish Ry. Co. v. Students Challenging Regulatory Agency Procedures (SCRAP) (1972). The railroads had filed for a rate increase, and SCRAP argued that this would further discourage the movement of recyclable goods in commerce and in turn lead to increased degradation of the environment by discarded, unrecycled goods. SCRAP objected to the ICC's failure to issue an impact statement evaluating the effect of the rate increase on shipments of recyclable materials. A three-judge district court held that the ICC decision not to suspend the rate increase while it looked into the environmental effect was a major federal action that would require an impact statement. On appeal, Chief Justice Burger, sitting as Circuit Justice, denied a stay of that order pending appeal.

It should be obvious from the foregoing that almost any federal project or important federal activity has environmental ramifications. In Anaconda Co. v. Ruckelshaus (D.Colo.1972), EPA itself was required to file an environmental impact statement with regard to a proposed emission limitation on a copper smelter. The court held that when Congress said all federal agencies had to comply, they intended no exceptions.

## § 10.  The Future of Environmental Controls

The crisis of the environment was the focus of major public concern during the 1960's and 1970's and resulted in substantial and far-reaching legislation during that period and on into the 1980's, as manifested by the discussion of hazardous wastes in particular.

To some degree, however, environmental activism was reduced and took a back seat in the 1980's and 1990's to concerns over government spending, the tax structure, the deficit and foreign affairs.

This seems to have come about for a variety of reasons. One was the national desire, manifested by individuals and corporations alike, to remove the national government as much as possible from regulative involvement in the lives of the people. This desire served well the aims of businesses engaged in pollution causing activities. But it cut across a wide front—from heavy industry to the agricultural use of pesticides. A second reason, interrelated with the first, was the perception that government spending was too high and government programs too extensive, expensive and wasteful. A further reason seems to have been the thought that federal taxes were overly burdensome and should be reduced. Again, this interrelated with the prior two concerns. Environmental programs thus became a visible, outward sign of what was perceived to be an inward, spiritual evil. They were involved with the lives of the people—private individuals and farmers as well as large corporations; they cost money (although a drop in the bucket compared to either national defense or entitlements); and they were supported by tax dollars. Such programs offended the powerful elite of the industrial establishment; and through such devices as an automobile emission control apparatus which necessitated more expensive gasoline, offended many ordinary citizens. The movement also occasionally bogged down in silliness, such as an over-concern for the possible extinction of the Tennessee snail darter, a problem which does not touch 99% of the public with the same concern as that over hazardous waste sites.

In this way, the great movement for a clean environment was substantially blunted. Aside from cutting funds and toning down the aggressiveness of EPA, there were reductions in technical assistance to the states and local governments and a softening of regulations in numerous areas of concern, including surface mining and protection of wetlands ecology.

The environmental movement, however, is probably only in remission. The problems mentioned previously will not go away and indeed are building up. Some day they will have to be addressed on a more forceful national scale. That seems likely to occur in the new millennium.

# CHAPTER XII

# TAXATION AND THE CONTROL OF LAND USE

## § 1.  Introduction

All of us know that taxation is not an isolated process having only the effect of raising revenue. Tax policy goes beyond that and affects the risk of investment through its benefits and burdens. It affects who will invest money in a particular venture and under what circumstances. As such, the taxing power becomes an extension of the police power in the sense that it becomes regulatory "for the general welfare."

It is obvious, then, that taxation can encourage or discourage the use of land. The difficulty in using it as a control on land development is that if it is focused on a particular parcel of land or seeks to promote or discourage a particular use, it is likely to be held invalid due to lack of uniformity of application or for related reasons. The power can be utilized for broader purposes, however, than simply taxation.

## § 2.  The Property Tax in General

Property taxes are ad valorem taxes, which means that they are based on the value of the property. Some states have classification schemes which allow property to be placed in different rational classifications for tax purposes. This leads to variations with regard to the tax burden, but where such schemes are constitutionally permissible, the courts have upheld rational classifications and have held them not to be a violation of the requirement of uniformity.

In addition to the general property tax, land may be subject to other taxation in the form of special assessments for the benefit of improvement districts, schools, and the like. This situation creates an uneven tax base within a community, and the variation within a metropolitan area may be even greater due to differences among the various suburban areas and the central city.

Differentiations are also produced by assessment ratios, particularly in jurisdictions in which the property can be assessed at less than 100% of value. Even in situations in which it is purportedly assessed at 100% of value, the recognition of what the true value is may vary among assessors. State tax equalization laws help in this regard, but deviations among neighboring cities or counties remain.

Obviously, this form of system leads to variations among communities in the quality of services and public facilities even within the same metropolitan area.

## § 3. The Effect of Zoning and Subdivision Restrictions

There are substantial variations in the tax treatment of land depending upon whether it is within an urban area or is rural and whether it is developed or undeveloped. Developers quite often follow the practice of subdividing and developing land on the fringe of a community and then petition to have the land annexed. This allows them to operate within a minimal tax structure for the maximum period of time, carry out the development with fewer controls being imposed, and still gain the benefit of city services following annexation. It also encourages land speculation. Moreover, this affords an opportunity to avoid subdivision exactions and other controls during the development process (although some exactions may later be imposed as a condition of annexation). This problem is controlled in some areas by extraterritorial zoning and subdivision regulations or by regional planning.

Aside from the foregoing situation, however, zoning and subdivision restrictions still have a major effect on taxes and on services. Large lots may result either from restrictive covenants or from zoning. Aside from the economic exclusion aspect, large-lot suburban areas mean that water and sewer lines and other utilities will have to be extended over substantial distances, that arterial streets into the subdivision may have to be widened, that schools will have to be provided, and that police and fire protection will have to be extended. Since there is not likely to be much commercial activity in the immediate vicinity and since many of these people work in the central city, the traffic problem is exacerbated by travel to and from shopping areas and places of business. All of these situations result in an increased economic burden, and even if the area in question is a separate municipal corporation, a portion of its burden (as, for example, the traffic problem) will fall upon the taxpayers of the central city. Even aside from the tax problem, the situation often leads to rezoning of lands on the periphery of the central city to accommodate the suburbs—sometimes leading to strip zoning for commercial purposes.

Of course, the situation cuts both ways in that a separate suburban community may elect to buy water and sewer services from the central city and thereby bear the cost of extending the lines into the area. This will likely result in a water and sewer district with the landowners paying for the services. Because the density of people in the area is relatively sparse, the cost to each landowner will be greater. On the other hand, if the subdivision is one which exists within the municipality or has been annexed and has its own water and sewer lines, the entire municipality will have to pay for extension of water and sewer lines into the area or for their enlargement unless a special improvement district is created.

Large lot restrictions have other effects as well. For one thing, it is doubtful even with relatively high property taxes being assessed in affluent subdivisions that those lots will bear their fair share of the community tax burden. Every time a new subdivision is created, a portion of the increased costs of services and facilities is passed off on the existing community. In addition, if the city is strapped for money (and most of them are), there is a tendency to zone for industry or commercial activities in order to increase the tax base in situations in which the land might be better devoted to some other activity. There is a similar tendency to take substantially less interest in government-financed low-income housing projects.

The property tax itself, of course, is an inhibitor. It discourages rehabilitation of existing structures which are deteriorating or have collectively become slums. If the landlord spends substantial sums renovating these structures, his property assessment goes up and his lower income tenants cannot afford to pay increased rent to cover the cost of renovation plus the increased taxes. If the owner of the structure is also its resident, he is usually unable to afford either the cost of renovation or the higher taxes.

Consequently, there is a certain interaction between zoning, restrictive covenants, and the property tax which serves to make planning more difficult and to place increased burdens on the cost of municipal services.

## § 4.  Regional Taxation

In 1971, Minnesota adopted a "Metropolitan Fiscal Disparities Act," Ex.Sess.L.1971, c. 24, Minn. Stat. 473F. This statute sought, in essence, to "even

out" any disparities which might exist in taxation
and tax expenditures in the seven-county area in
which Minneapolis and St. Paul are located. In
considering this statute, in Burnsville v. Onischuk
(1974), the Minnesota Supreme Court found the
formulas in the law to be extremely complex but the
objectives fairly simple. The act would avoid a
"competitive scramble" by local governmental units
for commercial and industrial development to improve their tax base. The units would instead pool
40% of the area-wide increase in commercial-industrial valuation subsequent to January 2, 1971. All
units of local government would receive some distri-
bution of the area-wide tax base, although some
units would contribute more to the pool than they
would receive. This amounted to a partial realloca-
tion according to need in inverse ratio to fiscal
capacity. The trial court relied on the uniformity
clause in the Minnesota Constitution to invalidate
this law, but the state supreme court reversed. The
court believed that units of local government which
contributed more to the pool than they received
were sufficiently benefited to meet the constitutional requirement. Thus, the benefits conferred on
residents of communities which were the site of
commercial-industrial development might exceed
the burdens imposed on it. They enjoyed direct
benefits from the existence of adjacent governmental units which provide open space, public facilities,
low-density housing, and the like.

It should be noted, as a dissenting judge did, that
the Minnesota act results in a diversion of funds

from commercial-industrial areas of the region to support bedroom communities which exclude such property. In effect, then, this law provided relief for the suburbs rather than coping with the need for providing relief for the central city. Nonetheless, the merit in the law was its regional approach, which recognized the regional effect of taxation on land use and the interlocking nature of the metropolitan area. What would probably be more desirable would be to utilize regional planning to locate industries within the metropolitan area and adjust the tax base throughout the region in such a way that it was fair to all of its component parts and was expended on a region-wide basis. This concept would probably not be legally feasible in many states, however, without changes in the taxation provisions of the state constitution.

What this amounts to is regional tax-sharing, a concept which is increasingly being considered. In Meadowlands Regional Redevelopment Agency v. State (1973), the New Jersey Court had under consideration a meadowlands reclamation and development act which involved regional activity and a pooling of the tax benefit and burdens among municipalities. One major issue involved the tax-sharing provisions. The sharing envisioned creation of an "intermunicipal account," into which municipalities would pay and from which they would receive benefits based on a statutory formula. The court stated that the tax-sharing provisions appeared to be rational and fair and did not appear arbitrary. The argument that some municipalities would be providing tax revenues for other municipalities was rejected on the basis that this was simply a cost of government imposed on all of the constituent municipalities.

A property tax involving Atlanta and its suburbs, which was specifically directed toward benefiting education in the county, was upheld in McLennan v. Aldredge (1968). It was argued that this was invalid because it was based on having a large city in the county and could only apply to Fulton County, because it discriminated against Atlanta taxpayers by requiring them to pay both this tax and city school taxes, and because a classification based on population does not bear a substantial relation to the taxing power. In rejecting these arguments, the Georgia Court stated that it was not unreasonable to impose some county school burdens on cities because cities are wealthier and that Atlanta would ultimately benefit from having good county schools in the areas it would eventually annex.

Despite these cases, many jurisdictions would probably find such schemes to be unconstitutional under either the uniformity clause of the state constitution or because tax revenue was being diverted from one municipality or one part of the region to another.

## § 5. Taxation Which Regulates Urban Growth

Taxes have not been used extensively for this purpose. In fact, as earlier mentioned, present property tax systems usually tend to spur land speculation and urban growth by encouraging subdivision development on the urban fringe. This is due to low, preferential assessment of agricultural or unimproved land.

Vermont did use the tax power to deter land speculation. It adopted a land gains tax to be imposed on the gain derived from the sale or exchange of land held for less than six years. The rate was high for property held a short time and sold at a high gain, but it went down significantly as the time during which the property was held increased and the gain itself diminished. Because this tax had been enacted to deter land speculation, it was argued that it was arbitrary, capricious and unconstitutional under the equal protection clause. In upholding the statute, the Vermont Court stated that legislation could serve more than one objective, that the aims of the legislature were a valid basis for acting, and that the tax scheme itself was reasonable. Andrews v. Lathrop (1974).

The end result of the Vermont act was not only to deter land speculation, but also to reduce subdivision of land without construction taking place. This tended to preserve land for agricultural uses. Essentially the same act was introduced in several legislatures. At the moment, however, most states have not attempted this scheme or some other plan which might reduce the proliferation of subdivisions immediately outside the boundaries of the municipality. In fact, tax preference for agricultural land or open space may be defended on the ground that it helps to preserve open space. If land value taxation, under which only raw land is taxed rather than improvements, came into widespread use, the high taxes would likely make it too expensive to maintain privately owned urban land in open space and would lead to increased construction and more intensive use. Moreover, the substantial increase in taxes in the central business area based on the land value of the area would likely deter new business construction.

Thus while developers benefit from low taxes on open land in the urban area or around the urban fringe, and while higher taxes might deter land speculation, higher taxes also could spur more sub-division and fringe-area commercial development rather than limit it. There is some benefit, there-fore, to be derived from this form of preferential taxation.

Other forms of preferential taxation or exemp-tions may be employed to encourage certain types of new construction. While some of these laws have fallen prey to strict interpretation of uniformity clauses, many of them have been sustained. See, *e.g.,* Opinion of the Justices (1960), which upheld a statutory exemption from taxation of urban renewal structures in Boston for a period of time.

Other ways which have been put forward to han-dle open land or farm land include deferred taxation and agreements limiting use of the land. Under the first method, agricultural land is valued only for agricultural use (as under the preferential method), but when it is sold for development there is an increased tax for that year and for a certain number of years prior to that time. Under the agreement method, the land is limited to agricultural use or open space by agreement between the owner and the local government for a specified number of years and, in return, the owner receives a low tax rate. Both of these methods tend to hold down land speculation and land development around the urban fringe, and the second method would obviously permit land use planning of a more meaningful nature.

## § 6. Integration of Land Use and Tax Policies

Hawaii has attempted to utilize tax policies and practices to a substantial extent to promote certain types of land use. The state land use commission establishes certain use classifications, and the director of taxation must consider those classifications in assigning land to one of the statutory categories. He also gives consideration to the districting established by the county in its zoning ordinance and to use classifications contained in the State's general plan. Various tax breaks result in certain situations. For example, if an owner makes improvements under an urban redevelopment project, his taxes do not increase for seven years. Repairs or improvements made to meet state health, sanitation or safety requirements do not increase taxes for a certain time period. Under certain situations, land may be dedicated to agricultural or ranching use and be assessed at that rate. The owner cannot change the use for a ten-year

period. Low and moderate-income housing projects
are exempt from taxes. The Hawaii statutes contain
various other provisions integrating tax and land
use policies.

No other state has gone to the extent of Hawaii in
interrelating property taxes with controls on land
use. In most of the mainland states, the uniformity
provisions of the state constitution would make it
difficult to emulate the Hawaii provisions to any
substantial degree.

## § 7.   A Summary of Problems with the Property Tax

Since the interrelationship of land development
and the property tax is clear, but since few states
have attempted to interrelate the two from a legal
standpoint, it is useful to summarize some of the
problems stemming from the property tax. With
regard to urban development and housing generally,
the tax reduces consumer demand for housing in
less affluent neighborhoods, reduces demand for
heavily taxed commercial property in the central
city thereby encouraging its deterioration, discourages owners of low cost housing from making improvements, affects land use planning due to fiscal
considerations, leads to land speculation and uncontrolled growth on the urban fringe, and results in
wide variations in the quality of public services due
to tax variations among communities in the same
general area. Moreover, it is essentially a regressive
tax up to a certain income level. With regard to

utilities, disproportionately high property taxes lead
to increased rates for consumers.

Solutions to this problem vary. One suggestion is
to rely less on the property tax to support local
funding and rely more on state sources. Some functions might be transferred to state government. The
land value or "Henry George" tax, previously discussed, has been mentioned as a possibility. Greater
reliance on other local sources of revenue also is a
possibility. Taxation of increases in land values
based upon unearned increment resulting from ex-
ternal activities of other landowners or from such
governmental action as new highways, rezoning,
and the like has been suggested. This latter possibility will be discussed briefly.

## § 8.  Recapture of Unearned Increment

The underlying thesis in this regard is that land
gains in value because governmental activities enhance it or because the land nearby is developed for
subdivision purposes or for similar reasons. One
way to recapture benefits to the land is through the
special assessment device. Certain types of public
facilities in an area enhance the value of the surrounding land. A special assessment would reduce
or even eliminate the cost of a facility to the government and recover some of the unearned enhanced
value. In Weitz v. Davis (1966), a formula for assessments for street improvements based upon the
front footage and other considerations was upheld.
By statute in California, land which receives special
benefit from being adjacent to a transit or rapid

transit district may be placed in a "special benefit district," if the voters approve, in situations involving acquisition, construction or repair of the facilities of the transit district. A scheme to pay for placing electric lines underground, to be financed by special assessments, was upheld in Citizens for Underground Equality v. Seattle (1972).

In addition to special assessments, an unearned increment tax has been suggested for application to situations involving rezoning or granting a permit for a development, or to the transfer of property which has greatly appreciated in value, or to persons who hold land for long time spans. It seems unlikely that such a tax would gain political favor, although the device of subdivision exactions bears a relationship to the unearned increment tax on development permits.

## § 9.  Federal Taxing and Spending

It requires no detailed discussion to illustrate the fact that federal taxing and spending policies also affect land use. The capital gains feature of federal income taxation leads to speculative investment in land around the urban fringe. Deduction of mortgage interest and property taxes by homeowners is an indirect subsidy to the building industry. Although the effectiveness of the real estate tax shelter as a tax avoidance device has been diminished, it still remains. Favored tax treatment is available to landlords who rehabilitate substandard housing occupied by low income tenants. These are only some of the ways federal tax policies affect urban development.

That they do have an effect is quite obvious. The fact that someone occupying rental housing cannot deduct his payments while a homeowner can deduct his mortgage interest and property taxes obviously leads most renters to purchase housing when they are able to do so. This in turn spurs subdivision development. While this is good for the economy, it obviously affects land use planning and the problem of urban growth. Moreover, while there should be tax incentives relative to repair of substandard housing, since most of these occupants will not be able to afford a house, there is a neglected class of individuals in between the low income group and the middle or upper middle income group. They do not usually live in true substandard housing, but they may not earn enough to eventually afford a house. Since the 1980's this group of people has been helped somewhat by low interest rate bond issues aimed at permitting first-time home buyers or persons earning less than a certain income to purchase a home with "bond money" at affordable monthly payments. But even then, there is a group of people just above the low income level who cannot qualify for such loans. Thus, federal tax and subsidy policies do not apply entirely evenly, just as the property tax fails in that regard also.

# CHAPTER XIII

# NEW INFLUENCING CONSIDERATIONS: ENERGY AND SPACE

## § 1. Introduction

Controls on the use of land continually take on new forms, and new problems continue to emerge. Devices utilized as tools of the planning process, such as planned unit developments, new forms of subdivision exactions, impact fees, transfer of development rights, and other such concepts will either become staples or provide the basis for new planning concepts or both. The ramifications of such cases as *Mount Laurel* and its progeny remain to be further explored in those jurisdictions which have adopted or may adopt that approach. The problem of exclusionary zoning, particularly with regard to racial and economic implications, will likely be developed more fully by case law in the years ahead. Perhaps the difficulty of zoning which relates to mobile homes and affordable housing in general will form an important part of that development. For local governments which have to assess the cost effects of zoning, the question of damages for unconstitutional land use regulations is likely to be determined and that area of the law will likely expand in the years ahead.

322

The nature of future planning and whether it will be on more of a regional or statewide scale than is the present norm remains a major issue. Local planning and zoning has been at least partly the reason that many courts have intervened in the process in an affirmative or coercive way, as witness *Arlington Heights, Gautreaux, Mount Laurel* and *Black Jack,* to name only a few. But the shortsightedness of most states in failing to go beyond purely local planning and land use controls in the light of increasing urbanization and the interlocking nature and complexity of metropolitan areas and surrounding satellite suburbs remains with us. The quality of life in the new millennium is being established now, and much of it is already fixed; but the planning process remains in most jurisdictions essentially as it was thirty or forty years ago.

The energy crisis of the 1970's came and passed with only a relatively minor ripple as far as law is concerned. Highway maximum speeds were reduced and more fuel efficient cars were produced. But when energy prices stabilized and gasoline shortages ended, people went back to business as usual. Some experts, however, predict more energy shortages in the 1990's as the current oil glut diminishes and as consumption catches up with the supply. This impacts to some extent on land use planning, particularly in cities without rapid transit systems and limited bus capacities. In considering how the city of the future might be restructured to respond to this problem, let us consider the allocation and utilization of space in American cities and how cities might develop in the future.

## § 2.   Airspace Utilization in American Cities

Many large American cities in all areas as well as smaller towns in the midwest and beyond were affected in their development by the railroad. By the latter part of the 19th century, the railroads had become essential to American commerce in the transport of goods and people. They ran into the heart of the downtown areas of all of the large cities, and their tracks and rail yards occupied large quantities of downtown land. As the cities grew outward from the core, as the value of commercial property grew, and as the property tax on such land increased, it became apparent that the tracks and rail yards were occupying valuable land which otherwise could be utilized for construction of business buildings.

The solution of the problem lay in the old common law maxim enunciated by Lord Coke, *cujus est solum, ejus est usque ad coelum et ad inferos,* which meant that the owner of the land surface owned the space above it up "to the sky" and the space below it down to the center of the earth. While the advent of aviation had provided reasonable limitations upon upward ownership, there seemed to be no question (as the cases later established) that the surface owner owned whatever airspace he might utilize. Airspace was a commodity which could be sold, leased, subdivided, and generally dealt with in the same manner as the surface. Thus, a way to create the modern condominium, which came to us from civil law sources, already existed in the common law.

Interestingly enough, an early environmental law lent impetus to the utilization of airspace over railroad facilities. Shortly after the turn of the century, the New York legislature passed an act requiring the railroads to operate on electricity in the Park Avenue area. There was also a need for larger facilities, and this gave rise to the construction of a two-level terminal yard which enlarged Grand Central Station and utilized the space over the tracks. This was followed in the same area of midtown Manhattan by the construction of the Biltmore Hotel and other hotels and public buildings over the tracks. Gradually, the tracks in the area of midtown Manhattan began to disappear and what appeared to be surface structures often had tracks running beneath them and involved ownership of the airspace with easements of support extending up from newly subterranean rights of way. Chicago pursued the same path in the late 1920's with the construction of the Merchandise Mart and the Chicago Daily News building. Numerous buildings, such as the Pan Am building, the Seagram's building, the Union Carbide building and many others in New York City, and the Prudential building, the Chicago Sun–Times building, Marina Towers and many others in Chicago, were constructed in airspace. The same pattern has been followed to a lesser degree in other large cities. (See generally, R.

Wright, *The Law of Airspace* 224–229, 261–271 (1968).)

The situation offers a potential for similar adaptation today in the case of large areas of urban space occupied by multi-lane highways. This has already occurred in a number of cities, although to a lesser degree than in the railroad situation, as buildings of various kinds extend across or occupy space over, below or along the side of major highways. This utilization was encouraged in the middle or late 1960's by the Bureau of Public Roads (now part of the Department of Transportation). This "joint development" concept was incorporated as federal policy in the Highway Assistance Act of 1968, P.L. 90–238, 81 Stat. 772, and it ultimately led to the promulgation of a Model Airspace Act by the American Bar Association. (Final Draft of Model Airspace Act, 7 *Real Prop.Prob. & Tr.L.J.* 353 et seq. (1972).)

Airspace over or around transportation rights of way offers potential use for various purposes. To planners, it offers the possibility of combining different kinds of commercial, recreational and residential uses in a location which would permit ready access to an individual's place of employment and permit most of his other needs to be satisfied without extensive travel. Such utilization might also alleviate the problem of displacement of large numbers of people due to public projects and permit the construction of new housing projects in approximately the same area of displacement. Through careful planning, in place of highway corridors becoming the sole occupant of otherwise wasted land, a carefully planned area of multi-family housing, parks, recreational facilities and shopping areas could develop. Some attention has already been given to such multi-use plans, and the potential of such plans in a time of shortage of fossil fuels should not be overlooked.

## § 3.  Utilization of Underground Space

Separate and apart from the possibility of air-space utilization in downtown urban areas to reduce dependence upon automobiles is the use of underground space to minimize energy consumption wherever the building may be located. Buildings in some areas have already gone to windowless arrangements and the use of earth berms against the sides. The design of such buildings necessitates some refinement, since these buildings often provide the appearance of huge bunkers of the World War II variety. Nonetheless, there is no question but that energy consumption can be reduced in this manner. It is known that substantially less energy is required to heat and cool an underground facility than is required for the equivalent facility above the surface. Underground temperatures vary much less from the average yearly temperatures than do surface temperatures.

Be that as it may, there are obviously certain amenities to be considered. People lived in caves during the Stone Age or occasionally occupied underground facilities in Europe during World War II out of necessity, but people prefer light and air.

Therefore, it seems more likely that architects and planners may develop structures in which a portion of the building is subsurface (bearing a relationship to our split-level housing of today) or in which portions of the house are earth-covered and some parts are exposed to sources of light and air. Properly designed, and perhaps designed in conjunction with the use of solar energy, such structures could retain the necessary amenities at very substantial savings in energy. While perhaps most useful in relation to residential housing, non-high rise commercial and industrial structures could also make use of such devices, as could public buildings such as schools and hospitals. Multi-family structures, grouped closely together to maximize energy-saving and to provide substantial open space for use by the residents, could also be adapted in this manner. For example, on several college campuses in recent years, new library construction has turned toward underground facilities.

## § 4.  Public Controls on Use of Space

The use of either airspace or underground areas should not present problems substantially different from those involving the land surface. In regard to airspace, there is no reason why zoning, for example, could not regulate the upward extension of space on the same basis as the surface, or for that matter, provide appropriate zones for different spatial levels. A parallel to this can be seen in condominiums, which are composed of cubicles of space sold to individual owners and which have certain common areas. The Merchandise Mart, which was developed under the common law rules pertaining to airspace, was segmented on a multi-dimensional basis as well.

## § 5. Energy Consumption and Land Planning

The foregoing has provided some insight into new architectural and planning concepts which may have a role to play in helping to alleviate the energy crisis. But these are only devices which may result in one way or another in reduction of energy consumption. Utilization of airspace reduces reliance upon the automobile for transportation over long distances as well as offers the energy-saving potential which results from a clustering of uses. Utilization of underground space offers direct reduction in consumption for heating and cooling purposes through innovative design processes. But solar energy offers even greater potential for reduced consumption whether used alone or in conjunction with these other devices. The problem as to solar energy is twofold: (1) designing efficient, low-cost systems for all types of new construction, and (2) designing efficient, low-cost systems for existing structures. The latter, once designed, will require tax benefits or government loans (or the underwriting of private lending) in order to come into widespread use.

None of these or other devices can be effective, however, until recognition of the energy problem translates itself into federal, state and local legislation having an impact upon the planning process. To be specific:

(1) The movement to save the downtown area of cities is desirable, but if the people who work there must travel many miles each day from their residences by automobiles, the result is highly wasteful from the energy standpoint. Planning, therefore, must provide for rapid transit systems for the surburbanite and must consider (a) renewal and revitalization of residential areas closer to the central core, and (b) provisions for multi-family housing of some attractiveness, including condominiums, close to the central city or to outlying business districts. Right at the turn of the new millennium the city of Atlanta is looking toward regional transportation controls to stem very serious urban sprawl.

(2) The not-so-new concept of a multiplicity of business and commercial centers forming a core, with housing of various kinds close by, should be encouraged in order to reduce travel distances. Some aspects of this can be found in younger cities. This provides a number of commercial centers, rather than one, and permits people to live closer to where they work. The same can be done with light industrial centers. Open space, parks and playgrounds can be interspersed at appropriate points in between.

(3) Zoning, building and subdivision ordinances should encourage and in some instances require or give priority to structures which utilize energy-

saving devices of the type discussed. This should reflect itself in something more than added thickness of insulation in the walls and ceilings of houses and apartments.

(4) Through regional and state planning, impetus can be given to promoting the development of new communities, new suburbs, or model neighborhoods which are planned for and intended to encourage energy conservation and which represent a mixture of residential, office and commercial components. This will require an entirely different approach for most states, however, and is unlikely to occur in many states very soon or with much effectiveness in the absence of a national land use policy mandating or offering incentives for state and regional planning.

(5) In addition to the development of rapid transit systems, more attention should be given to the efficiency of traditional highway, road and street travel in moving traffic at peak hours in congested areas.

These are obviously only a few of the major considerations which planners must face in this regard.

### § 6.  The Energy Problem and the Environmentalists

There have already been heated clashes between those concerned about the environment and those wishing to provide additional quantities of fossil fuels. To save the environment was an overwhelming issue of the 1970's with the result that environmental impact statements must now be filed and assessed in many situations in which boards administering traditional forms of land use controls have approved the proposed use. These clashes present the problem of weighing competing values which vary depending on the situation involved: the need to preserve and protect the environment; the need to proceed with land development projects which fall within the acceptability of the comprehensive plan and zoning and subdivision standards; and the need to create more energy sources or preserve existing ones. The standards of NEPA and related laws have generally been enforced or have prevailed or have, in some way, been satisfied. The result almost invariably has been delay.

It is safe to say that these conflicts may reoccur with a second energy crisis. People who are not used to being cold in the winter and hot in the summer when they are in their own homes or offices, and people who do not want to be laid off from work because an industry or business has had its energy source curtailed or reduced, are less likely to be sympathetic with environmental goals. The situation will increasingly cease to become a confrontation of environmentalists (the "good guys") with oil and utility companies (the "bad guys"), and will gradually develop into a situation involving the hard core environmentalists against average working people. Factory and business shutdowns would lead not only to reduced income for workers, but also to reduced profits for industries and businesses of all kinds, and in turn all of this would lead to a heightening of inflation and a reduction in living standards.

It seems unlikely that we will ever again ignore our environment or permit it to dissipate to the extent that we did in the period preceding the 1960's. Only a pending national catastrophe could lead to the repeal of basic environmental policies. It does seem likely, however, that the immediacy of environmental needs will become less immediate with the heightening of energy needs. It would, therefore, be in the best interest of the environmentalists to promote the development of safe, new forms of energy, such as solar energy and, for that matter, nuclear energy.

Another challenge to the core values of our political society is reflected in the increasing federalization and concomitant preemption of local and state power to regulate the conflicts of environmentalism and land development. In the late 1990's the Supreme Court undertook a re-examination of federalism issues under the Constitution. The current trend of decisions indicates the Court is bent on curtailing federal statutory control over issues deemed to be within the ambit of state powers. This basic constitutional problem has strong implications for land use and environmental regulation.

## § 7.  Control of Land and the Equitable Balance

In the last analysis, the control of land under the police power and all of the peripheral considerations which enter into a reconciliation of the legality or illegality of particular controls in specific situations come down to a single set of factors—reasonableness, or the lack of it; arbitrariness, or the lack of it; or doubt as between the two, which generally sustains the governmental determination. But more than any other factor, cases quite often come down to the simple principle of "balancing the equities." It is a judgment of values, and how those values fall on a particular scale in a specific situation and in a given moment will often determine the outcome. Patent or obvious deviations will not be tolerated on the part of government, nor will specious, self-interested challenges normally carry the day. But in those close cases involving important competing values, the tenor of the time, the jurisprudential values of a particular judge or jurisdiction, and the judge-made weight of one issue upon the scales of justice as opposed to another will generally be the ultimate determining factor. This is indeed the true "balancing of the equities," the choice in a specific situation among legitimate competing values.

And so the police power will prevail in a period and in a judicial body realizing the need for public controls to balance private irresponsibility and to prevent public harm. The police power will also prevail in a situation illustrating demonstrable or reasonable public need for regulation even without the creation of problems by private activity. Private rights will prevail in situations in which public actions fail to consider the fact that in America the ownership of private property is a constitutional right which, though not absolute in nature, is demanding of the utmost recognition when it does not contravene the public interest. The healthy public desire to preserve and purify the environment must be balanced against the somewhat ignored public essential for sufficient energy and commercial activity to house a nation and to permit it to be productive. The scales of justice do not usually weigh the sinner against the righteous or good against evil; they balance the accepted values of our civilization in a specific situation, at a particular time, in relation to a particular need, and with regard to the effects of a particular result.

It is so in this area of the law, and it is so in all areas of the law. Judges look to the problematic hills of a particular day, and if they are very good judges, to the hills beyond. This is what distinguishes poor judges from good ones and the good ones from the great ones. It is a matter of knowing the time and realizing the needs of this day and of the days to come.

*

# INDEX

**References are to pages**